Aquatic Stewardship Education in Theory and Practice

Aquatic Stewardship Education in Theory and Practice

Edited by

Barbara A. Knuth and William F. Siemer

Human Dimensions Research Unit
Department of Natural Resources
Cornell University
Ithaca, New York 14853, USA

American Fisheries Society Symposium 55

Proceedings of the Symposium
"The Theory and Practice of Aquatic Stewardship Education"
Held in Anchorage, Alaska, USA
September 14, 2005

American Fisheries Society
Bethesda, Maryland, USA
2007

Suggested citation formats are

Entire book

Knuth, B. A., and W. F. Siemer, editors. 2007. Aquatic stewardship education in theory and practice. American Fisheries Society, Symposium 55, Bethesda, Maryland.

Chapter in book

Fontaine, M. W., and M. P. Dunn. 2007. Overview of the recreational boating industry's aquatic stewardship through technology, innovation, and education. Pages 55–72 *in* B. A. Knuth and W. F. Siemer, editors. Aquatic stewardship education in theory and practice. American Fisheries Society, Symposium 55, Bethesda, Maryland.

Printed in the United States of America on acid-free paper.

Library of Congress Control Number 2007923418

ISBN 978-1-888569-90-2
ISSN 0892-2284

American Fisheries Society Web site: *www.fisheries.org*

American Fisheries Society
5410 Grosvenor Lane, Suite 110
Bethesda, Maryland 20814-2199
USA

Contents

Acknowledgments vii

Symbols and Abbreviations ix

PART I   Stewardship Definitions and Management Challenges

1   Improving Our Understanding of the Theory and Practice of Aquatic Stewardship
Education 3
Barbara A. Knuth

2   Reconciling Fishing and Boating Promotion with Safe, Sustainable Use 11
Bob Wattendorf and Jon Lyman

PART II   Fostering Stewardship: Theory and Practice

3   Fostering Aquatic Stewardship with the Help of Best Education Practices 25
Elaine Andrews

4   Developing Tomorrow's Anglers and Aquatic Stewards: Formative Evaluation of
MinnAqua's Leaders' Guide 33
Amy Grack Nelson and Jenifer Matthees

5   Environmental Communication for Aquatic Stewardship 45
Brian Day

6   Overview of the Recreational Boating Industry's Aquatic Stewardship through
Technology, Innovation, and Education 55
Monita W. Fontaine and Matthew P. Dunn

7   Fostering Boating-Related Aquatic Stewardship: Reaching the Boater 73
Ryck Lydecker

8   The Trout Unlimited Experience Teaching Aquatic Stewardship to Youth 79
Duncan Blair

9   Government, Nongovernmental Organizations, and Industry: Programs that Foster
Aquatic Stewardship 85
Annette L. Glick

10   Citizen Science: Stewardship Education in Washington State 93
Margaret Tudor and Michael O'Malley

11   Revisiting the Stewardship Concept: Faith-Based Opportunities to Bridge from
Principles to Practice 103
William F. Siemer and Gregory E. Hitzhusen

12   The Role of the American Fisheries Society in Fostering Aquatic Resources
Stewardship: Past Successes, Future Opportunities 117
Carl V. Burger and Michael E. Barnes

PART III Measuring Stewardship: Indicators and Outcomes

13 Measures of Aquatic Stewardship Behavior from the Boating Perspective 127
Andrew J. Loftus

14 Measures of Aquatic Stewardship from a Fisheries Perspective 137
Phil T. Seng and Gwen M. White

15 Does Angling or Boating Improve the Stewardship Ethic of Participants? 145
Steve L. McMullin, Karen S. Hockett, and Julie A. McClafferty

16 The Influence of Angler Value Orientations on Fisheries Stewardship Norms 157
Jeremy T. Bruskotter and David C. Fulton

17 A Test of Aquatic Education and Stewardship Relationships among Youth 169
Anthony J. Fedler

PART IV Future Directions for Aquatic Stewardship Education

18 Advancing the Theory and Practice of Aquatic Stewardship Education 179
Barbara A. Knuth and William F. Siemer

Acknowledgments

We thank the Recreational Boating and Fishing Foundation (RBFF), the Sport Fishing and Boating Partnership Council (SFBPC) through the United States Department of the Interior Fish and Wildlife Service, and Cornell University Department of Natural Resources for their generous financial support for this volume and for the American Fisheries Society symposium on which it is based. Bruce Matthews (RBFF) and William Taylor (SFBPC) merit particular thanks for their enthusiastic vision for this project.

Andrew Loftus provided important guidance in the overall design of this project and in focusing particular attention on aquatic stewardship within the recreational boating community. Carl Richardson made useful contributions to the design of the symposium.

We are grateful to the editorial staff of AFS, especially Aaron Lerner and Debby Lehman, for their assistance in completing this work.

We thank the following individuals who provided peer reviews for one or more of the chapters of this book:

Robin Abadia
Ira Adelman
Elaine Andrews
Stephan Carlson
Karen Dvornich
Ann Evans
Anthony Fedler
Gene Gilliland
Billy Higginbotham
Karen Hockett
Kevin Hunt
Robin Knox
Barbara Knuth
Andrew Loftus

Jon Lyman
Bruce Matthews
Julie McClafferty
Robert Muth
Paul Pajak
John Pierce
Charles Pistis
Stephen Quinn
William Siemer
William Taylor
Margaret Tudor
Doug Whittaker
Harry Zinn

Symbols and Abbreviations

The following symbols and abbreviations may be found in this book without definition. Also undefined are standard mathematical and statistical symbols given in most dictionaries.

A	ampere		i.e.	(id est) that is
AC	alternating current		IU	international unit
Bq	becquerel		J	joule
C	coulomb		K	Kelvin (degrees above absolute zero)
°C	degrees Celsius		k	kilo (10^3, as a prefix)
cal	calorie		kg	kilogram
cd	candela		km	kilometer
cm	centimeter		l	levorotatory
Co.	Company		L	levo (as a prefix)
Corp.	Corporation		L	liter (0.264 gal, 1.06 qt)
cov	covariance		lb	pound (0.454 kg, 454g)
DC	direct current; District of Columbia		lm	lumen
D	dextro (as a prefix)		log	logarithm
d	day		Ltd.	Limited
d	dextrorotatory		M	mega (10^6, as a prefix); molar (as a suffix or by itself)
df	degrees of freedom			
dL	deciliter		m	meter (as a suffix or by itself); milli (10^{23}, as a prefix)
E	east			
E	expected value		mi	mile (1.61 km)
e	base of natural logarithm (2.71828…)		min	minute
e.g.	(exempli gratia) for example		mol	mole
eq	equivalent		N	normal (for chemistry); north (for geography); newton
et al.	(et alii) and others			
etc.	et cetera		N	sample size
eV	electron volt		NS	not significant
F	filial generation; Farad		n	ploidy; nanno (10^{29}, as a prefix)
°F	degrees Fahrenheit		o	ortho (as a chemical prefix)
fc	footcandle (0.0929 lx)		oz	ounce (28.4 g)
ft	foot (30.5 cm)		P	probability
ft³/s	cubic feet per second (0.0283 m³/s)		p	para (as a chemical prefix)
g	gram		p	pico (10^{212}, as a prefix)
G	giga (10^9, as a prefix)		Pa	pascal
gal	gallon (3.79 L)		pH	negative log of hydrogen ion activity
Gy	gray		ppm	parts per million
h	hour		qt	quart (0.946 L)
ha	hectare (2.47 acres)		R	multiple correlation or regression coefficient
hp	horsepower (746 W)			
Hz	hertz		r	simple correlation or regression coefficient
in	inch (2.54 cm)			
Inc.	Incorporated		rad	radian

S	siemens (for electrical conductance); south (for geography)	Wb	weber
SD	standard deviation	yd	yard (0.914 m, 91.4 cm)
SE	standard error	α	probability of type I error (false rejection of null hypothesis)
s	second	β	probability of type II error (false acceptance of null hypothesis)
T	tesla		
tris	tris(hydroxymethyl)-aminomethane (a buffer)	Ω	ohm
		μ	micro (10^{26}, as a prefix)
UK	United Kingdom	$'$	minute (angular)
U.S.	United States (adjective)	$''$	second (angular)
USA	United States of America (noun)	$\circ$	degree (temperature as a prefix, angular as a suffix)
V	volt		
V, Var	variance (population)	%	per cent (per hundred)
var	variance (sample)	‰	per mille (per thousand)
W	watt (for power); west (for geography)		

PART I Stewardship Definitions and Management Challenges

American Fisheries Society Symposium 55:3–10, 2007

Improving Our Understanding of the Theory and Practice of Aquatic Stewardship Education

BARBARA A. KNUTH[1]

*Human Dimensions Research Unit, Department of Natural Resources
Cornell University, Ithaca, New York 14853, USA*

Abstract.—Patterns of human behavior, consumption, and resource use have contributed to declines in fisheries populations and degradation of aquatic habitat. Recreational anglers and boaters are among the key stakeholders who should be concerned about such changes and empowered to adopt behaviors that minimize adverse impacts on aquatic environments. Definitions of aquatic stewardship should include focus on human behaviors, which may be externally or internally motivated, and contribute to a local, regional, or global impact. The National Outreach and Communication Program, prepared and implemented through the collaborative efforts of the Sport Fishing and Boating Partnership Council and the Recreational Boating and Fishing Foundation, sets forth a vision for increasing sportfishing and boating participation and enhancing aquatic stewardship. Many other government and nongovernment organizations also strive to enhance aquatic stewardship. This proceedings volume results from a symposium on The Theory and Practice of Aquatic Stewardship Education, held at the 135th annual meeting of the American Fisheries Society in Anchorage, Alaska. The goal of the symposium and this text is to advance our understanding of (1) how stewardship is defined in theory and practice, (2) the approaches that are necessary to promote and foster desirable stewardship behaviors, and (3) how measures of aquatic stewardship might be used to evaluate progress toward goals. We emphasize the importance of including both recreational fishing and boating activities in discussions of aquatic stewardship.

The Call to Aquatic Stewardship Education

This proceedings volume results from a symposium on The Theory and Practice of Aquatic Stewardship Education, held at the 135th annual meeting of the American Fisheries Society in Anchorage, Alaska. The purpose of this symposium was to help organize the most current thinking about how to define, foster, and evaluate desirable aquatic stewardship behaviors as well as how to develop the educational programs and other motivating forces underlying such behaviors. This effort represents a partnership among academics, aquatic resource educators, fishery management professionals, and the fishing and boating industries to develop a shared understanding of desired characteristics of aquatic resource stewardship. An important component of this effort was to help elucidate what is known regarding the relationship between boating and fishing participation and aquatic stewardship attitudes and behaviors.

The concept of stewardship is not new; it plays a prominent role in Biblical passages (e.g., Siemer and Hitzhusen, 2007, this volume) and has been promoted in agricultural and watershed education efforts (e.g., Cole-Misch et al.1996; Boyle 1998). Applying the concept of stewardship to fisheries and aquatic resources is a natural outgrowth of concerned stakeholders observing trends indicating declining quality and quantity of these resources.

In 2002, the U.S. Fish and Wildlife Service's Fisheries Program Vision for the Future (http://www.fws.gov/fisheries/CAF/Vision.htm#status)

---

[1] E-mail: bak3@cornell.edu

summarized the status of fisheries and aquatic resources within the United States, reporting that

- Nearly 400 aquatic species require special protection due to declining populations (Williams at al. 1989; Moyle and Leidy 1992);
- At least 225 aquatic species are listed as federally threatened or endangered, including 115 fish species, 70 mussel species, 21 crustacean species, and 19 amphibian species;
- More than 50% of U.S. wetlands acreage has been lost (Dahl 1990); and
- A variety of habitat-related changes are linked to these declines in aquatic populations and communities, including changes in water flows, watershed modifications, and various forms of pollution, including chemical contaminants, sedimentation, and the introduction of nonnative and invasive species.

These changes are fundamentally human-induced. Thus, considerations of aquatic stewardship must include a focus on human behavior and the values and attitudes that relate to those behaviors. Aquatic stewardship has been defined as "the moral obligation to care for aquatic environments, and the actions undertaken to provide that care" (Knuth and Siemer 2004), emphasizing the importance of actions, or human behavior. Sia et al. (1986) examined predictors of responsible environmental behavior and concluded that responsible environmental behavior is a learned response. Holland and Carter (2005) demonstrated that an ideology of stewardship is important, but environmentally friendly actions are critical to demonstrating and fostering in others a commitment to environmental stewardship. Dixon et al. (2005) observed that increased public involvement in appropriate environmental management will require fostering both the motivation to care about the environment and environmental literacy. These studies suggest at least a twofold mission for aquatic stewardship education: fostering the motivation to undertake stewardship and empowering individuals with the skills to know what to do.

As the oldest and largest fisheries scientific and professional organization in the world, the American Fisheries Society has noted the importance of this issue by asserting aquatic steward-

ship as one of its three major focal areas within its strategic plan (www.fisheries.org/afs/about us/sp.pdf), emphasizing aquatic stewardship education among its main goals. Other organizations have adopted similar priorities. Prominent among these are two sponsors of this symposium, the Recreational Boating and Fishing Foundation (RBFF), and the Sport Fishing and Boating Partnership Council (SFBPC).

Anglers, Boaters, and Aquatic Stewardship

The 2001 National Survey of Fishing, Hunting, and Wildlife-Associated Recreation (www.census.gov/prod/www/abs/fishing.html) reported more than 34 million anglers fished in U.S. waters. In 2003, more than 69 million people participated in recreational boating (National Marine Manufacturers Association 2003). The extent of recreational participation related to aquatic and fisheries resources suggests an obvious focus for aquatic stewardship education programs, assuming recreational anglers and boaters clearly have a stake in the quality and quantity of aquatic resources available for their recreational pursuits. In addition, aquatic resource beneficiaries (who may or may not be anglers or boaters) hold an important stake in the future of aquatic resources' abilities to continue to provide societal benefits such as drought and flood mitigation, groundwater replenishment, nutrient cycling, and esthetic enhancements. Recognition of the benefits provided by healthy aquatic resources has stimulated citizen involvement in stewardship activities, particularly at local levels (Scarlett 2004).

The extent to which direct participation in aquatic resource-related recreation is linked to desirable aquatic stewardship behaviors is unknown (Fedler et al. 2001), although some contributions to this symposium volume begin to shed light on this issue (e.g., McMullin et al. 2007; Bruskotter and Fulton 2007; and Fedler 2007; all this volume). Previous researchers have noted a potential link between environmental sensitivity and environmentally responsible behavior (e.g., Sia et al. 1986; Sivek 1989), suggesting that sensitivity to or perceived importance of aquatic resources could be related to aquatic stewardship. Wells and Lekies (2006) reported a positive association between environmental behaviors and experiences with "wild nature" (such as an angler or boater might experience in the outdoors). Other work (Arlinghaus 2005) suggests that anglers may not be particularly receptive to long-term aquatic stewardship goals if pursuing those goals impinges on the angler's shorter-term interests and emphasizes the importance of comprehensive aquatic stewardship education to move beyond these potential barriers.

National organizations have recognized this potential link between resource users and the opportunity for promoting aquatic stewardship, including most prominently the SFBPC and RBFF. The SFBPC is a federally chartered advisory committee established in 1993 to advise the secretary of the U.S. Department of the Interior, through the director of the U.S. Fish and Wildlife Service, on recreational fishing and boating issues. The RBFF is a 501(c)(3) organization, established in 1998 to carry out the National Outreach and Communication Program, increase participation in fishing and boating, complement ongoing conservation efforts by government agencies, and foster a legacy of stewardship. In addition to these national-level organizations focusing on anglers, boaters, and stewardship, many local, state, federal, and nonprofit agencies and groups focus on some form of aquatic resource stewardship with their own stakeholders (e.g., watershed groups, environmental sustainability organizations, civic groups with an environmental focus). Many of the symposium presentations included in this volume provide insights into these stewardship-related organizations, their missions, and their activities. An overview of the SFBPC and the RBFF is provided here, given the importance of these organizations in promoting and, in some cases, helping to coordinate some of these regional, state, and local efforts, at least with recreational boaters and anglers.

The SFBPC (www.fws.gov/sfbpc/) exists to "conserve, restore, and enhance the quality, function, sustainable productivity, and distribution of aquatic resources that support and increase recreational fishing opportunities nationwide, and to increase public awareness of the importance of aquatic resources and the social and economic benefits of recreational fishing and boating." Its membership includes the director of the U.S. Fish and Wildlife Service, the president of the Association of Fish and Wildlife Agencies, directors from state agencies responsible for managing recreational fisheries resources, and stakeholders from the recreational fishing and boating industries, saltwater and freshwater recreational fishing organizations, recreational boating organizations, tourism, recreational fisheries resource conservation groups, and aquatic resource outreach and education groups. The council recommends policies and programs to increase public awareness and support for the Aquatic Resources (Wallop-Breaux) Trust Fund, suggests and supports activities and programs that will foster stewardship and ethics in recreational fishing and boating, identifies efforts to stimulate angler and boater participation in the conservation and restoration of aquatic resources through outreach and education, and fosters communication and coordination among government, industry, anglers, boaters, and the public. The council issued a key report, "A Partnership Agenda for Fisheries Conservation" (SFPBC 2002), which provided focused recommendations on aquatic species and habitat conservation and management, public use of aquatic resources, and leadership and cooperation. The council was instrumental in securing the political and financial support to create the Recreational Boating and Fishing Foundation and remains active in providing some oversight and guidance for the foundation's programs.

The mission of the RBFF (http://www.rbff.org/) is to implement an informed, consensus-based national outreach strategy that will increase participation in recreational angling and boating and thereby increase public awareness and appreciation of the need for protecting, conserving, and restoring this nation's aquatic resources. Explicitly, RBFF's mission is grounded in the assumption that recreational angling and boating relate to and support aquatic stewardship. RBFF national outreach campaigns have included "Water Works Wonders" and "Take Me Fishing" as part of efforts to implement the National Outreach and Communication Program. The strategic plan for the National Outreach and Communication Program is updated periodically, based on activities and achievements, evaluation of results, stakeholder input, and changing contexts related to recreational fishing and boating.

The focus of the RBFF is on boating as it relates to fishing and fishing as it relates to boating.

Components of Aquatic Stewardship Education

Aquatic stewardship, by definition, implies actions or behaviors undertaken to support or enhance the quality of the aquatic environment. What stewardship behaviors (and related skills, attitudes, and knowledge) should be the focus of aquatic stewardship education programs? Human-related activities having an impact on aquatic resources occur at all social and spatial scales: individual, family, local, national, and global; thus, it should be useful to focus aquatic stewardship education efforts at behaviors with ramifications along this spatial spectrum. Figure 1 provides examples for considering the spatial dimensions of aquatic resource-related behaviors. Some behaviors will have mostly a local impact (e.g., cleaning up one's own small pond); other behaviors contribute to a larger, collective impact on the global environment (e.g., driving a hybrid vehicle, with associated reduced emissions).

Because aquatic stewardship focuses on human behavior, questions arise whether the motivation for that behavior must be internal (from within the individual) or whether it can be external and still be sustainable. Knuth and Siemer (2004) address this issue in their discussion of ethics-based stewardship. See Figure 1 for examples of internally versus externally motivated behaviors. The concern with externally motivated behavior is centered on the potential for eventual

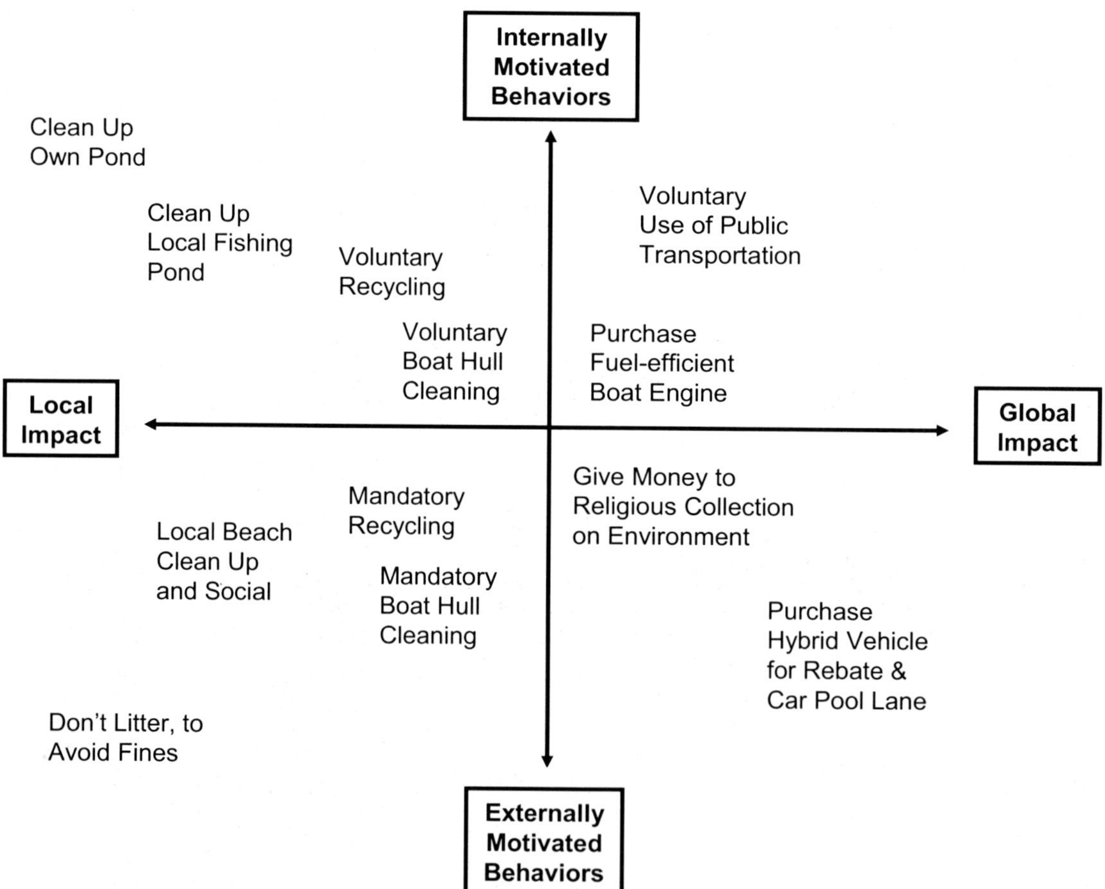

FIGURE 1. Examples of aquatic stewardship behaviors, demonstrating the components of scale (individual to global impact) and source of motivation (internal to external).

removal of the external stimulus. For example, if a tax rebate associated with purchase of hybrid vehicles is removed, would the behavior (buying and driving a hybrid vehicle) cease? More research is needed on the relative stability of internally versus externally motivated aquatic stewardship behaviors.

A large body of literature has addressed the general notion of determinants of behavior, resulting in several main theories, most prominently the theory of reasoned action (Fishbein and Ajzen 1975), the theory of planned behavior (Ajzen 1991), and the model of interpersonal behavior (Triandis 1977). Each of these theories notes, to varying degrees, the importance of motivations, intentions, knowledge, social norms, attitudes, and beliefs in relation to behaviors. A meta-analysis of behavior change empirical studies (Webb and Sheeran 2006) suggests that behaviors sustained over time do not necessarily have to be consciously internally motivated. Schaefer (2006) noted the importance of addressing motivations underlying stewardship actions. Wood et al. (2002) suggested that the likelihood of engaging in certain behaviors is enhanced with consistent cues or stimuli from one's surroundings. Sheeran et al. (2005) emphasized the importance of an individual understanding how to implement the specific steps required for a particular action. Hungerford and Volk's (1990) work on environmentally responsible behavior echoed a similar theme, noting the importance of entry-level variables, ownership variables, and empowerment variables; Siemer and Knuth (2001) applied these categories of variables to fishing education programs specifically. Zelezny (1999) conducted a meta-analysis of educational interventions and their relationship to environmental behaviors, concluding that (1) there are strong correlations between knowledge and behavior, (2) outreach interventions can improve environmental behavior, and (3) interventions that most effectively improve environmental behavior actively involve participants.

Collectively, these studies support the definition of aquatic stewardship education offered in the RBFF report, "Defining Best Practices in Boating, Fishing, and Stewardship Education" (Fedler 2001), as "a complex process by which related skills, attitudes, knowledge, and behaviors are enhanced, developed, and supported through a planned series of experiences." In the past decade, a variety of educational programs focusing on aquatic stewardship have been undertaken. The time is ripe to describe and evaluate those efforts, to improve our collective understanding of this complex process and identify next steps for the future.

Symposium Goals

Existing literature, empirical studies, and knowledge gained from implementation of on-the-ground stewardship education programs can provide insights about how to motivate individuals to wish to be good aquatic stewards (focusing on attitudes, intentions, and motivations) and how to empower individuals to be able to be good stewards (focusing on skills and behaviors). This symposium was intended to bring together a group of aquatic stewardship education practitioners and researchers to focus discussion on what is known about stewardship education programs and their results and to identify challenges, opportunities, and information needs.

The goal of the symposium and this proceedings volume is to advance our understanding of (1) how stewardship is defined in theory and practice, (2) the approaches that are necessary to promote and foster desirable stewardship behaviors, and (3) how measures of aquatic stewardship might be used to evaluate progress toward goals. We designed the symposium content to include a mix of theory, empirical data, and practice (through case studies). We also designed the content to focus largely on programs related to fishing and boating in recognition of these groups as critical stakeholders in aquatic resource management, although we included some broader watershed conservation programs as well. It is important for fisheries professionals and aquatic resource educators to be involved in many types of outreach, with many audiences and partners, if societal goals for aquatic resource management and conservation are to be achieved.

The symposium included three main topics: issues in defining stewardship, issues in fostering stewardship, and issues in evaluating stewardship. Part I, Stewardship Definition and Management Challenges, presents an overview of concerns related to aquatic stewardship education (this chapter) and describes the tensions that exist between theory and practice, particularly at the state management agency level when confronting the potentially opposing missions of fostering participation in consumptive recreational activities (fishing, boating) and at the same time managing to maintain, restore, protect, and conserve sometimes fragile fisheries resources (Wattendorf and Lyman 2007, this volume).

Parts II and III were designed to include attention to both theory and practice (through case studies of particular stewardship education programs). Part II, Fostering Stewardship: Theory and Practice, considers how best education practices can be applied in stewardship education programs (Andrews 2007, this volume) and how government and nongovernment boating, fishing, and watershed interests can be involved in fostering aquatic stewardship. Grack Nelson and Matthees focus on Minnesota's pioneering efforts, in "Developing Tomorrow's Anglers and Aquatic Stewards: Formative Evaluation of MinnAqua's Leader's Guide" (Grack Nelson and Mathees 2007, this volume). Day (2007, this volume) synthesizes concepts from environmental education theory and practice generally and offers suggested approaches specifically for aquatic stewardship education programs. Fontaine et al. (2007, this volume) provide insights not readily available in the published literature because recreational boating has often been ignored in discussions of aquatic stewardship. Similarly, Lydecker (2007, this volume) provides practical suggestions for working with boating audiences to encourage stewardship. Blair (2007, this volume) provides insights on the role of nongovernmental organizations in stimulating aquatic stewardship, in this case focused on youth. Glick (2007, this volume) summarizes the goals and activities of a diverse set of aquatic stewardship programs, illustrating the important roles that may be played by different sectors. Tudor and O'Malley (2007, this volume) emphasize the opportunities to engage citizens more broadly (beyond anglers and boaters) in aquatic resource stewardship, focusing on efforts in Washington State. Siemer and Hitzhusen (2007) also move beyond the angling and boating clientele to illustrate opportunities to partner with faith communities in achieving goals for aquatic steward- ship education and behavior

among a broader citizenry. Finally, Burger and Barnes (2007, this volume) describe the efforts of fisheries professionals to foster aquatic stewardship and suggest avenues for new partnerships to increase the impact of these efforts.

Part III, Measuring Stewardship: Indicators and Outcomes, suggests potential measures of desirable outcomes and impacts of aquatic stewardship education programs and provides examples of how elements of the outcomes and impacts of these programs may be evaluated. Loftus (2007, this volume) suggests a series of aquatic stewardship indicators that could be used to measure the extent of stewardship behaviors and impact within the recreational boating sector. Seng and White (2007, this volume) provide a similar analysis, applied to aquatic stewardship in the recreational fisheries sector. McMullin et al. (2007) offer initial data from a larger study designed to address one of the fundamental assumptions that prompted this symposium, whether participation in recreational angling or boating is positively associated with aquatic stewardship. Bruskotter and Fulton (2007) apply social science theory on value orientations to improve understanding of factors that influence the prevalence of aquatic stewardship. Fedler (2007) evaluates an aquatic stewardship outreach program targeted towards youth.

The symposium concluded with a panel discussion to help draw conclusions across these topics, and to address several important questions, including what is being accomplished and what more should be done to

- encourage the use of best practices in aquatic stewardship education,
- strengthen partnerships (government and nongovernment),
- develop acceptable and appropriate measures of aquatic stewardship,
- conduct and fund evaluation and improvement of stewardship education programs,
- foster greater dialogue among fisheries professional about methods and venues to promote stewardship, and
- stimulate American Fisheries Society members to be involved in stewardship education and outreach.

Part IV, Future Directions for Aquatic Stewardship Education, synthesizes the panel's discussion of these topics and provides suggestions and recommendations for future efforts by fisheries professionals, aquatic resource educators, and researchers in support of aquatic stewardship education theory and practice (Knuth and Siemer 2007, this volume).

References

Ajzen, I. 1991. The theory of planned behavior. Organizational Behavior and Human Decision Processes 50:179–211.

Andrews, E. 2007. Fostering aquatic stewardship with the help of best education practices. Pages 25–32 *in* B. A. Knuth and W. F. Siemer, editors. Aquatic stewardship education in theory and practice. American Fisheries Society, Symposium 55, Bethesda, Maryland.

Arlinghaus, R. 2005. A conceptual framework to identify and understand conflicts in recreational fisheries systems, with implications for sustainable management. Aquatic Resources, Culture, and Development 1(2):145–174.

Blair, D. 2007. The Trout Unlimited experience teaching aquatic stewardship to youth. Pages 79–84 *in* B. A. Knuth and W. F. Siemer, editors. Aquatic stewardship education in theory and practice. American Fisheries Society, Symposium 55, Bethesda, Maryland.

Boyle, J. 1998. Cooperative agriculture leads the way on environmental stewardship. National Council of Farmer Cooperatives, American-Coop, Washington, D.C.

Bruskotter, J. T., and D. C. Fulton. 2007. The influence of angler value orientations on fisheries stewardship norms. Pages 157–167 *in* B. A. Knuth and W. F. Siemer, editors. Aquatic stewardship education in theory and practice. American Fisheries Society, Symposium 55, Bethesda, Maryland.

Burger, C. V., and M. E. Barnes. 2007. The role of the American Fisheries Society in fostering aquatic resources stewardship: past successes, future opportunities. Pages 117–123 *in* B. A. Knuth and W. F. Siemer, editors. Aquatic stewardship education in theory and practice. American Fisheries Society, Symposium 55, Bethesda, Maryland.

Cole-Misch, S., L. Price, D. Schmidt, D. Smith, S. Fields, and R. Goto. 1996. Sourcebook for watershed education. Kendall/Hunt Publishing Company, Dubuque, Iowa.

Dahl, T. E. 1990. Wetland losses in the U.S. 1970's to 1980's. U.S. Department of the Interior, Fish and Wildlife Service, Washington D.C.

Day, B. 2007. Environmental education for aquatic stewardship. Pages 45–53 *in* B. A. Knuth and W. F. Siemer, editors. Aquatic stewardship education in theory and practice. American Fisheries Society, Symposium 55, Bethesda, Maryland.

Dixon, S. P., A. C. Birchenough, S. M. Evans, and M. P. Quigley. 2005. Children's knowledge of birds: how can it be improved and cat it be used to conserve wildlife? Transactions of the Natural History Society of Northumbria 64 (Part 3):121–133.

Fedler, A. J. 2007. A test of aquatic education and stewardship relationships among youth. Pages 169–175 *in* B. A. Knuth and W. F. Siemer, editors. Aquatic stewardship education in theory and practice. American Fisheries Society, Symposium 55, Bethesda, Maryland.

Fedler, A. J. 2001. Defining best practices in boating, fishing, and stewardship education. Recreational Boating and Fishing Foundation, Alexandria, Virginia.

Fedler, A. J., W. F. Siemer, B. A. Knuth, and B. E. Matthews. 2001. Developing aquatic resource stewards. Taproot (Coalition for Education in the Outdoors) 12(4):9–15.

Fishbein, M., and I. Ajzen. 1975. Belief, attitude, intention and behavior: an introduction to theory and research. Addison Wesley, Reading, Massachusetts.

Fontaine, M. W., M. P. Dunn, and D. Lijana. 2007. Overview of the recreational boating industry's aquatic stewardship through technology, innovation, and education. Pages 55–72 *in* B. A. Knuth and W. F. Siemer, editors. Aquatic stewardship education in theory and practice. American Fisheries Society, Symposium 55, Bethesda, Maryland.

Glick, A. L. 2007. Government, nongovernment organizations, and industry: programs that foster aquatic stewardship. Pages 85–91 *in* B. A. Knuth and W. F. Siemer, editors. Aquatic stewardship education in theory and practice. American Fisheries Society, Symposium 55, Bethesda, Maryland.

Grack Nelson, A., and J. Matthees. 2007. Developing tomorrow's anglers and aquatic stewards: formative evaluation of MinnAqua's leaders' guide. Pages 33–43 *in* B. A. Knuth and W. F. Siemer, editors. Aquatic stewardship education in theory and practice. American Fisheries Society, Symposium 55, Bethesda, Maryland.

Holland, L., and J. S. Carter. 2005. Words v. deeds: a comparison of religious belief and environmental action. Sociological Spectrum 25:739–753.

Knuth, B. A., and W. F. Siemer. 2004. Fostering aquatic stewardship: a key for fisheries sustainability. Pages 243–255 *in* E. E. Knudsen, D. D. MacDonald, and Y. K. Muirhead, editors. American Fisheries Society, Symposium 43, Bethesda, Maryland.

Knuth, B. A., and W. F. Siemer. 2007. Advancing the theory and practice of aquatic stewardship education. Pages 179–187 *in* B. A. Knuth and W. F. Siemer, editors. Aquatic stewardship education in theory and practice. American Fisheries Society, Symposium 55, Bethesda, Maryland.

Loftus, A. J. 2007. Measures of aquatic stewardship behavior from the boating perspective. Pages 127–135 *in* B. A. Knuth and W. F. Siemer, editors. Aquatic stewardship education in theory and practice. American Fisheries Society, Symposium 55, Bethesda, Maryland.

Lydecker, R. 2007. Fostering boating-related aquatic stewardship: reaching the boater. Pages 73–77 *in* B. A. Knuth and W. F. Siemer, editors. Aquatic stewardship education in theory and practice. American Fisheries Society, Symposium 55, Bethesda, Maryland.

McMullin, S. L., K. S. Hockett, and J. A. McClafferty. 2007. Does angling or boating improve the stewardship ethic of participants? Pages 145–155 *in* B. A. Knuth and W. F. Siemer, editors. Aquatic stewardship education in theory and practice. American Fisheries Society, Symposium 55, Bethesda, Maryland.

Moyle, P. B. and R. A. Leidy. 1992. Loss of biodiversity in aquatic ecosystems: evidence from fish faunas. Pages 127–170 *in* P. L. Fiedler and S. K. Jain, editors. Conservation biology: the theory and practice of nature conservation, preservation, and management. Chapman and Hall, New York.

National Marine Manufacturers Association. 2003. 2003 recreational boating abstract National Marine Manufacturers Association, Chicago.

Scarlett, L. 2004. Citizen stewardship and the environment. Society 41(6):7–11.

Schaefer, V. 2006. Science, stewardship, and spirituality: The human body as a model for ecological restoration. Restoration Ecology 14(1):1–3.

Seng, P. T., and G. M. White. 2007. Measures of aquatic stewardship from a fisheries perspective. Pages 137–143 *in* B. A. Knuth and W. F. Siemer, editors. Aquatic stewardship education in theory and practice. American Fisheries Society, Symposium 55, Bethesda, Maryland.

Sheeran, P., T. L. Webb, and P. M. Gollwitzer. 2005. The interplay between goal intentions and implementation intentions. Personality and Social Psychology Bulletin 31:87–98.

Sia, A. P. H. R. Hungerford, and A. N. Tomera. 1986. Selected predictors of responsible environmental behavior: an analysis. Journal of Environmental Education 17:31–40.

Siemer, W. F. and G. E. Hitzhusen. 2007. Revisiting the stewardship concept: faith-based opportunities to bridge from principles to practice. Pages 103–116 *in* B. A. Knuth and W. F. Siemer, editors. Aquatic stewardship education in theory and practice. American Fisheries Society, Symposium 55, Bethesda, Maryland.

Siemer, W. F., and B. A. Knuth. 2001. Effects of fishing education programs on antecedents of responsible environmental behavior. Journal of Environmental Education 32(4):23–29.

Sivek, D. 1989. An analysis of selected predictors of environmental behavior of three conservation organizations. dissertation Abstracts International 49(11):3222-A.

SFBPC (Sport Fishing and Boating Partnership Council). 2002. A partnership agenda for fisheries conservation. U.S. Fish and Wildlife Services, Washington, D.C.

Triandis, H. C. 1977. Interpersonal behavior. Brooks/Cole, Monterey, California.

Tudor, M., and M. O'Malley. 2007. Citizen science: stewardship education in Washington State. Pages 93–101 *in* B. A. Knuth and W. F. Siemer, editors. Aquatic stewardship education in theory and practice. American Fisheries Society, Symposium 55, Bethesda, Maryland.

Wattendorf, B., and J. Lyman. 2007. Reconciling fishing and boating promotion with safe, sustainable use. Pages 11–21 *in* B. A. Knuth and W. F. Siemer, editors. Aquatic stewardship education in theory and practice. American Fisheries Society, Symposium 55, Bethesda, Maryland.

Webb, T. L., and P. Sheeran. 2006. Does changing behavioral intentions engender behavior change? A meta-analysis of the experimental evidence. Psychological Bulletin 132(2):249–268.

Wells, N., and K. Lekies. 2006. Nature and the life course: pathways from childhood nature experiences to adult environmentalism. Children, Youth, and Environments 16(1):1–24.

Williams, J. E., J. E. Johnson, D. A. Hendrickson, S. Contreras-Balderas, J. D. Williams, M. Navarro-Mendoza, D. E. McAllister, and J. E. Deacon. 1989. Fishes of North America endangered, threatened, or of special concern: 1989. Fisheries 14(6):2–20.

Wood, W., J. M. Quinn, and D. Kashy. 2002. Habits in everyday life: the thought and feel of action. Journal of Personality and Social Psychology 83:1281–1297.

Zelezny, L. C. 1999. Educational interventions that improve environmental behaviors: a meta-analysis. Journal of Environmental Education 31:5–14.

American Fisheries Society Symposium 55:11–21, 2007

Reconciling Fishing and Boating Promotion with Safe, Sustainable Use

BOB WATTENDORF[1]
Florida Fish and Wildlife Conservation Commission
620 South Meridian Street, Tallahassee, Florida 32399, USA

JON LYMAN[2]
Alaska Department of Game and Fish
1255 West 8th Street, Juneau, Alaska 99801, USA

Abstract: Fishery management agencies face the potentially opposing missions of fostering participation in consumptive recreational activities (fishing, boating) and, at the same time, managing to maintain, restore, protect, and conserve sometimes fragile fisheries resources. We discuss how two conservation agencies representing states as geographically, biologically, demographically, and climatically different as Florida and Alaska address the challenges of promoting recreational fishing use, while trying to sustain fragile fisheries resources and provide quality fishing opportunities for all types of anglers. In both cases, promotion of recreational fishing within appropriate constraints and with well-tailored outreach and conservation education messages are considered justified and necessary to the future of healthy fisheries and their continuing management.

Introduction

It is well known that the Grand Banks cod fishery was one of the enabling commercial ventures that allowed the original American colonies to survive and thrive. Similarly, both Native Americans and colonists exploited freshwater fisheries for their subsistence. What is perhaps less well known is that in North America, there was recognition of the value of recreational fishing as a way to renew the human psyche as far back as colonial days. In 1739, Reverend Seccombe wrote that fishing is the best way to renew oneself for the Lord's work on Sunday in his sermon *Business and Diversion Inoffensive to God* (Seccombe 1743). Thaddeus Norris, in his 1864 publication *The American Angler's Book,* specifically referred to the need for conservation (Norris 1864). Thus, recreational, subsistence, and commercial fishing are deep-rooted American traditions, requiring an empowered conservation stewardship ethic to be sustainable. Stewardship

requires self restraint and an ethic devoted to sustaining the resource. Those needs have grown over the years as human populations have expanded and uses of our aquatic resources have intensified.

As the 13 original colonies multiplied and expanded across the continent, citizens took the desire to fish with them, making it a part of the American tradition. From the beginnings of state-level fisheries management, agencies have been faced with reconciling the competing demands of use and protection of fisheries resources.

The Challenges

Fisheries resources occur within a human context that is much more complex for the manager than simply regulating the limited act of fishing or stocking fish. In addition to the resource-related impacts potentially posed by harvest activities, fisheries resources are affected by a multitude of human-related impacts.

Czech and Pfister (2005) introduced a series of articles in *Fisheries* entitled "Economic Growth, Fish Conservation, and the American Fisheries So-

---

[1] E-mail: Bob.Wattendorf@MyFWC.com
[2] E-mail: jon_lyman@fishgame.state.ak.us

ciety." They contended that neoclassical economists, especially many of the policy makers pursuing a macroeconomic goal of increasing gross domestic product, fail to recognize that pursuing economic growth is at the competitive exclusion of fish and wildlife in the aggregate. Whitehead et al. (2005) responded that many economists, at least those knowledgeable about conservation issues, agree that there is a conflict between economic growth and environmental protection, but analyze the underlying problem differently and therefore reach different conclusions. Whitehead et al. (2005) cite the economic analysis of pollution (Pigou 1920) and of market failures due to overharvesting fisheries (Gordon 1954) as examples of how economic and market principles can be utilized to optimize long-term cost-benefits and as conservation tools to help achieve sustainability. Hartman and Northcote (2005) emphasized the need to focus more on the population growth component of economic impacts, due to its effect on ecosystems and specifically energy scenarios.

The rate of human population growth is continuing. Between 2000 and 2004, for example, Alaska's population expanded by 4.5% to more than 655,000 (Quick Facts 2005), with more than half concentrated in and around Anchorage. Meanwhile, Florida's population grew by 8.8%, exceeding 17 million. Population density in Alaska is 3 people/km^2 in Alaska, and in Florida, 767 people/km^2. Their simple presence is a challenge to conservation agencies trying to protect native habitats and ensure water quality, quantity, and schedules that support native fish communities.

We add the impact on freshwater use to the overall concerns about human population growth. Although people want to live on shorelines and near the water, they seek to tame nature to prevent their properties from flooding or being left high and dry and to use that water for farming, industry, and personal use.[3] People further seek to customize the scenery to their own liking by altering the

flora and fauna, including importing exotic species—all of which can wreak havoc on natural fisheries. As human populations grow, demand on freshwater supplies and habitat alterations increase, adversely affecting fish and other aquatic wildlife. Those impacts are independent of fishing or boating pressures and must be mitigated by proactive management to conserve the resource.

Direct impacts from anglers and boaters have also increased over time, although not proportionally to the human population. In 2003, Alaska certified for Federal Aid in Sport Fish Restoration (Federal Aid)[4] a total of 442,474 paid license holders; 59% of those were sold to nonresident tourists (USFWS 2003). Alaska's certifications have increased 8% since 1999. The same year, Florida certified 1,045,564 paid license holders, with 29% of the sales going to nonresidents. Since 1999, Florida's certifications have dropped 13% and now represent 3.7% of licenses certified nationally, versus 5.9% in 1999. Much of the reduction in this percentage of certified paid license holders is due to other states beginning to charge license fees for senior citizens, reducing the age at which youth purchase licenses, and removing other exemptions, rather than an actual change in fishing participation.[5] The results in Florida include less direct license-based revenue for fisheries management and less Federal Aid for conservation (Wattendorf 2000).

Fishing pressure may also be measured based on anglers/km^2 of inland water.[6] In Alaska, 13

---

[3] Per capita water use in North America is 1,280 m^3/d of water, which is seven times more per person than in Africa (see information regarding current water resources conditions on the U.S. Geological Survey Web site: http://water.usgs.gov/waterwatch/?m=real&r=fl), dramatically changing water availability, quality and schedules.

[4] Federal Aid in Sport Fish Restoration (also known as Dingell-Johnson or Wallop-Breaux) collects excise taxes on sportfishing-related products, motorboat fuel taxes, and import duties on pleasure vessels and returns them to the states based on a formula that includes paid-fishing-license holders (individuals not licenses) and the area of the state for fisheries conservation work.

[5] The amount being the consequence of an allocation formula based on the size of the state's land and water area and number of paid fishing license holders granted.

[6] Permanent inland water surface, such as lakes, reservoirs, and ponds having an area of 40 acres or more; streams, sloughs, estuaries, and canals one-eighth statute mile or more in width; deeply indented embayments and sounds, and other coastal waters behind or sheltered by headlands or islands separated by less than 1 nautical mile of water, and islands under 40 acres in area. The figure excludes areas of oceans, bays, or sounds lying within U.S. jurisdiction but not defined as inland water.

people/km^2 use the resource, whereas in Florida, 238 anglers share each square kilometer of inland water. However, in Alaska, the majority of sportfishing activity takes place in the limited areas accessible by road, with approximately one-third of all sport fishing pressure occurring on Kenai Peninsula streams and rivers.

The combination of societal pressures on aquatic resources generally, and the magnitude of fishing activity on fisheries resources specifically, provide important challenges to fishery managers. There is the need to reduce adverse impacts on fishery and aquatic resources while, at the same time, preserving the revenue stream of the agencies and fostering a human population that recognizes the importance of good stewardship of aquatic resources.

Fishing and Anglers—Source of Both Revenue and Impacts

A major difference between habitat pressures caused by overall human population growth, economic development, and commercial uses of water, versus resource pressures caused by recreational fishing, is that anglers pay directly for conservation. In addition, sport fishers may also better understand their impacts on fisheries resources and may seek to mitigate those impacts through stewardship behaviors. Therefore, anglers appear to have more direct potential to be part of the solution to problems caused by their impacts than do other users.

In Alaska, during fiscal year 2004, license sales generated $13.1 million toward fisheries resources management, and Federal Aid provided $14.7 million in matching funds. In Florida, fishing license sales generated $22.4 million for conservation, but Federal Aid provided only an additional $7.9 million, due to the funding equation being based on the area of the state and number of paid license holders.

An important consideration when evaluating fishing pressure is the ratio of resident to nonresident anglers and the average amount of time each spends fishing annually. Even though Florida is the leading nonresident angling destination in the United States, Florida sells more than twice as many fishing privileges to residents ($12/year) as to nonresidents ($15 for 7 d or $30/year), and residents average 21 d fishing/year, versus 6 d fishing/year for out-of-state visitors (USFWS 2001). With a year-round fishing season, residents generate significantly more fishing pressure for a lower per-unit return than do nonresidents who buy licenses. In Alaska, residents ($24/year) average 13 d fishing/year, while nonresidents ($55 for 7 d or $145/year) averaged only 4 d fishing/year. The ratio of residents to nonresidents, coupled with license fee costs, is therefore especially important when balancing return on investment and the impact of increased license sales on fisheries and the state's economy.

In the context of expanding human populations adversely affecting aquatic resources through impacts on water and habitats coupled with the direct effect on fish populations that anglers cause through harvest, why promote fishing at all? First, we note the value of the personal, esthetic, and spiritual benefits that individual anglers and their fishing partners derive from the sport. Second, we as fisheries managers believe that anglers convey some of those values to society and thereby increase the desire to conserve and restore natural resources, fostering a stewardship ethic that benefits fisheries. Third, over our careers as fisheries managers, we have observed the feeling of involvement and ownership anglers experience from paying for their sport, either through license fees or into the general economy (e.g., purchasing tackle, bait, ice, fuel), generating a further commitment to protect the resource.

Reconciling the "Ugly Money" Issue

We concur with the position taken by Whitehead et al. (2005) that solid market research and economic analysis can help pave the way to ensuring adequate funding and sustainable resources. It is critical that this be done in a way that emphasizes conservation of all species, healthy populations of important recreational and commercial species and is consistent with the public's preferences and the common good.

State-based tax systems provide some funds for general environmental quality initiatives, but the vast majority of fisheries and aquatic resource management in the United States is funded through a user-pays/user-benefits scenario to finance most habitat protection and restoration, as well as research and other specific fisheries management programs (Congressional Sportsmen's Foundation 2001). Fishing license sales and excise taxes on fishing tackle and motorboat fuel taxes pay for the majority of conservation programs. Relatively little general tax monies typically go towards sustaining the future of the resource or recreational activities. In 2003, Alaska's Division of Sport Fish spent approximately $35 million, of which $26 million (74%) came from user-pay sources, including the sale of fishing licenses, stamps, and federal taxes on sportfish-ing-related equipment and fuel (Table 1). Given the overall economic impact of sport fisheries in Alaska was more than a billion dollars, that represents just a 3.3% reinvestment of the overall economic value of recreational fisheries (Table 2).

In Florida,[7] approximately $40 million is available annually for fisheries conservation, with

____

[7] Due to a recent restructuring in Florida, there are now Freshwater and Saltwater Fisheries Management Divisions that each receives about $4 million annually. The Florida Wildlife Research Institute receives about $39 million for all of the agency's research needs covering fish and wildlife including sport, nongame, and imperiled species and their habitats. About 40% of that goes to fisheries related work and much of that comes from specific grants. The Division of Habitat and Species Conservation gets about $61 million to do a similar array of restoration work, with perhaps 30% going to fisheries. Documentary stamps are a significant additional revenue source for this work.

$30.4 million (75%) coming from license sales and Sport Fish Restoration. The reinvestment in the resource related to the value of recreational fishing ($7.4 billion) is 0.5%. In Florida, the legislature is pushing the agency to be more self-sufficient and reducing the amount of general revenue available for conservation.

Flather and Hoekstra (1989), in analyzing the future of fishing on U.S. Forest Service properties, stated that "Important social implications are associated with fish and wildlife resources including cultural, psychological, physiological, and societal aspects of public welfare. Declining inventories and use restrictions infringe on the lifestyles of certain cultural groups and reduce or eliminate a recreational outlet for which few substitutes exist." Americans participate in a wide range of outdoor recreation activities, and outdoor recreation remains a pervasive leisure-time use across the nation with 87% participating in an outdoor recreational activity during 2003 (RoperASW 2004). Fishing ranked fifth-most popular, with 28% of Americans participating, behind fitness walking, pleasure drives, swimming and picnicking, but ahead of biking, running and camping. Fishing had more participants than golf and tennis combined. Consequently, we suggest that it is in the public interest to continue to provide recreational fishing opportunities.

So then, how do agencies as diverse as the Alaska Department of Fish and Game and the Florida Fish and Wildlife Conservation Commission address their missions while accommodating growth and fishing pressure? Both agencies

TABLE 1. Fishing pressure is only partially represented by license sales, but those sales and the resulting draw from Federal Aid in Sportfish Restoration account for the vast majority of fisheries conservation funding (USFWS 2003).

Fiscal year 2003	Fisheries budget	License revenue	Sportfish Restoration match	Total user revenue	Percentage of budget from users
ALASKA	$35,000,000	$13,067,536	$13,262,060	$26,329,596	74%
FLORIDA	$40,000,000[a]	$22,448,453	$7,422,277	$29,870,730	75%

[a] Florida Fish and Wildlife Conservation Commission recently underwent an internal restructuring. There are now Freshwater and Saltwater Fisheries Management Divisions that each receives about $4 million annually. However, the Florida Wildlife Research Institute receives about $39 million for all agency research, and the Division of Habitat and Species Management gets about $61 million for restoration work. Our best estimate, to compare to activities covered in Alaska, is $40 million is dedicated to fisheries.

TABLE 2. Recreational fishing provides a variety of emotional and social benefits to anglers. Additionally, the economic contribution anglers make to the local community is immense, yet only a minimal amount is reinvested into resource conservation (USFWS 2001).

Fiscal year 2003	Fisheries budget	Retail sales	Total economic effect	Wages	Sales and motor fuel taxes	Jobs	Percent invested
ALASKA	$35,000,000	$640,000,000	$1,047,000,000	$260,000,000	$3,000,000	12,065	3.3%
FLORIDA	$40,000,000[a]	$4,061,000,000	$7,353,000,000	$1,967,000,000	$224,000,000	78,849	0.5%

[a] The Florida Fish and Wildlife Conservation Commission recently underwent an internal restructuring. There are now Freshwater and Saltwater Fisheries Management Divisions that each receives about $4 million annually. However, the Florida Wildlife Research Institute receives about $39 million for all agency research, and the Division of Habitat and Species Management gets about $61 million for restoration work. Our best estimate, to compare to activities covered in Alaska, is $40 million is dedicated to fisheries.

have similar missions[8] that speak first to sustaining and enhancing the fish and wildlife resources and then specifically to the "benefit of people." Clearly, neither agency, both of which used stakeholder input processes to create their strategies and mission statements, believes that preservation of the resource by excluding public use is appropriate. But is there a limit regarding how many people should have access to fisheries resources, or a preference for which people have different types of access, use, and harvest ability? Should we promote recreational fishing to ensure a grassroots base for conservation issues and to help solidify funding for important conservation research and management purposes? Or, should we simply build the opportunities and let those who want to and know how to fish do so without encouraging others to participate?

Core Services and Goals of the Alaska Department of Game and Fish point to the importance of providing opportunities to utilize fisheries resources, keeping the public informed and involved with decision making, and optimizing economic benefits and public participation. Arguably then, it is an agency function to recruit anglers and conservation stewards while optimizing economic

considerations. Alaska's Board of Fisheries allocates fisheries resources among commercial, subsistence, personal use, and sport-user groups according to a seven-step rationale. The process considers historic use, group sizes, an emphasis on resident subsistence, alternate choices, state and local economic concerns, and recreational use.

Similarly, the Florida Fish and Wildlife Conservation Commission's long-term objectives specify (1) to provide for increasing or stable fish and wildlife populations, and (2) to increase the number of customers and continue to provide customer satisfaction. So even more directly in Florida, there is a clear challenge to build the customer base and ensure satisfaction, while providing sustainable fisheries. At the same time, a major concern exists about our ability to do both simultaneously.

Within Florida's Division of Freshwater Fisheries Management budgets have been very limiting; angler involvement in sociopolitical issues has been minimal and diffused, and there is a belief that we can spread the pressure among various water bodies and species without impacting negatively customer satisfaction and fishing quality. Consequently, the Division of Freshwater Fisheries Management has a marketing plan to promote safe, sustainable participation and generate revenue and support for conservation stewardship.

On the other hand, Florida's Division of Marine Fisheries Management has major concerns about the impact of concentrating fishing on key species, locations, and times, such as the Boca Grande tarpon season. Their funding is somewhat more di-

---

[8] —Alaska Department of Fish and Game Mission: To protect, maintain, and improve the fish, game, and aquatic plant resources of the state, and manage their use and development for the maximum benefit of the people of the state, consistent with the sustained yield principle.
—Florida Fish and Wildlife Conservation Commission Mission: To manage fish and wildlife resources for their long-term well-being and the benefit of people.

verse, and having been supplemented by license sales for the first time in 1990, they are less dependent than freshwater programs on angling revenues. Moreover, saltwater anglers and guides are well organized and vocal, and along with a statewide marine recreational fishing publication, have the potential to affect attitudes and help to communicate about important conservation issues. As a consequence, there is less focused effort in the marine sector on promoting recreational fishing.

Florida freshwater and saltwater license sales vary compared to population growth, which has reached 17 million (Figure 1).[9] In general, saltwater licenses have increased and kept pace with population growth. However, freshwater license sales declined in 1989/1990 when saltwater licenses were first sold, which also coincided with a 50% price increase in freshwater license sales, and a media-fueled scare regarding mercury in Florida fish (Florida Department of Health 2005). Although freshwater license sales never fully recovered, they have shown some gradual increase. This further emphasizes the rationale for the saltwater division being comfortable with participation rates, while the freshwater division is interested in increasing participation to generate both public support and revenue to meet existing conservation needs.

Alaska has experienced steady human population growth, with the population reaching two-thirds of a million people. Generally, license sales follow overall population growth, even though typically about 59–75% of sales are to nonresidents (Figure 2).[10] Tourists have been the growth sector in Alaska, but education programming seeks to promote more resident sportfishing.

---

[9] Florida began selling saltwater fishing licenses about half-way through fiscal year 1989/1990, at the same time that annual resident freshwater license fees increased from $7 to $12 (same as the new saltwater license, and other fees increased proportionally). Since that time, license fees have not changed significantly, so there has been nearly a 50% loss in spending power. Saltwater license sales have more closely approximated population increases than have freshwater license sales.

[10] Alaska's population has steadily increased, and thanks to nonresident license sales, fishing license sales have increased correspondingly. Periodic adjustments to the cost of licenses have kept the value of the licenses increasing.

Approaches to Stewardship Education in Alaska and Florida

Alaska has made stewardship education a significant initiative. They also engage strategies involving information dissemination related to recreational fishing opportunities and sponsor kids and family fishing "days" to develop skills, knowledge, and attitudes needed to be responsible anglers and stewards. Alaska furthermore has one of the most intense public regulation processes in the country, with a citizen board that hears more than 400 public proposals annually.

The cultural mixes of attitudes toward fish prevent establishing a single stewardship ethic in Alaska, where "Fish are Food." They have always been at the heart of native cultures, at the core of the Alaskan economy, and a primary reason sportfishers spend huge sums of money. Each of these groups must be treated fairly and appropriately apportioned a part of the resource.

Sport anglers remain largely harvest-oriented, although nonresident sport anglers bring different patterns of behavior with them to Alaska, including in some recreational fisheries a catch-and-release philosophy that can be very controversial with natives (Lyman 2002). Commercial fisheries still harvest the vast majority of fish. In Alaska, subsistence fishing is much more than just the taking of fish as food. Fish are at the heart of most native cultures where "cutting and hanging" fish is essential to their life style.

Since behavior toward the fish resource is central to many varied cultural norms, Alaska Fish and Game focuses communication messages on natural history and the needs of fish for habitat throughout their life cycle. These education programs support the broadest variety of cultural responses toward fish and fishing possible, while teaching the essential science needed for the public to participate in the Board of Fisheries public input process and to make informed decisions. The Alaskan program looks for the "teachable moment" to expand people's understanding of stewardship, without seeking to change their culture.

Alaska's size dictates that its educational programs be regionally based. Formal education programs in the schools avoid becoming a series of only threshold experiences by employing repeat

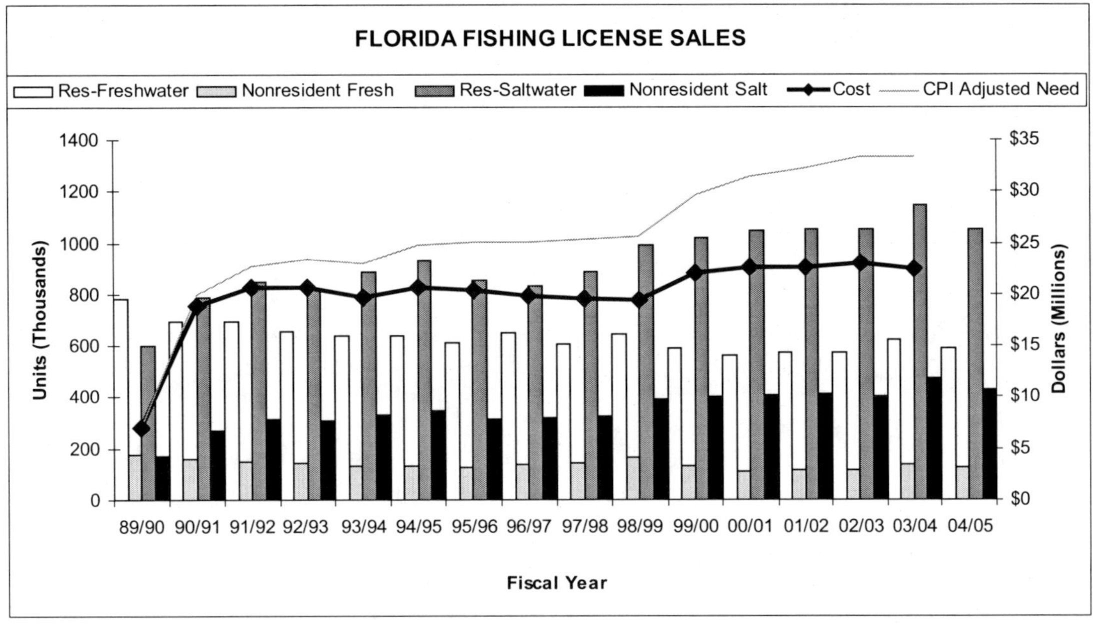

FIGURE 1. Florida fishing license sales, 1989–2005.

contact throughout the school year. The Alaska Water Watch program in the Southeast involves students in activities from water quality monitoring to fly tying, as well as providing access to angler education by supporting 4-H outdoor skills clubs and rod-loaner sites.

In much of Alaska, the Salmonids in the Classroom program teaches salmon biology, life cycles,

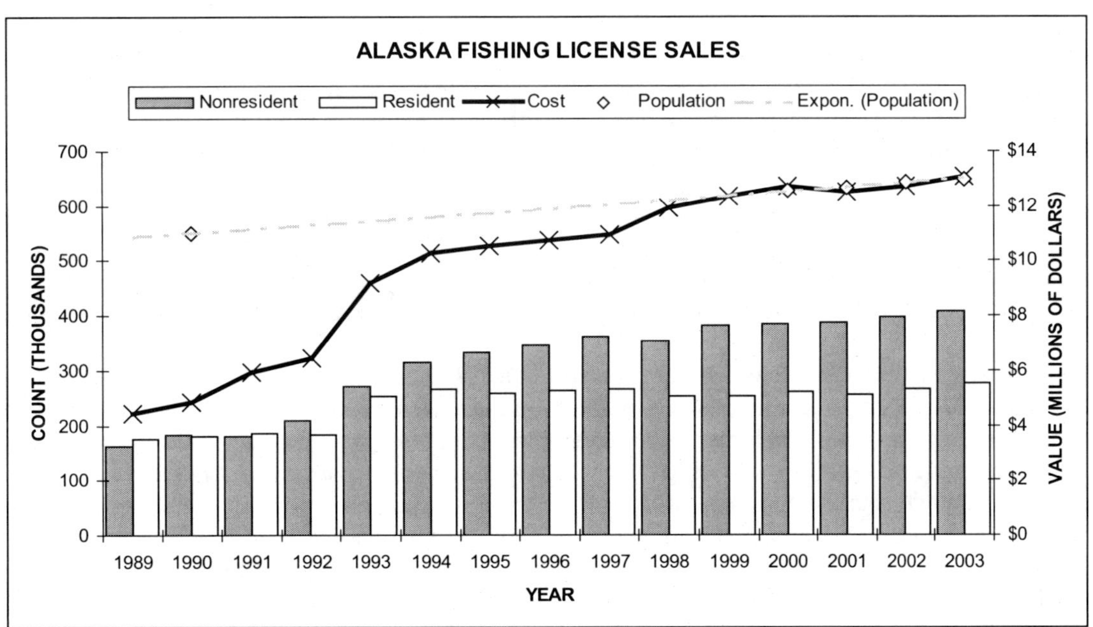

FIGURE 2. Alaska fishing license sales, 1989–2003.

stream health, and ice fishing. The program is delivered to more than 200 schools statewide. In the Interior, the Salmonids in the Classroom program is supplemented with village visits that focus on stream habitat and fish biology. Village residents also seem intrigued by sportfishing with a fly and request access to fly tying lessons, which is part of the educational effort.

Planning for education programming emphasizes resident angler recruitment. Accordingly, in Alaska the public looks to the Sportfish Division to support development of angler education Web sites, volunteer-led mentoring activities and additional angler access programs. The division also proposes additional support for long-term angler education efforts, including 4-H clubs, tackle loaner sites, Becoming an Outdoors Woman, Hooked on Fishing – Not on Drugs, and the Recreational Boating and Fishing Foundation's (RBFF) Physical Education Grants (administered by the Future Fisherman Foundation).

Florida approaches stewardship education and outreach issues in a similar way, adjusting to their own unique mix of cultures. Unfortunately, the Fish and Wildlife Conservation Commission has confronted a series of budget cuts in recent years that specifically targeted education and outreach programs that are not located within the Department of Education (a separate agency). Consequently, there have been serious cutbacks in these activities, in spite of the fact that both internal and external stakeholder surveys indicate these are some of the most important activities the agency performs. For instance, a recent survey of Floridians indicated that educating the public about fish and wildlife was the fifth most important thing the agency could do and ranked it 8.5 on a scale of 10 (Duda 2005a). Surprisingly, that is higher than the importance they assigned to items such as restoring native fish and wildlife, managing fisheries, or protecting the public from wildlife.

The Marine Fisheries Management Division has a well-established Outreach and Education section that uses a proactive approach to increase public participation in management of these resources. Saltwater fishing is encouraged along with ethical angling and boating practices by using a variety of methods, such as kids' fishing

clinics, women's fishing clinics, teacher workshops, marine field activities, and interactions at fishing-related shows and events.

Freshwater Fisheries continues to operate the Joe Budd Aquatic Education Center, where students participate in aquatic programs, ranging from studying pond life to wetland surveys that complement classroom learning. Intensive fisheries management and outreach programs are conducted in four urban communities around the state that produce family fishing events, especially around free-fishing weekend in April and National Fishing and Boating Week in June. However, most of the historic fishing clinics to teach youth about resource conservation and engage them in fishing were curtailed, as part of the legislative education cut backs and general budget shortfalls. Fish Orlando! is the biggest of the community-based programs, seeking to provide quality fishing for families; their premier event can attract 4,000 people. In all cases, Florida communications messages focus on safe and sustainable use and stewardship conservation. The Florida Fish and Wildlife Conservation Commission also supports use of Aquatic Wild, Hooked on Fishing – Not on Drugs, Teen Anglers, Becoming an Outdoors Woman, and the RBFF Physical Education Grants. Ladies, Let's Go Fishing is a saltwater program that the Marine Division helps finance.

In Florida, the marketing solution is to actively promote freshwater fishing and marginally promote saltwater. Overall, as one of the RBFF's focus states, Florida seeks to leverage the "Take me Fishing" theme. Florida also uses the theme of "Fishing Capital of the World." By encouraging anglers who fish without a license to purchase one, emphasizing up-selling current anglers, attracting nonresidents, conveying a message of ethical angling, and focusing on underutilized resources that can handle more pressure, Florida hopes to increase revenue and customer satisfaction and generate funds for resource conservation, while minimizing the increase in actual fishing pressure.

In Florida it is estimated that approximately half of the anglers using state fisheries resources do not buy fishing licenses. They are over 65 years old, under 16 years of age, fish in saltwater from shore or a licensed vessel or fishing pier, are disabled, or simply do not know they need a license or choose not to buy one. Adjusting exemptions and enforcing licensing requirements would greatly increase revenues, while not increasing fishing pressure and likely decreasing it. Similarly, it is possible to adjust license fees based on elasticity of demand and willingness to pay to either optimize revenues or to use as a tool to marginally decrease participation (Southwick et al. 2005). Use of tags or permits for high profile fish species can have similar beneficial effects by both raising funds for conservation and moderating fishing pressure and harvest. Recent efforts to evaluate and report public support for removing or altering exemptions or adjusting fees via the legislature have thus far been unsuccessful, since they are viewed as taxes. However, there will be an ongoing effort to understand more fully the preferences of Florida anglers and general public regarding fees and to better inform them of how license monies are used for conservation and how they affect Sportfish Restoration Funds. For instance, only 12% of the public know that fishing licenses fund conservation and only 1% are aware of Federal Aid in Sportfish Restoration (Duda 2005b), and 76% did not support giving exemptions to shoreline anglers. A similar series of online surveys and focus groups reiterated the need for enhanced communication of what the agency does and how it is funded (Group Solutions 2005).

Therefore, Florida seeks to encourage anglers who fish but do not buy a license to purchase one, either as a voluntary contribution or by making them more aware of their legal obligation to have a license. One such advertising campaign is directed at exempt seniors encouraging them to voluntarily purchase a license to support conservation and to help reclaim some of the Federal Aid taxes that they pay into Wallop-Breaux.

Similarly, by up-selling avid anglers to purchase a 5-year or lifetime license, Florida increases and stabilizes its funding without actually increasing pressure. Simultaneously, Florida develops better partners in the industry because they benefit from direct marketing to this targeted audience, and angler satisfaction is enhanced by giving them something for free.

Such promotions can dramatically affect sales (Figure 3),[11] in spite of anecdotal prejudices that say promotions do not work with regulatory products such as licenses. In addition, increased awareness from advertising may help increase the base level of sales.

The theme "Fishing Capital of the World" is based on statistics from the National Survey of Fishing, Hunting and Wildlife-Associated Recreation (Table 3), from International Game Fish Association records (more than 700 species and line class world records) and license-sales data. Florida ranks number one in overall economic impact ($7.4 billion), nonresident economic output ($1.5 billion), number of anglers (3.1 million), nonresident anglers (1 million), retail sales ($4.3 million), and recreational fishing-related jobs (80,000) (USFWS 2001; Southwick 2002). It is perceived as the ideal message to use in promoting to the nonresident audience because it enables Florida to tie in the privatized state tourism agency (VISIT FLORIDA). As mentioned previously, selling licenses to nonresidents provides a larger revenue stream ($30 for an annual, or $15 for a 7-d nonresident license versus $12 for an annual resident) and generates less fishing pressure and harvest than selling to residents. Hence, it is another way of reconciling fishing promotions with safe and sustainable use.

All of the Florida angler education programs, whether in house or piggy-backed with national programs, stress ethical fishing, stewardship skills, and safety. By using RBFF best practices, Florida anticipates developing a more stewardship-oriented fishing clientele, who are active spokes people and leaders in conservation issues.

Finally, Florida endeavors to promote use of underutilized fish species, techniques, and locations to divert pressure away from the most popular species and locations, while maintaining a high

---

[11] Florida's 5-year freshwater fishing license promotions have dramatically increased sales and awareness, while fostering good will with both industry partners and avid anglers. It is generated with virtually no increase in fishing pressure, since only avid anglers switch from annual to 5-year licenses, while substantially increasing revenue and helping to reduce churn.

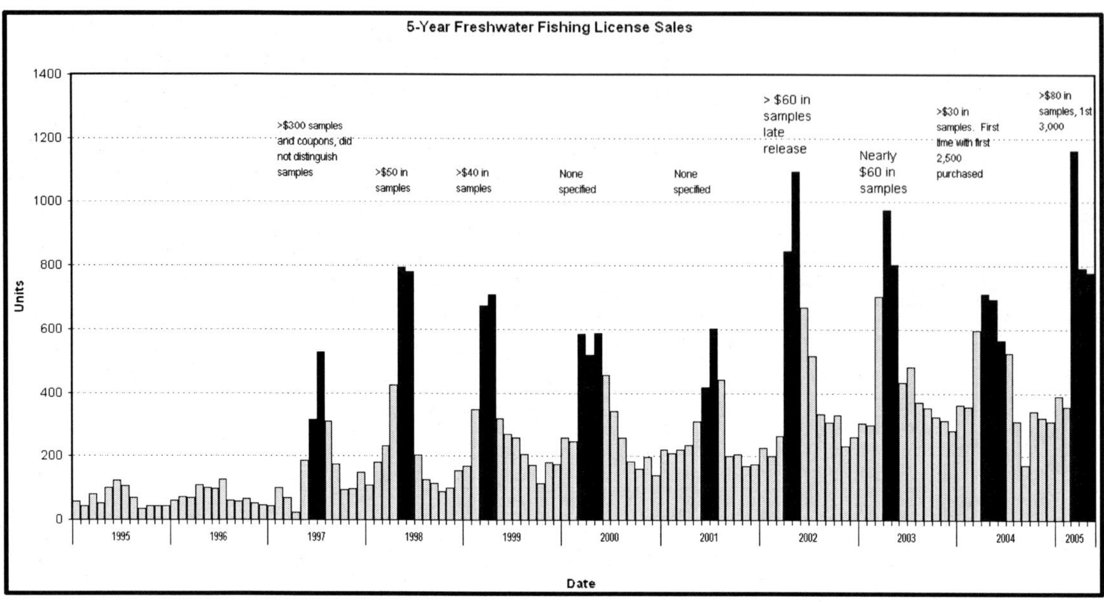

Figure 3. Florida 5-year freshwater fishing license sales, corresponding to active promotion period. Gray bars represent normal sales. Black bars represent periods of special promotions involving a free bonus package (values varied from $30 to $80 between years) of samples and premiums donated by the industry that are available when anglers upgrade to a 5-year freshwater fishing license.

level of customer satisfaction. For instance, catfish or gar in freshwater, or permit *Trachinotus falcatus* or bonefish in saltwater are species that provide recreational enjoyment but are not in jeopardy of overharvest.

Conclusions

Both Alaska and Florida, as different as the states are, have not only seen the value of promoting safe and sustainable fishing, but recognize that it is necessary for agencies to fulfill their missions. Education, outreach, and marketing are legitimate and useful tools to accomplish this task. Messages should convey the proactive management done by the conservation agencies, how they are funded, and what individuals can do to help ensure the future of the resource.

When encouraging additional use, effective educational programs emphasize people, places, species, and techniques that minimize fisheries impacts and optimize revenues for conservation. It is very important to meet customers' diverse cultural stewardship norms and not force one standard on everyone, just as it is to segment markets according to local customers' needs and fishing preferences.

Acknowledgments

The authors appreciate the Recreational Boating and Fishing Foundation support for this

Table 3. Fishing is tourism: top 4 fishing destinations ranked by nonresident economic output (Southwick 2002).

State	Nonresident economic output	Nonresident anglers	Nonresident fishing days
Florida	$1,535,730,679	1,050,515	6,432,800
North Carolina	$716,318,246	467,665	2,298,119
New York	$584,764,500	307,129	2,884,003
Alaska	$575,727,045	239,092	1,147,344

symposium and their focus on quality research-driven marketing, education, and outreach efforts on behalf of the fishing, boating, and conservation-stewardship communities. Review comments by Brett Boston, Anne Glick, and Rob Southwick are appreciated.

References

Congressional Sportsmen's Foundation. 2001. The American sportsman—take a closer look. Congressional Sportsmen's Foundation, Washington, D.C. Available: www.sportsmenslink.org/Sportman/body.html (August 2006).

Czech, B., and P. Pfister. 2005. Economic growth, fish conservation and the American Fisheries Society: introduction to a special series. Fisheries 30(1):38–40.

Duda, M. 2005a. Public opinion on fish and wildlife management issues and the reputation and credibility of fish and wildlife agencies in the southeastern United States. Available: responsivemanagement.com/download/reports/SEAFWA_Regional_Report.pdf (August 2006).

Duda, M. 2005b. Public opinion on fish and wildlife management issues and the reputation and credibility of fish and wildlife agencies in the southeastern United States—Florida. Available: responsivemanagement.com/download/reports/SEAFWA_Regional_Report.pdf (August 2006).

Flather, D., and T. Hoekstra. 1989. An analysis of the wildlife and fish situation in the United States: 1989–2040. U.S. Forest Service, Rocky Mountain Forest and Range Experiment Station, General Technical Report RM-178, Fort Collins, Colorado.

Florida Department of Health. 2005. Your guide to eating fish caught in Florida. Florida Department of Health, Tallahassee. Available: www.doh.state.fl.us/environment/community/ fishconsumptionadvisories/Fish_consumption_guide.pdf (August 2006).

Gordon, H. 1954. The economic theory of a common property resource: the fishery. Journal of Political Economy 62:124–142.

Group Solutions. 2005. FWC financial impact study: phase II. Final report. Group Solutions, Inc., Hialeah, Florida.

Hartman, G., and T. Northcote. 2005. Economic growth and fish conservation: we need more emphasis on the population component. Fisheries 30(10):36–38.

Lyman, J. 2002. Cultural values and change: catch and release in Alaska's sport fisheries. Pages 29–36 in J. A. Lucy and A. L. Studholme, editors. Catch and release in marine recreational fisheries. American Fisheries Society, Symposium 30, Bethesda, Maryland.

Norris, T. 1864. The American angler's book. S. Low, Philadelphia.

Pigou, A. 1920. The economics of welfare. Macmillan, London.

Quick Facts. 2005. United States Census Bureau. Available: quickfacts.census.gov (August 2006).

RoperASW. 2004. Outdoor recreation in America 2003: recreation's benefits to society challenged by trends. American Recreation Coalition, Washington D.C. Available: http://www.funoutdoors.com/files/ROPER%20REPORT%202004_0.pdf (August 2006).

Seccombe, J. 1743. Business and diversion inoffensive to God. University of New Hamshire Library, Milne Special Collections and Archives, Durham. Available: www.izaak.unh.edu/dlp/seccombe/pages/SEC_cover.htm (August 2006).

Southwick, R. 2002. Sportfishing in America, values of our traditional pastime. American Sportfishing Association, Alexandria, Virginia. Available: www.asafishing.org/asa/images/statistics/participation/sportfishing_america/fish_eco_impact.pdf (August 2006).

Southwick, R., T. Allen, and M. Teisl. 2005. State fishing licenses: pricing and maximizing revenue. Produced for the American Sportfishing Association via Multi-State Conservation Grant #M-9-R. American Sportfishing Association, Alexandria, Virginia.

USFWS (U.S. Fish and Wildlife Service). 2001. National survey of fishing, hunting, and wildlife-associated recreation. Government Printing Office, Washington, D.C.

USFWS (U.S. Fish and Wildlife Service). 2003. National fishing license report. U.S. Fish and Wildlife Service, Division of Federal Assistance, Arlington, Virginia. Available: federalaid.fws.gov/license%20holders/Fishing%20License%20Data.pdf (August 2006).

Wattendorf, B. 2000. A history of sport fish restoration's impact on Florida's freshwater fisheries. Celebrating 50 Years of the Sport Fish Restoration Program: Supplement to Fisheries. American Fisheries Society, Bethesda, Maryland.

Whitehead, J., D. Lipton, F. Lupi, and R. Southwick. 2005. Economic growth and environmental protection. Fisheries 30(4):32–34.

PART II   Fostering Stewardship: Theory and Practice

American Fisheries Society Symposium 55:25–32, 2007

Fostering Aquatic Stewardship with the Help of Best Education Practices

ELAINE ANDREWS[1]

University of Wisconsin, Environmental Resources Center
1545 Observatory Drive, 210 Hiram Smith Hall, Madison, Wisconsin 53706, USA

Abstract.—Practicing good education means knowing your goal, how to achieve the goal, and how to measure effectiveness. This paper describes the state-of-the-art for conservation best education practices. Findings are based on extensive work by educators working with the Recreational Boating and Fishing Foundation, the Institute for Learning Innovation, and the University of Wisconsin as part of a national facilitation project for water outreach. Concepts include environmentally responsible behavior, essential best education practices, choice of outreach focus, understanding target audiences, implementing best education practices and free-choice learning principles, and the role for agencies in promoting conservation education. Recommendations suggest themes that have potential in building stewardship when applied to programs or experiences. These are organized according to community norms, instruction content, learner needs, learner self-confidence, program context, and program quality.

Introduction

Aquatic stewardship education is benefiting from a progressive professional effort to develop practices that have an impact on citizens. Applying best education practices could be the next step toward improving the effectiveness and enjoyment value of stewardship education experiences. Many authors have described the need for quality aquatic stewardship education (Fedler 2001a; Siemer and Knuth 2001) and have identified elements required to improve its effectiveness (Fedler 2001b; Zint et al. 2002). Among these, effective outreach planning requires that education lead toward a specific purpose and that educators have an opportunity to develop and apply essential skills. This chapter provides thoughts about the importance of specific goals for aquatic stewardship education and describes significant national initiatives to identify and implement conditions for success. It suggests how these efforts might be synthesized to establish basic guidelines that fit a variety of aquatic stewardship needs and scenarios.

What Do We Mean by Best Practices?

In the simplest terms, applying best practices means: knowing your goal, knowing how to achieve that goal, and knowing how to measure effectiveness. The concept of best practices can easily be demonstrated through a fishing analogy. Visualize a young man, fishing pole in hand, lying on his stomach at the edge of a hole in the ice. It is clear to the observer that the young man has a goal—he is determined to catch a fish. He knows something about how to achieve the goal— he has dipped his line into the cold lake waters, through a hole in the ice. Finally, we can measure the effectiveness of his technique, and whether he picked the best spot, by noting whether or not he catches a fish. If his goal is simply to have fun on a winter's day in Wisconsin or to exercise his curiosity, his strategy for how to achieve each of those goals and how to measure their effectiveness might be different.

In aquatic education, we are challenged by how to apply fundamental best practices. Our answers need to be specific. We will not be able to develop evidence for our effectiveness unless we establish, specifically, what we are trying to ac-

---

[1] E-mail: eandrews@wisc.edu

complish and how. Goals we often discuss when thinking about aquatic stewardship include increasing knowledge, increasing sensitivity, encouraging stewardship, building ownership and empowerment, or encouraging environmentally-responsible behavior. Questions arise about each of these goals. Will training for any one of these stated goals lead to enhanced stewardship practices? Are there specific training techniques for each goal that are more likely to lead to success than others?

Definitions of stewardship[2] certainly provide guidance, but leave educators with the task of determining the details for exactly which skills and actions are needed to "care for the environment" and how to motivate youth or adults to apply the skills in selected settings. Environmentally responsible behavior (ERB) is one concept that might help clarify what factors may be important to consider in efforts to foster desirable aquatic stewardship. ERBs were suggested by John Disinger (1985) to characterize research findings about what leads a person to take action about the environment. Disinger identified several components that provide a foundation for achieving ERBs, including knowledge of issues, ecology, and actions; skill in taking actions; group locus of control (empowerment); individual locus of control; intention to act; environmental sensitivity; and sense of personal responsibility. Over time, the significance of these components has been confirmed by others (Hines et al. 1987; Hungerford and Volk 1990; NAAEE 2000), but there has been minimal testing of the effectiveness of these concepts when applied as a group.

When effectively presented, each ERB component is also a best education practice. That is, attention to one component, "skill in taking actions" for example, will result in measurable learning because a focus on skills is likely to motivate learners to achieve (see Essential BEPs of the National Extension Water Outreach Education Web site, http://wateroutreach.uwex/beps/essential.cfm). While the efficacy of an ERB model as a grouping of components significant to stewardship education is yet to be proven, at least one study indicates its potential. In an evaluation of Chesapeake Bay education programs, Zint et al. (2002) showed that when training is designed so that all seven ERB elements are addressed together, students and teachers are more likely to demonstrate competence in each of the individual ERB characteristics. When one or more of the elements is eliminated from the education experience, overall competency in ERB components is reduced. In the more limited education design, the students might retain knowledge of issues or actions for example, but not demonstrate personal responsibility or individual locus of control.

The Zint study findings seem to confirm that education programs should be focused, but provided as part of multiple experiences over extended periods of time, and offered in coordination with other interventions in order to reach their full potential in promoting environmentally responsible behaviors. ERB components suggest a comprehensive model that at least provides a checklist to help refine objectives that aquatic educators could systematically apply towards achieving stewardship goals.

Applying best practices to determine education or outreach goals also requires decisions about the focus and the audience for each effort. A stewardship education initiative might focus on individuals, groups, communities, or government agencies. Audiences can vary widely (e.g., policy makers/leaders, property owners, sports enthusiasts, students/youth, teachers, recreational water users). Though, it may seem obvious to an educator that best practices should be identified based on the program focus and target audience, educators should not underestimate the value of explicit planning documentation that identifies the program's purpose and target audience, to ensure that all important linkages and assumptions are identified. Making those decisions clear is a first step toward selecting the means of education that will help reach your program goals with the intended audience.

---

[2] "Stewardship is the moral obligation to care for the environment and the actions undertaken to provide that care. Stewardship implies the existence of an ethic or personal responsibility, an ethic of behavior based on reverence for the Earth and a sense of obligation to future generations." (Dixon et al. 1995, as reported in Fedler 2001a)

Development Of Best Practices: Four Examples

To take "best practices" a step further, several professional groups have launched efforts to identify best practices and provide training on techniques that educators can use to create environmental understanding and to encourage stewardship behaviors (see, for example, MacPherson and Tonning 2003; NAAEE 2004; Paul F-Brandwein Institute 2005). This section describes four of those efforts: the Recreational Fishing and Boating Foundation (RBFF) Best Practices Initiative, the Association of Fish and Wildlife Agencies (AFWA) Conservation Agenda, the "Free-Choice Learning" collaboration, and the U.S. Department of Agriculture (USDA) water outreach initiative.

The RBFF Best Practices initiative[3]

Beginning in the late 1990s, the RBFF Education Task Force worked to develop research-based guidelines for boating and fishing education. The Education Task Force asked, "Which processes provide the best experiences for conveying knowledge, developing skills, and changing attitudes and behaviors?" Experts summarized research and made recommendations (Fedler 2001b).

The RBFF Education Task Force defined "best practice" as a program or practice that has been clearly defined, refined through repeated delivery, and supported by a substantial body of research. The group outlined components of effective programs as well as specific opportunities to enhance programs. RBFF implemented the task force's recommendations by developing the *Best Practices Workbook* (Seng and Rushton 2003), a leader training resource that provides guidance on program development and implementation, professional development, program evaluation, and using research to support programs. The workbook also includes chapters with guidance on specific needs (i.e., programming to serve ethnic minorities or persons with disabilities, boating programs, fishing programs, and aquatic stewardship education).

RBFF invested significant resources in the process of developing and pilot testing the *Best Practices Workbook* and accompanying support resources. The Education Task Force reviewed multiple drafts of the workbook and accompanying training guide to assure that practices identified from the research were appropriately captured and described in the training materials. The Education Task Force also encouraged RBFF to make the information available in a simpler, fact sheet format to make it easier to promote the principle ideas to supervisors, policy makers, and others who would not have the time to read a lengthy guide. Pilot testing opportunities were identified and funded through a competitive process.

Immediately following the development of the workbook, RBFF launched an extensive effort to train the trainers and to promote use of the resource at meetings where fishing, boating, and stewardship educators might be gathered. A related effort to launch an electronic newsletter for information sharing among trained and potential users was less successful. Creating an effective vehicle for supporting a best practices "community of practice" remains as a challenge.

AFWA conservation agenda[4]

An interesting development growing out of RBFF's work is an initiative to enhance support for conservation education by AFWA. AFWA members are state and provincial government agencies responsible for North America's fish and wildlife resources. In December 2004, the AFWA Board approved and promulgated a Conservation Education Resolution that promoted "a national agenda for wildlife and conservation education" (AFWA Executive Committee 2004). The agenda referenced by the resolution generally incorporated RBFF best practices recommendations and specifically encouraged the use of best practices to achieve the highest quality of educational programs (AFWA 2004). The agenda included actions to move toward the following goals:

- A definition of conservation education in the context of agency missions and goals.

---

[3] The RBFF Web site (http://www.rbff.org/) provides details about the organization's mission, initiatives, and other educational resources.

[4] The Web site for the Association of Fish and Wildlife Agencies (http://www.fishwildlife.org/) provides details about the organization's mission and activities.

- Support at all levels of agencies, among partners, and by key decision makers for the concept that conservation education is mission critical.
- Conservation education funding that is significant and stable.
- Strong partnership support and collaboration to realize the full potential of conservation education in state/provincial fish and wildlife agencies.
- Conservation education that is responsive to, integrated with, and/or correlated to all applicable professional and learning standards based on sound educational theory.

This vote of confidence in best practices fosters aquatic stewardship by building a constituency for their comprehensive application in fish, wildlife, and forestry education.

The "free-choice learning" collaboration

"Free-choice learning" is the concept underlying a second national research-based initiative that describes how people learn in multiple settings and across generations. A partnership between the Institute for Learning Innovation (ILI)[5] and the U.S. Environmental Protection Agency (U.S. EPA) engages national scholars and stakeholders in interpreting research findings to incorporate new understandings about how people learn into environmental stewardship and conservation education. The ILI investigates learning in zoo, museum, and aquarium settings; supports and documents efforts to create effective free-choice learning experiences; and helps professionals develop and build their skills and capacities.

The ILI/U.S. EPA partnership had not completed its proposed tasks as of the writing of this chapter, but the underlying concepts are well established and can inform the current discussion. Falk and Dierking (2000) described "free-choice learning" as the type of learning that takes place outside of schools and the workplace, such as learning from museums, libraries, the Internet, television, film, books, newspapers, radio, and

magazines. They defined it as the most common type of learning: self-directed, voluntary, and guided by an individual's needs and interests. People have control over what and how they learn. They can choose to learn in appropriate and supportive contexts. People engage in free-choice learning throughout their lifespan, so it is a process relevant to educators whether they work with youth or adults.

Falk and Dierking (2000) organized the results of their research about free-choice learning in terms of a Contextual model of Learning. This model describes factors that influence learning related to the personal context, sociocultural context, and physical context of the individual. Personal context factors highlight motivation and expectations, interest, prior knowledge and experience, and choice and control. Sociocultural context refers to within-group sociocultural mediation, facilitated mediation by others, and culture. The physical context refers to advance preparation, setting, design, and subsequent reinforcing events and experiences.

Falk and Dierking (2000) asserted that each context contributes to and influences the interactions and experiences that people have when engaging in free-choice learning activities. Aquatic educators can easily identify examples from their own work for how each of these three context factors may have affected the outcome of an initiative.

USDA water outreach initiative

The USDA Water Outreach coordination project is a third national initiative to identify best education practices (BEPs) that relate to water and stewardship education. This project produced a Web site that lists research-based best education practices and provides resources to facilitate their application (National Extension Water Outreach Education Web site, http://wateroutreach.uwex.edu). Users can investigate target audience studies or classic education theory; they can apply a decision-tree to help choose appropriate best practices; they can review processes for teaching and facilitating learning; and they can search an online library for resources and outreach practices on a particular water topic.

---

[5] The Institute for Learning Innovation Web site (http://www.ilinet.org/) provides details about the organization's mission and activities.

The Water Outreach Web site presents BEPs in two ways. Essential BEPs groups classic education theory according to typical ways that the educator may approach learners. There are essential BEPs for working directly with individuals and for work with groups, with communities, or with units beyond the size of a single community. Target audience BEPs are research-based study findings about a particular audience, such as a recreational water user. Results for each audience are grouped according to a program planning question that an educator might be trying to solve. The educator may want more information about the audience itself, message content that interests that audience, an effective method for delivering the message, outreach strategies that are more likely to work with this audience, public participation techniques effective with this audience, or particular evaluation strategies to try (BEP Research of the National Extension Water Outreach Education Web site, http:// wateroutreach.uwex.edu/beps/research.cfm). Study-specific recommendations for 14 audiences are reported on the water outreach Web site. Other audiences reported in the study include, for example, business and industry water users, local decision makers, households, and landowners.

Best Practices that Foster Aquatic Stewardship Education

Aquatic educators are uniquely positioned to apply much of the best advice generated through these best practice initiatives. Because of the hands-on, real-life, and outdoor nature of aquatic subject matter, educators can provide youth and adults with opportunities to be curious, have a direct experience with aquatic resources, address authentic problems, develop solutions to problems, and have fun while doing so. Each of these is a demonstrated "essential" best education practice (Essential BEPs of the National Extension Water Outreach Education Web site, http:// wateroutreach.uwex.edu/beps/essential.cfm).

For a suggestion about how to frame this collection of best practices, we look to Knuth and Siemer (2004) who have summarized research about instilling stewardship behaviors in a way that has led to important conclusions about what

to emphasize. Their recommendations are built on the findings of numerous researchers and refer to models developed by others who have also analyzed multiple studies (such as Hines et al. 1987 and Hungerford and Volk 1990). In their summary, Knuth and Siemer suggest that programs could focus on (1) awareness and knowledge of aquatic systems and their importance to overall ecosystem functions, (2) knowledge among individuals of the consequences of their specific behaviors related to the aquatic environment, and (3) knowledge and skills needed to implement aquatic stewardship behaviors. They suggest that implementation practices are more likely to lead to successful efforts if they are learner-centered, engaging, and cognizant of the cultural and environmental contexts of those engaged.

The Knuth and Siemer summary could be refined to suggest application of these principles at different intensities, depending on the experience of the participant. Hungerford and Volk (1990) describe major and minor variables for three levels of environmentally responsible behavior that lead to environmental citizenship. These levels may help aquatic educators choose what to emphasize with each particular audience. For example, among entry-level variables, environmental sensitivity is the most significant, but knowledge of ecology, androgyny, and attitudes toward pollution, technology, and economics may have a role. Among ownership variables, in-depth knowledge of issues is the most significant, but knowledge of consequences of behavior, both positive and negative, and a personal commitment to issue resolution, may have a role. Among empowerment variables, knowledge of and skill in using environmental action strategies, locus of control, and intention to act are important, but in-depth knowledge about issues may also have a role.

An additional perspective for identifying best education practices derives from extensive work by social psychologists to provide more detail about variables that have been shown through research to affect a person's likelihood of adopting environmentally significant behaviors. These can be grouped according to attitudinal variables, personal capabilities, contextual factors, and habit and routine (Stern 2000) (see

Figure 1). Each variable can affect behavior on its own or in interaction with other variables. Stern's summary adds to and confirms free-choice learning parameters defined by Falk and Dierking (2000), but also serves to illustrate the complexity of the task ahead for aquatic educators.

A synopsis of the theories and best practices presented in this chapter suggest several themes to guide aquatic stewardship education planning and implementation. When planning any program or initiative, educators could take into account community norms, recommended instruction content, learner needs, learner self-confidence, program context, and program quality. If properly considered, these themes can result in programs or activities that have potential to build stewardship among participants.

Table 1 summarizes parameters for each theme that were identified by the programs described in this chapter. This summary is intended to help the educator by providing a shorter list of things to remember—six themes instead of hundreds of suggestions. But the summary is not meant to replace careful professional preparation guided by training resources such as those developed by the Recreational Boating and Fishing Foundation.

Conclusions

Best practice lists, such as those presented in this paper, are helpful in summarizing what we know about what works. These new research-based findings are providing wonderful insights about what educators can do that they may not have tried in the past. But ultimately, what matters is whether aquatic educators understand the implied concepts and whether they have the skill and the support of their organization to apply them. The next step in fostering aquatic stewardship is to support those on the front-line of education and outreach with best practices training, reinforcing experiences, and organizational commitment.

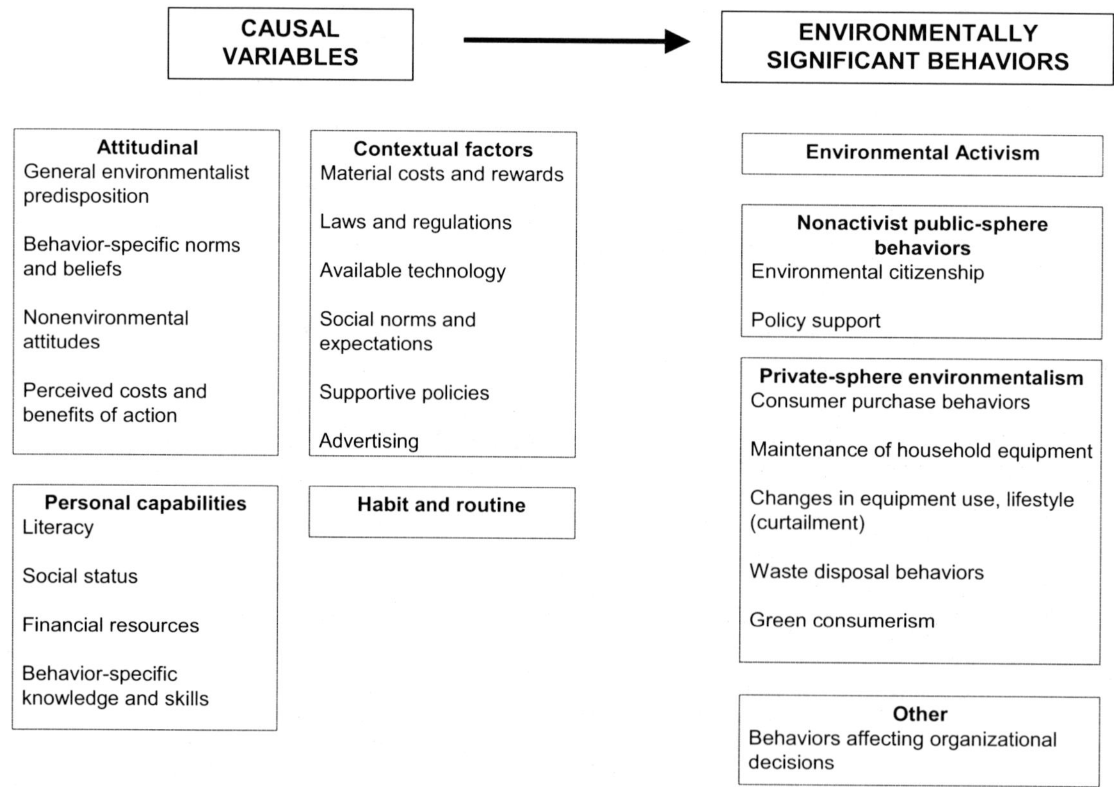

FIGURE 1. Behavior is determined by multiple variables, sometimes in interaction (Stern 2000).

TABLE 1. Aquatic Stewardship Best Education Practices.

Theme	Parameters
Community norms	• Attend to building local or group support for the new behaviors, especially as they relate to community expectations and practices.

Instruction content	• Provide a program or experience that addresses the following topics at a depth appropriate to the individual's previous experience:
	  o Awareness and knowledge of aquatic systems and their importance to overall ecosystem functions;
	  o Knowledge among individuals of the consequences of their specific behaviors related to the aquatic environment; and
	  o Knowledge and skills needed to implement aquatic stewardship behaviors.

Learner needs	• Investigate and provide programs or experiences that address social and personal qualities about the target audience, including
	  o attitudinal variables,
	  o personal capabilities,
	  o contextual factors, and
	  o habits and routines.
	• Provide a program or experience that is
	  o learner-centered,
	  o engaging, and
	  o cognizant of the cultural and environmental contexts of those engaged.
	• Provide the learner with authentic problems and with problem-solving experiences.
	• Implement other best practices for enhancing learning, as educator training and outreach opportunity permit.

Learner self-confidence	• Provide opportunities for the learner to develop self-confidence in applying skills, and in encouraging a commitment to try the new skill. • Offer education or outreach initiatives that are part of a repeated opportunity and provide long-term reinforcement for appropriate application of skills.
Program context	• Attend to the context for the learning experience itself—including advanced preparation, setting, design, and subsequent reinforcement. • Provide learning experiences in the setting where stewardship behaviors will be applied (e.g., in an aquatic setting).
Program quality	• Rely on instructors trained in best education practices. • Use effective program planning, especially to engage the target audience in the planning process, to pilot test outreach strategies, and to revise efforts based on evaluations.

References

Disinger, J. F. 1985. What research says: environmental education's definitional problem. School Science and Mathematics 85(1):59–68.

Dixon, D. O., W. F. Siemer, and B. A. Knuth. 1995. Stewardship of the Great Lakes environment: a review of literature. Cornell University, Department of Natural Resources, HDRU Series Publication No. 95–5, Ithaca, New York.

Falk, J. H., and L. D. Dierking. 2000. Learning from museums: visitor experiences and the making of meaning. AltaMira Press, Oxford, UK.

Fedler, A. J. 2001a. An examination of the relationship between recreational boating and fishing participation and aquatic resource stewardship. Recreational Boating and Fishing Foundation, Alexandria, Virginia.

Fedler, A. J. 2001b. Fishing, boating, and aquatic stewardship education: framework and best practices recommendations. Pages 4–17 in A. J. Fedler, editor. Defining best practices in boating, fishing, and stewardship education. The Recreational Boating and Fishing Foundation, Alexandria, Virginia.

Hines, J. M., H. Hungerford, and A. Tomera. 1987. Analysis and synthesis of research on responsible environmental behavior: a meta-analysis. Journal of Environmental Education 18(2):1–8.

Hungerford, H. R., and T. L. Volk. 1990. Changing learner behavior through environmental education. Journal of Environmental Education 21(3):8–21.

AFWA (Association of Fish and Wildlife Agencies). 2004. An agenda for conservation education in state fish and wildlife agencies, December 9, 2004. Available: www.iafwa.org/conservationeducation/docs/IAFWA%20Education%20Agenda.pdf. (April 2006).

AFWA (Association of Fish and Wildlife Agencies) Executive Committee. 2004. Resolution of support for conservation education. Available: www.iafwa.org/conservationeducation/summit_resolution.htm. (April 2006).

Knuth, B A., and W.F. Siemer. 2004. Fostering aquatic stewardship: a key for fisheries sustainability. Pages 243–255 *in* E. E. Knudsen, D. D. MacDonald, and Y. K. Muirhead, editors. Sustainable management of North American fisheries. American Fisheries Society. Symposium 43, Bethesda, Maryland.

MacPherson, C., and B. Tonning. 2003. Getting in step: a guide to effective outreach in your watershed (a web-based training module from EPA's Watershed Academy). Available: www.epa.gov/watertrain/gettinginstep/step1a.html. (October 2005).

NAAEE (North American Association for Environmental Education). 2004. Nonformal environmental education programs: guidelines for excellence. North American Association for Environmental Education, Washington, D.C. Available: www.naaee.org/pages/npeee/nonformal.html. (October 2005).

The Paul F-Brandwein Institute. 2005. The Conservation Learning Summit: resources at risk. Available: www.brandwein.org. (October 2005).

Seng, P. T., and S. Rushton, editors. 2003. Best practices workbook. Recreational Fishing and Boating Foundation, Alexandria, Virginia.

Siemer, W. F., and B. A. Knuth. 2001. Effects of fishing education programs on antecedents of responsible environmental behavior. Journal of Environmental Education 32(4):23–29.

NAAEE (North American Association for Environmental Education). 2000. Excellence in environmental education-guidelines for learning (K-12). NAAEE Publications and Membership Office, Rock Spring, Georgia. Available: www.naaee.org/pages/npeee/learner_guidelines.html. (April 2006).

Stern, P. C. 2000. Toward a coherent theory of environmentally significant behavior. Journal of Social Issues 56(3):407–424.

Zint, M., A. Kraemer, H. Northway, and M. Lim. 2002. Evaluation of the Chesapeake Bay Foundation's conservation education programs. Conservation Biology 16(3):641–649.

American Fisheries Society Symposium 55:33–43, 2007

Developing Tomorrow's Anglers and Aquatic Stewards: Formative Evaluation of MinnAqua's Leaders' Guide

AMY GRACK NELSON[1]

4750 Nicols Road, Eagan, Minnesota 55122, USA

JENIFER MATTHEES[2]

Minnesota Department of Natural Resources, Division of Fish and Wildlife
500 Lafayette Road, St. Paul, Minnesota 55155, USA

Abstract.—MinnAqua, a program of the Minnesota Department of Natural Resources' (DNR) Division of Fish and Wildlife, educates the state's youth about angling and aquatic resources. In 2001, MinnAqua began developing a leaders' guide so educators could carry out MinnAqua activities in their own setting. As part of the development process, a formative evaluation was undertaken to answer two questions: (a) to what extent are MinnAqua's rewrite guidelines addressed in individual lessons and the leaders' guide as a whole?, and (b) to what extent does the leaders' guide meet the educational needs of intended users in both formal and informal education settings? Evaluative feedback was gathered from a variety of individuals over two stages of data collection, with revisions occurring after each stage. During stage one, formal and informal educators pilot tested lessons in their respective educational settings and provided input through surveys, critiques, and focus groups. DNR Fisheries staff also critiqued lessons to ensure the scientific accuracy of the biological information. Stage two involved instructional design experts verifying educational content in the lessons, educational outreach partners commenting on how the leaders' guide could be used to support their outreach efforts, and an accessibility expert determining how to adapt MinnAqua lessons for use with individuals with physical disabilities. The evaluation results were used to verify the incorporation of the rewrite guidelines, identify ways to strengthen the extent to which the guidelines were addressed, and modify the leaders' guide to more fully meet educators' needs.

Introduction

Minnesota is known for its "10,000 lakes" and the fishing opportunities these waters hold. The Minnesota Department of Natural Resource's (DNR) Division of Fish and Wildlife is responsible for managing the state's aquatic resources to ensure that fishing continues to be a popular recreational activity. In the late 1980s, in response to a request from the Fisheries Roundtable,[3] a needs assessment was conducted that identified the need for a division angling and aquatic education program to educate Minnesota's citizens about the state's aquatic resources, fisheries management activities, and fishing regulations (Bilitz 1989). From this, MinnAqua was created. MinnAqua's mission is to "provide life-long educational programming that will increase people's knowledge and understanding about aquatic ecosystems, management, and resource issues; help acquire skills related to aquatic recreation, careers, and teaching; and foster a better stewardship of the state's natural resources" (Matthees 2003:3). MinnAqua achieves its mission through various educational programs, interpretive displays, educational trunks, publications, and a leaders' guide

---

[1] E-mail: grac0019@umn.edu

[2] E-mail: jenifer.matthees@dnr.state.mn.us

[3] The Fisheries Roundtable brings together individuals and organizations to listen, talk, and learn about issues related to angling in Minnesota and the state's fisheries.

that contains various angling and aquatic resource education activities. The MinnAqua staff consists of a coordinator, four regional education specialists, nine seasonal interns, and one staff member at each area Fisheries office to act as a MinnAqua Liaison by devoting 5% of their time to education outreach.

Over the years, MinnAqua has striven to improve their programs and products to strengthen the impact they have on fostering stewardship of Minnesota's aquatic resources. In 2000, the MinnAqua coordinator was involved with the Recreational Boating and Fishing Foundation as a reviewer for their newly developed *Best Practices Workbook for Boating, Fishing, and Aquatic Resources Stewardship Education* (*Best Practices*; Seng and Rushton 2003). *Best Practices* was "designed to help educators build, enhance, and evaluate their programs based on research and practices shown to be effective" (Seng and Rushton 2003:Intro–2). Through this involvement, it was evident that MinnAqua could be improved by looking at the effectiveness of their programs and products in terms of the research-based *Best Practices*.

MinnAqua decided to focus their program improvement on rewriting and redesigning the leaders' guide to better align with *Best Practices*. One of the best practices states that effective programs are developmentally appropriate for participants (Seng and Rushton 2003). The original leaders' guide contained activities labeled as beginner, intermediate, or advanced without age levels identified. MinnAqua created a new leaders' guide specifically for grades 3–5. Focusing on specific grades was intended to help ensure that concepts in the lessons were appropriate for the developmental levels of the students. MinnAqua also decided to expand their outreach to formal education settings by making activities more classroom-appropriate, since the leaders' guide had primarily been used in informal education settings. Expanding their outreach to formal classroom environments was also supported by a 2001 environmental education survey administered by the DNR and Minnesota Department of Education, which found an interest among formal educators in utilizing aquatic education materials in their classrooms (Minnesota Department of Natural Resources and Minnesota Department of Education 2001).

In 2001, MinnAqua began creating a leaders' guide that could be effectively utilized by educators working with grades 3–5 in both formal and informal education settings. MinnAqua's goals for the new leaders' guide were that educators would use it to (a) teach about Minnesota fish, aquatic resources, and resource management; (b) lead students outdoors and initiate self-sustaining programs such as volunteer monitoring projects, shoreline restoration, and other service learning projects; (c) connect students to their local aquatic resources through the recreational activity of angling; and (d) promote lasting stewardship of Minnesota's aquatic resources. To reach these goals, MinnAqua needed to ensure that the leaders' guide contained quality lessons that met educators' needs.

Before the leaders' guide was rewritten, MinnAqua wanted to gain a clear understanding of what constitutes a quality educational product. One of the best practices is to align educational products with national and state standards (Seng and Rushton 2003). To ensure that concepts presented in lessons were developmentally appropriate for grades 3–5, MinnAqua reviewed the National Research Council's *National Science Education Standards* (NRC 1996), North American Association for Environmental Education's *Excellence in Environmental Education: Guidelines for Learning* (K–12) (NAAEE 2004), American Association for the Advancement of Science's *Benchmarks for Science Literacy* (AAAS 1993), and the Minnesota Academic Standards. *Best Practices* also emphasizes using educational research in product development (Seng and Rushton 2003). MinnAqua did an extensive review not only of educational research, but other educational products as well to become familiar with learning theory, developmentally appropriate concepts and skills for students in grades 3–5, and features of a lesson plan. Some examples of research and other resources reviewed include biology and earth science textbooks; educational products similar to the leaders' guide, such as Project WET and Project WILD; and literature on topics such as inquiry-based learning, authentic assessment, multiple intelligence theory, and child development. In addition, MinnAqua staff spoke directly to various educational professionals to gain insight into what features were necessary for the leaders' guide to be useful in both formal and informal education settings.

As a result of reviewing a variety of resources, talking to educational professionals, and considering *Best Practices*, MinnAqua created a set of rewrite guidelines to help ensure the development of a quality leaders' guide that would meet the needs of both formal and informal educators. Rewrite guidelines for individual lessons included (a) adding background biology information for each lesson, (b) better defining steps and procedures for lesson implementation, (c) aligning with the 2004 Minnesota Academic Standards and Minnesota's Environmental Literacy Scope and Sequence[4] (Landers et al. 2002), (d) including measurable objectives, (e) adding authentic assessment ideas, (f) ensuring activities and concepts are developmentally appropriate and build on students' prior knowledge, (g) accommodating multiple learning styles in lesson activities, and (h) including ideas on how to adapt lessons for use with grades K–2. Rewrite guidelines for the leaders' guide as a whole included (a) ensuring concepts, environmental issues, and problems are addressed with accuracy and fairness; (b) featuring content specific to Minnesota culture, natural resources, and fisheries management; (c) making connections to students' everyday lives; (d) adding more indoor classroom activities; (e) including self-directed, student-centered learning opportunities; (f) incorporating individual and group activities; (g) including interdisciplinary, hands-on, and inquiry-based lessons; (h) adding service-learning ideas; (i) modifying lessons to stand alone or be used as part of a unit; (j) improving the appearance of graphics and copy pages; (k) creating a glossary of terms used in lessons; and (l) developing related reading lists for students.

The resulting leaders' guide had 39 lessons divided into six chapters: aquatic habitats, Minnesota fish, water stewardship, fish management, fishing equipment and skills, and safety and the fishing trip. Each chapter contributes to a better understanding of Minnesota's aquatic systems

---

[4] The Environmental Literacy Scope and Sequence takes a systems approach to environmental education. It describes key concepts about the interaction of natural and social systems and a sequence in which they can be taught to learners at each grade level.

and basic fishing skills. The lessons were structured in a lesson plan format to provide educators with the variety of information necessary to successfully carry out an activity. Key features included vocabulary words, Minnesota Academic Standards, Minnesota's Environmental Literacy Scope and Sequence, measurable learning objectives, extensive biology background for the educator teaching the lesson, authentic assessments, K–2 options, and extensions for added learning on the lesson topic. MinnAqua's hope is that the leaders' guide will enhance opportunities for students to have authentic experiences in their local surroundings, leading to a deeper understanding of their role in their environment and ultimately helping to guide them toward a path of stewardship.

This paper focuses on the formative evaluation process undertaken to create a quality leaders' guide that will meet the needs of both formal and informal educators. The formative evaluation was carried out January 2003 to May 2005.

The Evaluation

Best Practices emphasizes the importance of evaluation during educational product development (Seng and Rushton 2003). Moreover, carrying out a formative evaluation can improve the learning effectiveness of educational products significantly when compared to educational materials that have not undergone any type of evaluation (Nathenson and Henderson 1980; Tessmer 1993). For this reason, a formative evaluation of the leaders' guide was carried out upon completion of the first draft. Formative evaluation is "designed and used to improve an object, especially when it is still being developed" (Joint Committee on Standards for Educational Evaluation 1994:206). In the case of MinnAqua, the goal of the formative evaluation was to improve the leaders' guide during its development by ensuring that the rewrite guidelines were addressed and the needs of intended users were met. The guiding evaluation questions were (a) to what extent are MinnAqua's rewrite guidelines addressed in individual lessons and the leaders' guide as a whole?, and (b) to what extent does the leaders' guide meet the educational needs of intended users in both formal and informal education settings?

The evaluation was designed to address the evaluation questions by verifying that the rewrite guidelines were incorporated, identifying how to strengthen the extent to which the guidelines were addressed, and recognizing means to increase the utility of the leaders' guide. Figure 1 provides an illustration of the evaluation design, which took place in two stages. During stage one, formal and informal educators pilot tested lessons in their respective educational settings. Expertise of DNR Fisheries staff was also drawn upon to ensure the scientific accuracy of lesson content. Input during stage one was used to make necessary revisions to the leaders' guide before stage two of the

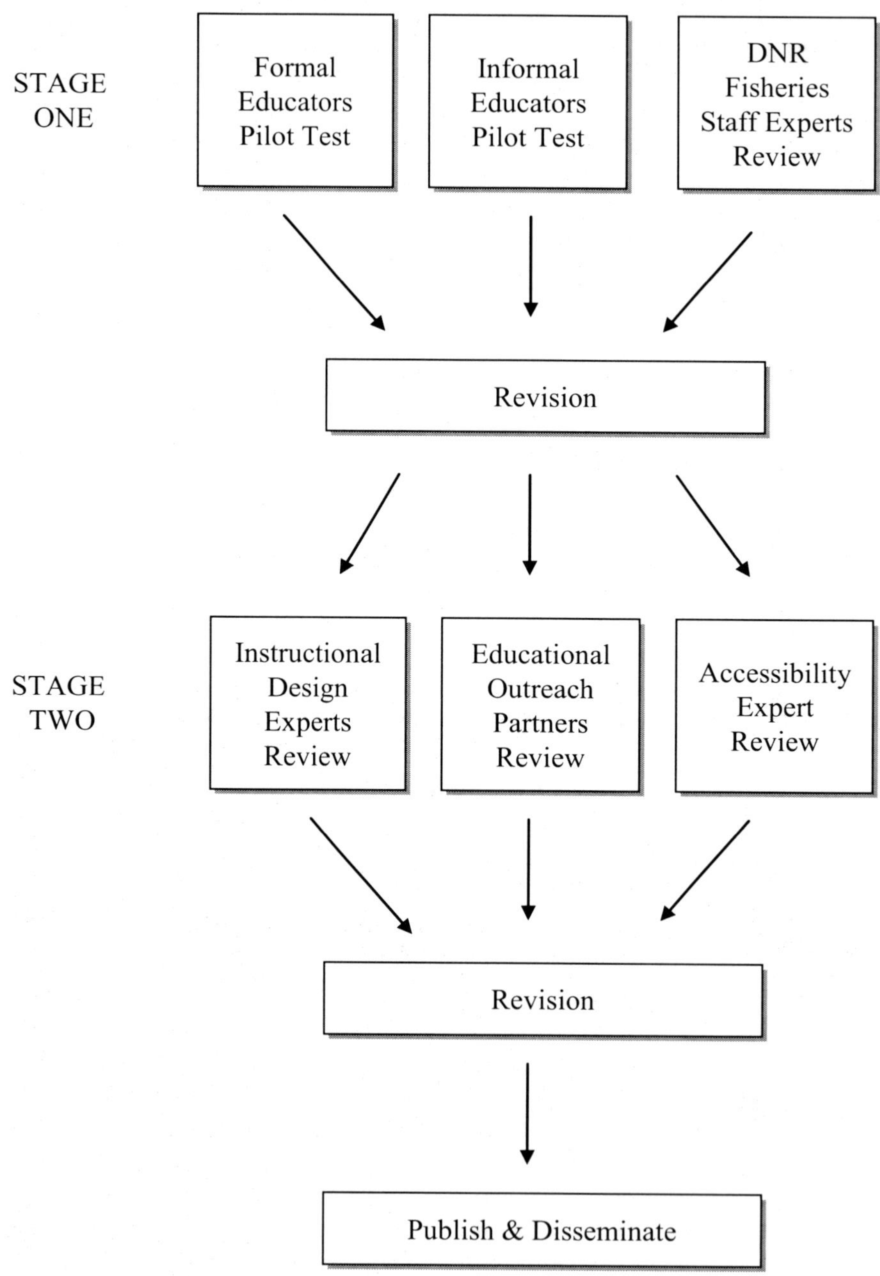

FIGURE 1. Leaders' guide formative evaluation process.

evaluation. Stage two involved three types of reviews. Instructional design experts verified specific educational content in the lessons. In addition, educational outreach partners provided feedback on how the leaders' guide could be used to support their outreach efforts. Finally, an accessibility expert was consulted to determine the best method to ensure activities were inclusive of individuals with physical disabilities. MinnAqua then made additional revisions based on these reviewers' comments. Upon completion of stage two, the leaders' guide was ready for layout, graphics, and final editing.

Stage One Methodology

Formal and informal educator pilot test

The purpose of pilot testing is to see first-hand how well a product works in its intended settings with intended users (Beyer 1995; Weston et al. 1995). For this reason, the leaders' guide was piloted by educators who taught grades 3–5 in both formal and informal education settings. The goals of the pilot test were to determine the usefulness of the leaders' guide in various educational settings, identify the leaders' guide's strengths and needed improvements, and obtain suggestions for dissemination and training.

A purposive sampling technique was used to choose the pilot testing sample. Using this sampling technique, individuals who are considered "information-rich cases" are selected to provide a deep understanding of the object under study (Patton 1990). In the case of the piloting of the leaders' guide, a diverse mix of formal and informal educators were chosen in order to obtain the depth of information needed to understand how the materials worked with various intended users and guide revisions. Recruitment efforts focused on obtaining third, fourth, and fifth grade educators from various types of formal and informal education settings spread throughout the state in urban, suburban, and rural areas. As illustrated in Table 1, the sample included a broad representation of educators from a wide variety of educational settings in which the leaders' guide is intended to be utilized. Fewer informal educators reviewed the guide because many of the lessons were written and used by MinnAqua education specialists whose experience was in informal education. Incentives for pilot testing included aquatic education teaching materials, a set of rods and reels, acknowledgment in the leaders' guide, and a copy of the leaders' guide upon publication.

Educators attended an introductory meeting to learn about the MinnAqua program, the new leaders' guide, and the evaluation process in order to clearly define their role in relation to the goals of the evaluation. At the meeting, educators selected six lessons, one from each chapter if possible, to pilot test at their site. Educators chose their own lessons to allow for easier integration into their regular curriculum. Each lesson was piloted by a minimum of one formal educator at each grade level (third, fourth, and fifth) and one informal educator, who in most cases piloted the lesson with various grade levels.

Educators were given 3 months to pilot test

TABLE 1. Characteristics of pilot testing sample.

Formal educators ($n = 17$)	Informal educators ($n = 5$)
Educational setting	Educational setting
• Public[a] school: 14	• 4-H: 2
• Private school: 2	• Nature center: 1
• Homeschool: 1	• Cub Scouts: 1
Geographic location	• Tribal Community Waste Management: 1
• Twin Cities metro area: 5	Geographic location
• Outside metro area: 12	• Twin Cities metro area: 1
Grade taught	• Outside metro area: 4
• Third grade: 9	
• Fourth grade: 4	
• Fifth grade: 8	

[a]Public schools included a fine arts public school, tribal community school, and Montessori school.

lessons. More than one data collection method was utilized to gain the variety of information necessary to assist in the identification of problem areas and possible solutions, specifically in relation to the rewrite guidelines. For each lesson piloted, educators completed a questionnaire and critiqued the lesson. The questionnaire asked for feedback about lesson content, delivery, and adaptations made to lessons. Critiquing lessons involved critically reviewing each component of a lesson and providing targeted suggestions for improvement. Upon completion of pilot testing, educators participated in a 2-h focus group. The purpose of the focus group was to gain a deeper understanding of the pilot testing experience, understand how students reacted to lessons, gain additional feedback on how to improve the leaders' guide, and discuss ideas for dissemination.

Fisheries staff expert review

One of MinnAqua's rewrite guidelines, based on *Best Practices*, was to present environmental information with fairness and accuracy (Seng and Rushton 2003). For this reason, an expert review was carried out by various DNR fisheries staff. Thirty-eight MinnAqua liaisons each reviewed two lessons to verify the scientific accuracy of the lesson content. Using a questionnaire, they identified any necessary changes to the lesson and commented on their ability to use the lesson in their educational outreach.

Stage one data analysis

Current literature lacks clear direction on how to present and interpret results obtained for individual lessons from a pilot test, so a question was posted on the American Evaluation Association's listserv. Responding evaluators recommended presenting the data to MinnAqua and letting them decide what feedback to incorporate as opposed to generating recommendations for each lesson. To facilitate processing questionnaire and critique data from stage one, feedback was compiled for each lesson by color-coded pages corresponding to the type of reviewer (informal educator, formal educator, fisheries staff). This allowed MinnAqua to easily compare input from the various reviewers for a single lesson.

Focus group transcripts were analyzed and responses were coded by themes. Focus group data were presented separately from the compiled lesson data, and major findings and recommendations were structured around the various themes. However, both formal and informal educator comments related to specific lessons were pulled out of focus group transcripts, color-coded by type of educator, and included with the questionnaire and critique feedback for each lesson.

A 2-d meeting was held with MinnAqua staff to discuss the compiled lesson results and recommendations from stage one. Recommendations were generated to draw attention to frequent concerns educators and fisheries staff had with certain lessons, provide suggestions for changes to the overall leaders' guide, and discuss educator ideas for future dissemination of the leaders' guide. After the meeting, it was up to MinnAqua staff to decide what changes and additions would be made before stage two of the evaluation.

Stage One Findings and Recommendations

Addressing the rewrite guidelines

Educators responded positively to characteristics of the leaders' guide that were incorporated based on the rewrite guidelines. Educators felt the lessons built on students' prior knowledge, made connections to students' daily lives, and accommodated students' variety of learning styles. They contributed the hands-on nature of the lessons to the high level of student engagement and ease of use with students of varying abilities. Additionally, educators felt the inclusion of both individual and group activities helped ensure the success of all students, particularly students with disabilities and English language learners, by providing opportunities for students to work together and learn from one another.

As planned for in the rewrite guidelines, MinnAqua lessons listed the Minnesota Academic Standards that aligned with the lesson content. Educators appreciated the inclusion of the standards because it saved them the work of having to align the lessons with the standards themselves. The variety of standards made it easy for educators to teach across disciplines, providing evidence for the inclusion of the rewrite guideline, "including interdisciplinary lessons." Additionally, educators felt the inclusion of academic standards would help gain administrative support to integrate MinnAqua lessons into their regular curriculum.

MinnAqua was provided with recommended changes to increase the extent to which the rewrite guidelines were addressed. Example recommendations included

1. Developing rubrics to increase the utility of the authentic assessment ideas added to the lessons per the rewrite guidelines.
2. Creating matrices to make it easier for educators to develop units out of MinnAqua lessons based on standards, topics, and seasons. The matrices will help to address the guideline "creating lessons to stand alone or be used as part of a unit."

Meeting the needs of intended users

Educators provided feedback to confirm that the leaders' guide was successful in addressing the needs of intended users. Most educators thought the lesson format was easy to follow, the lessons would fit into their regular curriculum, and they would use MinnAqua lessons again in the future. Educators were excited about the new knowledge they acquired, even those who considered themselves avid anglers. Educators unfamiliar with angling did not find their lack of experience a barrier to implementing lessons, but an opportunity to bring in guest speakers to assist with a topic.

MinnAqua was provided with a number of recommendations in order to more fully meet the educational needs of formal and informal educators. Example recommendations included

2. Making leaders' guide information available either online or on a CD-ROM. Information accessible digitally could include links referred to in lessons, lesson updates, and online support from educators and Minn Aqua staff.
1. Assisting educators in obtaining resources for lesson implementation through means such as providing grants for educators to obtain their own supplies or creating kits of materials for educators to check out or purchase.

Stage Two Methodology

Upon completing revisions to the leaders' guide, a second round of reviews was carried out. The goals of stage two were to verify the educational content of the leaders' guide, gain support from various educational outreach partner organizations and identify future partnership opportunities, and address inclusion of individuals with physical disabilities in MinnAqua lessons. Valuing the reviewers' time, these reviews took place during stage two when a more complete product was available.

All reviewers during stage two were given approximately 2 months to review. Reviewers were provided with background information about MinnAqua, the new leaders' guide, and the evaluation process in order to make sure they had a clear understanding of the evaluation's purpose and the importance of their role in the review. Incentives for reviewers during stage two were either a $100 honorarium or $100 in fishing supplies for their program use, acknowledgment in the leaders' guide, and a copy upon publication. The specifics of the three types of reviews are described below.

Instructional design expert review

To create a quality leaders' guide, it was important that the educational content was accurate. For this reason, the first goal of the evaluation during stage two was verification of instructional content in the leaders' guide by instructional design experts. Experts were asked to focus their review on educational content specific to their area of expertise. Content areas verified by experts aligned with the rewrite guidelines, as illustrated in Table 2.

A purposive sampling technique was used to choose instructional design experts based on their expertise in a specific educational content area. In some cases, more than one expert was chosen for a content area because the review involved delving into all 39 lessons, which would have been a substantial task for one reviewer in

TABLE 2. Instructional design expert reviewers and rewrite guidelines addressed.

Content area of review	Rewrite guideline addressed	Expert's title
Service-learning components	Adding service-learning ideas.	• Service-learning specialist, Minnesota Department of Education
K–2 options	Including ideas on how to adapt lessons for use with grades K–2.	• Kindergarten teacher • Second grade teacher, Minnesota Science Teachers Association elementary representative, president of Society of Elementary Presidential Awardees, member of Quality Teaching Network
Objectives, assessments, rubrics	Including measurable objectives. Including authentic assessment ideas.	• Two science assessment specialists, Minnesota Department of Education • Two language arts assessment specialists, Minnesota Department of Education • Two math assessment specialists, Minnesota Department of Education
Minnesota Science Academic Standards	Aligning with the 2004 Minnesota Academic Standards.	• District science chair, member of Quality Teaching Network • Catalyst science coach, member of Quality Teaching Network
Minnesota Social Studies Academic Standards	Aligning with the 2004 Minnesota Academic Standards.	• Former social studies specialist for Minnesota Department of Education
Minnesota Math Academic Standards	Aligning with the 2004 Minnesota Academic Standards.	• Principal, member of Quality Teaching Network
Minnesota Language Arts Academic Standards	Aligning with the 2004 Minnesota Academic Standards.	• Second grade teacher, member of Quality Teaching Network • Middle school lead • English teacher, president of Minnesota Council of Teachers of English
Environmental Literacy Scope and Sequence	Aligning with Minnesota's Environmental Literacy Scope and Sequence.	• Education specialist, Minnesota Office of Environmental Assistance

the allotted time. The number of experts was limited to no more than three individuals per content area to help avoid contradictory and counterproductive suggestions, as recommended in both Weston (1987) and Tessmer (1993).

Educational outreach partners' review

Best Practices stresses involvement of stakeholders throughout program development, with an emphasis on developing partnerships to strengthen a program (Seng and Rushton 2003). As mentioned earlier, stakeholders are an important part of any formative evaluation since these individuals can influence the decision for their organization to utilize an educational product (Beyer 1995). To increase the likelihood that the leaders' guide would be a useful tool for various organizations MinnAqua had partnered with in the past, they recognized the value of including these partner organizations as part of the formative evaluation process. For this reason, the goals for the educational outreach partner review were to gain approval and support for the leaders' guide, identify future partnership opportunities, and give partners an opportunity to provide feedback if they desired.

For the partner reviews, MinnAqua identified the organizations they wanted to review the leaders' guide and gave suggestions of individuals within these organizations. Suggested reviewers were individuals who would most likely be responsible for utilizing the leaders' guide with their organization. See Table 3 for listings of educational outreach partner reviewers.

Reviewer tasks varied depending on the stakeholder. MinnAqua created correlation matrices for Junior Girl Scouts, Cub Scouts, and 4-H, which identified correlations between MinnAqua lessons and the organizations' activity requirements. The intent was that MinnAqua would be used as a supporting tool, not a replacement for their educational materials. Individuals from these organizations were asked to review the matrix created for them to verify it was easy to use, comprehensive, and accurate. Great Lakes Aquarium, Cabelas, Gander Mountain, and the University of Minnesota Water Resources Center all reviewed the leaders' guide and provided documentation on how it could be used to strengthen their outreach efforts and future partnerships with MinnAqua. The Recreational Boating and Fishing Foundation was asked to review the leaders' guide and provide supporting documentation of how MinnAqua addressed *Best Practices* throughout the leaders' guide.

Accessibility expert review

Best Practices states that effective programs strive to be inclusive of individuals with disabilities by decreasing constraints to involvement (Seng and Rushton 2003). To address *Best Practices* and ensure that MinnAqua lessons were inclusive of all intended users, an expert familiar with making environmental education and outdoor recreation activities accessible was contacted. The expert was asked to review the leaders' guide and determine how best to address accessibility in individual lessons and/or the leaders' guide as a whole.

Stage two data analysis

Each instructional design expert provided feedback specific to their educational content area, so their feedback was not compiled for each lesson as in stage one. Instead, the data from each lesson were given directly to the MinnAqua education specialist responsible for incorporating comments for specific educational content areas. After reviewing feedback from their assigned instructional design experts, MinnAqua education specialists scheduled one-on-one follow-up meetings to clarify suggestions and ask additional questions.

Two types of feedback were received from educational outreach partners. Some partners commented on the correlation matrices developed for their organization. The MinnAqua education specialist responsible for the matrix reviewed the feedback and met with the reviewer to ensure the utility of the matrix for the partner organization. Other educational outreach partners provided letters of support for the leaders' guide and future partnership efforts. This feedback was given directly to MinnAqua for follow-up with the organizations to identify ways to strengthen partnerships.

The accessibility expert had extensive experience in adapting lessons to be inclusive of individuals with physical disabilities in informal education settings. Based on this experience, he created planning documents for the leaders' guide to aid educators in adapting any MinnAqua lesson for use with individuals with physical dis-

TABLE 3. Educational outreach partner reviewers.

Partner organization	Reviewer's title
Junior Girl Scouts	• Director of Council Services, Girl Scouts Peacepipe Council
Cub Scouts	• Cub Scout leader, Indianhead Council
4-H	• Extension educator, University of Minnesota Extension Center for 4-H Youth Development
University of Minnesota's Water Resources Center	• Water Resources Education coordinator, University of Minnesota Water Resources Center & Sea Grant Program
Great Lakes Aquarium	• Director of Education, Great Lakes Aquarium
Sporting Goods Stores	• Aquarium curator, Cabela's • Retail marketing coordinator, Gander Mountain
Recreational Boating and Fishing Foundation	• President, Recreational Boating and Fishing Foundation

abilities. MinnAqua reviewed the documents and set up a follow-up meeting with the expert to discuss any questions and proposed changes before including the documents as an appendix in the leaders' guide.

Stage Two Findings and Recommendations

Addressing the rewrite guidelines

Each of the instructional design experts reviewed the lessons based on one of the rewrite guidelines. Their positive feedback provided evidence for the successful incorporation of the guidelines, with some reviewers also offering suggestions to strengthen the extent to which guidelines were addressed. For example, the variety of experts reviewing the Minnesota Academic Standards appreciated the interdisciplinary nature of the lessons, while the science experts' provided specific suggestions to make lessons more inquiry-based. This feedback provided evidence that the rewrite guideline, "incorporating interdisciplinary, hands-on, and inquiry-based lessons," was addressed during the expert review.

After stage two, MinnAqua was provided with additional recommended changes to increase the extent to which the rewrite guidelines were addressed. Example recommendations included

1. Revising a variety of lessons where the reading level and concepts were too advanced for students in grades 3–5. This recommendation was based on concerns from instructional design experts, who echoed educator feedback received during pilot tests. This re vision would help to more fully address the rewrite guideline, "ensuring activities and concepts are developmentally appropriate and build on students' prior knowledge."
2. Removing K–2 options where experts felt the lesson's concepts were too advanced to appropriately adapt for younger ages. This would help to more accurately address the rewrite guideline, "including ideas on how to adapt lessons for use with grades K–2," since experts felt it would be inappropriate to try to adapt every lesson to a younger grade level.

Meeting the needs of intended users

Educational outreach partners provided overall positive feedback about the usefulness of the leader's guide. The reviews of the Junior Girl Scouts, Cub Scouts, and 4-H confirmed the utility of the correlation matrices for their organizations' activities. In addition, they provided a few suggestions to better align their organizations' requirements to MinnAqua lessons and strengthen the usefulness of the matrices. The Great Lakes Aquarium saw value in the lessons' information and activities and recognized a variety of ways the leader's guide could be useful to their setting. Representatives from sporting goods stores gave mixed reactions about the usefulness of the leader's guide, with one unsure of its utility and the other excited about the possibility of using the guide to build mentoring opportunities.

Recommendations were generated after stage two to more fully meet the needs of the variety of intended users of the leader's guide. Example recommendations included

1. Writing out the Minnesota Academic Standards and associated benchmarks addressed by a lesson, instead of using letter and number indicators. Instructional design experts felt this would save educators the time of having to cross-reference standards themselves.
2. Working with sporting goods stores to identify how the leader's guide can be used to address their unique educational needs.

Future Directions

Future evaluation efforts to continue to improve the leader's guide include tracking educator use of the leader's guide and the impact MinnAqua activities have on student learning and behaviors. MinnAqua plans to disseminate the leader's guide through workshops and track its use by educators. This will provide an understanding of how lessons are being utilized and aid in future revisions. MinnAqua also intends to carry out a longitudinal study to track student involvement in both MinnAqua activities and angling in general. The study would focus on MinnAqua's ability to reach their long-term student outcomes of aquatic stewardship, participation in angling, and purchase of a fishing license upon turning 16.

Conclusions

Formative evaluations are an integral part of the development of new educational products. The formative evaluation of the leader's guide brought forth its strengths but most importantly identified areas for improvement. The two-stage evaluation design provided the opportunity for lessons to receive multiple reviews from a variety of intended users and stakeholders. The diversity of reviewers provided the depth and breadth of feedback necessary to adequately address the evaluation questions by verifying the incorporation of the rewrite guidelines, identifying ways to strengthen the extent to which the guidelines were addressed, and modifying the leader's guide to more fully meet educators' needs.

The formative evaluation not only gathered feedback to improve the MinnAqua leader's guide; it has value on a larger scale. The evaluation process described in this chapter adds to the literature another formative evaluation design for educators, evaluators, and other professionals wishing to evaluate the development of new educational materials.

Acknowledgments

This evaluation was funded by the Minnesota Department of Natural Resources Division of Fish and Wildlife's MinnAqua program with support from Federal Aid Sportsfish Restoration funds. This chapter is based on a Master's Plan B paper detailing the formative evaluation of the MinnAqua leader's guide (to obtain a copy, contact Amy Grack Nelson). The authors thank Stephan Carlson, who provided valuable support and feedback during the development of the Masters Plan B paper on which this chapter is based. We also extend special thanks to Travis Nelson, Maureen Hawes, and Anne Barthel who provided feedback on this chapter.

References

AAAS (American Association for the Advancement of Science). 1993. Benchmarks for science literacy. Oxford University Press, New York.

Beyer, B. K. 1995. How to conduct a formative evaluation. Association for Supervision and Curriculum Development, Alexandria, Virginia.

Bilitz, S. 1989. Needs assessment for a comprehensive aquatic resources education program. Minnesota Department of Natural Resources, Division of Fish and Wildlife, St. Paul.

Joint Committee on Standards for Educational Evaluation. 1994. The program evaluation standards, 2nd edition. Sage Publications, Thousand Oaks, California.

Landers, P., M. Naylon, and A. Drewes. 2002. Environmental literacy scope and sequence: providing a systems approach to environmental education in Minnesota. Minnesota Office of Environmental Assistance, St. Paul.

Matthees, J. 2003. Annual Funding Agreement (AFA) Minnesota Sports Fish Restoration proposal for aquatic education program-MinnAqua. Minnesota Department of Natural Resources, St. Paul.

Minnesota Department of Natural Resources and Minnesota Department of Education. 2001. Environmental education survey. Minnesota Department of Natural Resources, St. Paul.

Nathenson, M., and E. S. Henderson. 1980. Using student feedback to improve learning materials. Croom Helm, London.

NRC (National Research Council). 1996. National science education standards. National Academy Press, Washington, D.C.

NAAEE (North American Association for Environmental Education). 2004. Excellence in environmental education: guidelines for learning (K–12). North American Association for Environmental Education, Washington D.C.

Patton, M. Q. 1990. Qualitative evaluation and research methods, 2nd edition. Sage Publications, Newbury Park, California.

Seng, P. T., and S. Rushton, editors. 2003. Best practices workbook for boating, fishing, and aquatic resources stewardship education. Recreational Boating and Fishing Foundation, Alexandria, Virginia.

Tessmer, M. 1993. Planning and conducting formative evaluations: improving the quality of education and training. Kogan Page, Philadelphia.

Weston, C. 1987. The importance of involving experts and learners in formative evaluation. Canadian Journal of Educational Communication 16(1):45–58.

Weston, C., L. Mc Alpine, and T. Bordonaro. 1995. A model for understanding evaluation in instructional design. Educational Technology Research and Development 43(3):29–48.

American Fisheries Society Symposium 55:45–53, 2007

Environmental Communication for Aquatic Stewardship

BRIAN A. DAY[1]

Environmental Communication & Training, LLC
1917 Greenbrier Drive, Charlottesville, Virginia 22901, USA

Abstract.—Although educators like to feel that awareness changes behavior, data suggests otherwise. Managers have some tools that educators can also use for directing communication toward changed behavior. Both education and communication are often seen as soft and optional. Because nearly every problem faced in aquatic stewardship is caused by human behavior, this paper is aimed at introducing the tools that can change behavior. It is mostly a measurable scientific approach, but its design and implementation requires good behavioral research. The suggested approach is meant to help aquatic professionals understand and learn the steps of applying behavior change strategies to accomplish their objectives. A simple model of the process and an introduction to social marketing are important components. Most often professionals face aquatic resource management problems to which they can apply well-developed planning, management, engineering, and scientific principles to develop problem solutions. The emerging field of environmental communication brings together a set of behavior change tools that can help address problems related to aquatic stewardship behavior and focus on environmental enforcement, changing behavior when no policy or law exists to force that behavior or helping to drive compliance with existing regulations. Regardless of the aquatic stewardship problem, people need to be engaged in its solution, and behaviors need to change.

Introduction

There is a critical relationship between aquatic stewardship and human behavior. The behaviors of individuals and groups form the interface between the natural and social systems. Since nearly all environmental problems are caused by human behavior, the only long-term solution to these problems is to change human behavior.

Aquatic stewardship has been defined as "the moral obligation to care for the aquatic environment and the actions undertaken to provide that care" (Knuth and Siemer 2004). These actions are behaviors. For most people, these behaviors need to change if we are going to become aquatic stewards.

What is behavior? Behavior is the collective pattern of decisions, practices, and actions of people. Behavior is defined according to what humans perceive to be in their best interests, and is based on their values, socioeconomic situation, as well as many other factors such as experiences, culture, and religion. People interact with their environment through their behavior, decisions, practices, and actions. Successful conservation requires integrating the values, interests, and actions of many stakeholders at a number of different levels, local to global.

Changing behavior is much more difficult than many people think. Long-standing wisdom suggests that if you educate, you change behavior. Although educators like to feel that awareness changes behavior, decades of data suggest this relationship is tenuous at best (Festinger 1964; Haskins 1964; Krugman 1965; Schram 1971; Day and Smith 1996; Hough and Day 2000). The largest gap in human behavior is between what we know and what we do (Festinger 1964; Haskins 1964; Krugman 1965; Day and Smith 1996; AED 2002b). Awareness is not enough. Education is not enough. Instructors need to seriously focus on people's behavior and learn how to change it if

______
[1] E-mail: brian@dayinternet.com

we are going to protect the environment. This cannot be done haphazardly. Some of the people in every community are carrying out good behaviors already. If it is known why people are doing what they do, achieving behavioral goals becomes much easier.

Factors Influencing Behavior

Decisions about which behaviors are to be targeted for change through an aquatic stewardship program need to be technically informed, but also must be socially, culturally, and economically viable for stakeholders, the beneficiaries of these programs. The diverse set of stakeholders should be involved in selecting the desired new behaviors. Stakeholders should be asked to review the potential behaviors and indicate whether they are viable within the community of interest. When identifying what is possible, stakeholder concerns must be addressed. Behaviorists refer to real barriers to carrying out new behaviors as "external determinates;" those barriers that are perceived are equally important and are called "internal determinates." Hernandez and Monroe (in Day and Monroe 2000) have called this process "Making it possible by making it easy – Removing barriers!"

The critical elements of barriers to achieving desired behaviors are often rooted in values, ethics, culture, and religious beliefs. Value barriers may arise when considering what is more important to the individual or community, financial rewards of harvest or conservation for future generations. Ethical norms, or judgments of right and wrong, may vary between communities that share a resource. Culture barriers may have to do with passed-down trades or skills such as fishing practices and rights. Religious beliefs often affect the way that resources are perceived, with some religious traditions considering that humankind has dominance over other species, while other religious traditions hold that there is a human commitment to sharing the earth.

Communication programs aimed at establishing or reinforcing a sense of aquatic stewardship may aim at educating a population or at building new skills for individuals, such as preparing them to negotiate in a resource allocation process. At other times communication bypasses the educa-

tion process altogether and aims to stimulate a new behavior based on appealing to emotional or cultural values and then providing the education after the initial behavioral commitment is made.

Education/skills

Education is an important factor in determining a person's behavior. The type, quality and amount of education will determine the way a person behaves and the way he or she perceives, values, and interacts with others and the environment. An important element is people's confidence to act. Self-efficacy refers to what people think about their ability "to organize and execute courses of action required to attain designated types of performance" (Bandura 1977). To create effective behavior change programs, educators need to build confidence in being able to take on new behavior(s). This can be done by both providing verbal persuasion and by creating opportunities within education programs to allow building skills through guided practice and/or corrective feedback.

Social norms, mores, and peer pressure

Our societies create a system of social norms that humans follow in their daily lives. These social norms are tempered by the values and ethics of that society. When a person strays from the social norms or mores of society, they are often ostracized or punished. There is peer pressure from society to follow the norms or mores that are considered to be in the best interest of all citizens of that society. Human behavior is therefore very often molded and guided by social norms and peer pressure.

As we develop educational programs that call for changes in behavior, there is a need to be consistent with the overall sociocultural norms of the community. Changing these norms is more than an aquatic stewardship program can be expected to do in many cases. The new behavior sought must be consistent with the basic norms of the community if there is any hope of it being adopted. The pressure to fit in is sometimes offset by those who want to be special or a leader or first to do something new. These early adopters are whom educators need to reach to create an alternative norm in the community. Educators can use assessments of the audience and the community to identify these potential early adopters (Hernandez 2000).

Social marketing (Kotler and Zaltman 1971; Day and Monroe 2000; AED 2002a) is a set of communication tools designed to address not only the communications needs for behavior change, but also to put the product or idea (e.g., of aquatic stewardship) into circulation as a part of bringing out this behavior change. Thus, social marketing targets and involves both the individual and the community.

Politics and law

Politics and law have a large influence on the behavior of people. Law serves to standardize behavior and to regulate relations between individuals and groups. Conformance and obedience to laws results in some type of reward or social acceptance for the individual and deviance results in punishment. A person's behavior is greatly defined by the political system and laws they live under; politics likewise is heavily influenced by people's values, ethics, culture, and economic system. When an effective enforcement mechanism is in place, laws and regulations can be very efficient ways of changing behavior. However, when there is no enforcement, laws and regulations are just paper documents. Often behavior change campaigns can be used to enforce laws (for an example, see Day and Monroe 2000, Chapter 14).

Economics

An aquatic stewardship program that promotes behavior change in conflict with economic realties will be ignored or unsuccessful. Most often, if real effort is put into addressing human needs and stewardship at the same time, there is real potential for long-term change. Facilitating these efforts is a difficult and critical job.

A Five-Step Process for Changing Behavior

An emerging group of communication professionals who draw from academic research in social sciences and commercial marketing experience (Day and Monroe 2000; AED 2002b) have introduced new techniques that, used together, will not only raise awareness but will actually persuade both citizens and policymakers to change behavior. The field is called social marketing and can provide the tools to systematically approach the problem with well-tested techniques. The goal of environmental social marketing is to promote behaviors that will improve the environment with social benefits (Kotler and Zaltman 1971; Day and Monroe 2000).

Social marketing techniques include thorough assessment of the potential audiences, a clear definition of the objectives, development of key messages, and an overall strategy that makes sure messages are consistent while also uniquely persuasive to each audience. Social marketing practitioners believe it is often barriers—real or perceived—that prevent people or institutions from changing their behaviors. Traditional marketing tools are used to remove those barriers. Social marketing also provides positive incentives to motivate people to change. Effective marketing campaigns are not strictly a function of how much money is spent. Strategic social marketing with limited resources can be effective.

Defining terms

Social marketing is a step-by-step approach to motivate specific people (often referred to as "stakeholders" or "key audiences" or "target audiences") to take some specific, measurable action or actions for the good of the community. "Social marketing is a process for influencing human behavior on a large scale, using marketing principles for the purpose of societal benefit rather than for commercial profit" (Smith 1999).

Public awareness or public education has the task of making people aware of a certain set of facts, ideas, or issues. Social marketing often utilizes public awareness or education campaigns to inform key audiences and predispose them to appropriate action, but takes this process further to prompt people to act on their new awareness. All too often, campaigns that are intended to cause specific changes in a community stop at simply informing people. This is rarely enough to promote the kinds of specific actions needed to protect the environment.

Social marketing in five steps

Successful social marketing involves creativity and fun, but it also involves more detailed data collection, analysis, and interpretation than most people realize. The five steps depicted in Figure 1 involve a process for collecting information from people on their concerns, attitudes, actions, and reactions. By listening carefully, thinking critically and creatively, and checking and re-checking his/her impressions, a social marketing campaign planner discovers what will work for this audience, in this campaign, at this time (Day and Monroe 2000; AED 2002b).

Step 1: conduct an initial assessment.—The success of any social marketing effort depends largely on the quality of its initial assessment. This critical stage will determine future activities. Campaign managers must ensure that their own biases do not distort strategies. Often, communicators think they know what people think and allow that to influence their work. Communicators need to be objective when doing the assessment. The assessment step makes sure that the perspectives of all stakeholders are considered when identifying the key issues.

Market research will serve as a guide to all marketing decisions and be the basis for tracking the impact of the campaign. Without consumer-based market research, marketing campaigns are guaranteed to miss their mark. Many large commercial and social marketing campaigns have had little impact or, even worse, have triggered major backlashes because their strategies were based solely on the thinking of experts claiming to know what is best for their target market. The target audience(s) must be actively involved in campaign development through market research. Of course experience is important, but research data are critical in veri-

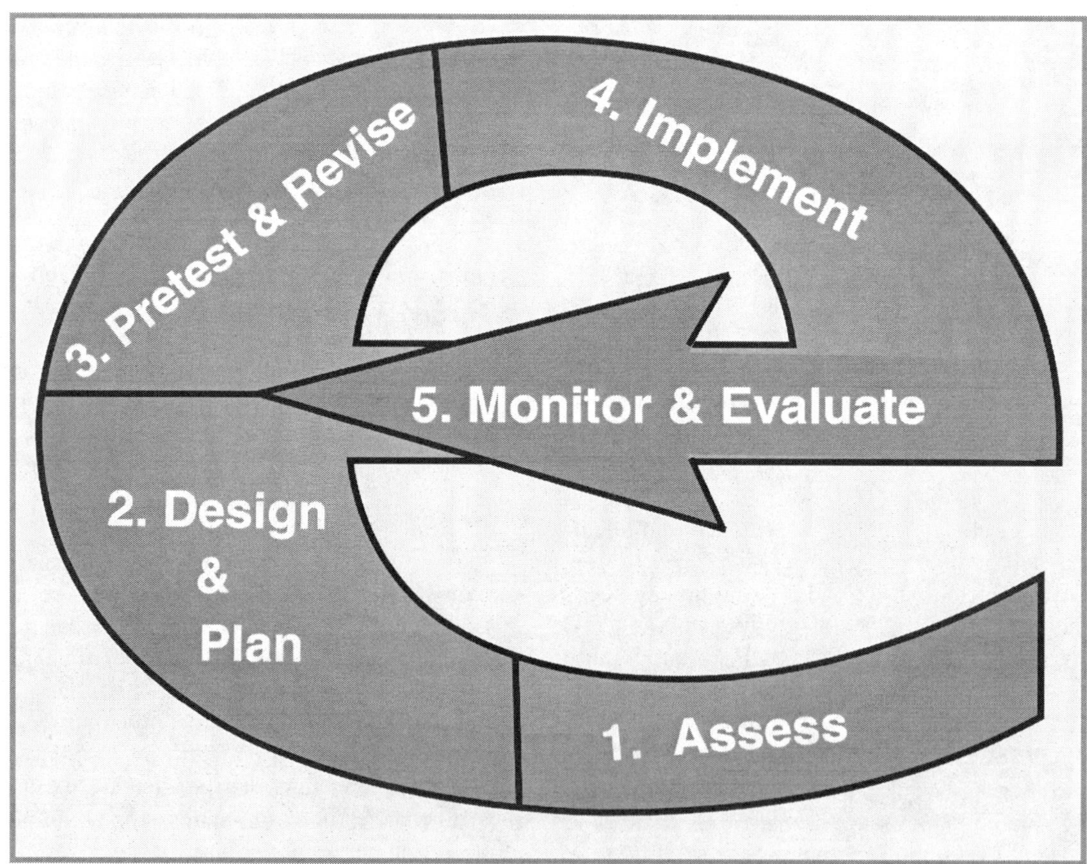

FIGURE 1. The five steps of social marketing for creating behavior change.

fying or dispelling assumptions and conventional wisdom.

The scope of research can be modified to match the resources available. Keep in mind, though, that if an effort lacks the funds to conduct minimally adequate research, the first task is to build the case for new funding. Also, remember that the reluctance to invest in meaningful research may very well be the primary cause of failure in most behavior change campaigns.

Questions such as the following should help campaign planners collect the necessary information and perspectives (Hernandez 2000):

- What is/are the concerns to be addressed by this campaign? What are environmental, social and economic impacts as seen from the perspective of each stakeholder?
- Is the problem ongoing or is it the result of past demands of the local people? Is it passive and unintentional?
- Are the environmental, economic, social, or other perceived benefits gained by those who adopt the new behavior, or do benefits accrue to some other individuals or groups?
- What are the laws and policies that govern the problem? Who is responsible for their enforcement?
- What work on the problem has been done to date? What was their approach? Did they produce data that would be useful to the new campaign? What were their achievements, obstacles and failures? What worked?
- What are the specific behaviors that will contribute to solving the problem?
- Who are the "doers" (i.e., those who have adopted the desired behavior) and "nondoers"? Is there a need to change, improve, or maintain certain behaviors in each group?
- For each stakeholder, what is their "media diet?" What radio do they listen to? Do they watch any television? Can and do they read and if so what? Who do they find a credible source of information?

In trying to answer these and related questions, educators will clearly define the problem and the key issues for each stakeholder and will probably identify several important unknowns that will require further investigation.

Each stakeholder (or a sampling from each group of stakeholders) must be interviewed either individually or collectively (via focus groups) to determine what incentives or benefits and potential obstacles to behavior or policy changes need to be addressed in the social marketing program. Relevant information must be gathered about the current or potential effects of the problem on the lives of stakeholders. Each will have a different perspective and level of knowledge related to the problem that must be taken into consideration.

Educators conducting an assessment should be sure to talk with both men and women and understand who might be impacted by the behavior change plan. Information channels and motivations are often different for men and women. This can be key to a final communication plan. Mitigation strategies should be identified for the negatively impacted parties. Attention to this element is critical for achieving broad support for the goals of the program and for implementing the necessary behavior change.

The final aquatic stewardship assessment document should include

- Situation analysis—a clear and concise summary of the status of the problem, including a statement of the problem, objectives, and strategic options for achieving objectives. Summaries of interviews with representatives from each group of stakeholders (anglers, boaters, electric utilities, etc.) to understand their particular perspective on or interest in the problem.
- An assessment of the potential for partnerships among stakeholders to address the problem.
- Key issues—the problems and opportunities that will be encountered in addressing the problem (specific for each group). These issues are identified in the assessment and will be addressed by the marketing strategies. It is important to clearly define what can be done on the supply, demand, and policy levels to control the problem and which stakeholders can potentially have an impact by taking certain actions. These stakeholders will be your target group. All other groups

that influence the behavior of these stakeholders become channels through which targeted groups can be reached.

- Potential channels of communication and influence on stakeholders (interpersonal—who do they listen to, electronic and print).
- Finally, the assessment should include a comprehensive list of recommendations and potential strategies drawing on outside technical assistance if necessary.

Step 2: design and plan.—Educators should define the objective(s) of the campaign. Objectives should be SMART: specific, measurable, ambitious, realistic, and time-bound. They must clearly describe the desired outcomes of the proposed campaign. Will the education team be content in raising awareness about the problem if no real action is taken? What progress will be made in phases toward the ultimate goal? The draft strategy will define the target audiences. It will also address each of the four elements of the social marketing campaign. Often, when social marketing or behavior change strategies are taken up by anyone in the environmental field, they think of only the promotion portion of the social marketing approach. But there is much more. Among formal social marketers, these are called the "Four P's" (i.e., product, price, promotion, and place)

Product.—What is the behavior the program is trying to encourage? Will the intended behavior change involve use of particular products? Will people perceive the use of those products as being in their interest? How will use of particular products benefit them and their community? For example, if a program is designed to reduce unintended catch of sea turtles, the program sponsor should ask questions such as where will commercial fisherman buy turtle exclusion devices, are the devices readily available, and do fishermen see it as consistent with their self-interest to use the devices.

Price.—What will it cost the target consumer in money, time, or psychological terms to adopt the desired behavior? Will people have to spend free time in their community contributing to the effort? (Again, from an aquatic stewardship perspective, an example might be, is the mooring buoy close enough to where I want to dive to make it worth my time to use it instead of drop-

ping my anchor at a dive site?) Will that mean giving up something else? Ultimately the target group will have to be convinced that what they are being asked to do is relevant to their welfare and worth the price they are being asked to pay and/or time they are being asked to give.

Promotion.—The social marketer should ask questions such as the following. What are the key messages for each target audience? What content and approaches may best influence the decisions and behaviors of the specific stakeholder? What are the most cost-effective means of getting those messages to the key audiences, interpersonal, print media, television, radio, or electronic media? Messages should be relevant, well focused, and, ultimately, must influence behavior change. Messages will vary depending on prior knowledge and understanding of the issue, and concerns of the target groups. The messages will change over time as the target audiences evolve in their perceptions and behavior: initially, the focus may be on raising awareness, but later may change to a call to action. Once people are convinced to adopt the desired behavior, the message must be modified to focus on the maintenance of the new behavior. Both the environment and people's behaviors are dynamic. Never assume that things will stay the same for very long.

Place.—Where is the consumer expected to act on the call to action? Sometimes it is necessary to select a place and create an event where people can get involved. People will be asked to take action within their communities to identify, report, purchase, or carry out some new behavior. (In aquatic stewardship, for example, an appropriate question may be, are there stations convenient to the target audience to unload onboard sewage systems?)

Based on the assessment carried out in Step 1, it is now time to develop the initial communication strategy. It is important that educators actually involve stakeholders in this process. To the degree that people feel this is coming from the outside, they will feel that it is imposed on them and may not take any ownership. To the degree that they feel a part of developing the campaign and strategy, they will feel pride and ownership and the degree of internalization and potential adoption of new behaviors will be much higher.

It bears repeating that people will not adopt

the new behaviors promoted by an aquatic stewardship program unless they believe that such behavior is in their own best interest. This is why one should involve stakeholders directly in the program development process. In the process of doing the assessment, discussed in step one, each of the stakeholders communicates what he or she feels are the barriers to carrying out the desired new behavior. The campaign must remove these perceived or real barriers. This may mean changing people's understanding or addressing specific pieces of their livelihoods. This is where social marketing gets a lot bigger than just communication (product, price, and place). Sometimes there are real economic and social issues that need to be addressed, not just talked about. These issues are critical to success. People must feel they can overcome those barriers if communicators are going to be successful in bringing about behavior changes.

Part of designing the campaign is determining how to measure success. This means turning the results of the step one assessment into a baseline against which success can be measured. The evaluation in step five requires this baseline. This evaluation measure can then be used to report back to program donors and supporters and provides an element of accountability.

A basic approach to establishing a quantitative, repeatable measure of the community's problem is a knowledge, attitudes, and practices (KAP) survey. KAP surveys query a statistically representative sample of the targeted consumers via telephone interviews, written questionnaires, and/or interviews (for environmental examples of KAP studies, see AED 1998, 1999). Focus groups are another standard tool for gathering information from a range of individuals representing the target community. A range of expert consultants, private market research firms, and academic institutions can assist in conducting this research.

A part of the communication plan may address training needs related to building the skills or knowledge of stakeholders, building the skills of the communication/education team, and fostering important skills in participants.

The success of a social marketing program will depend on the degree to which all key stakeholders are willing to join forces based on common and mutually beneficial objectives. Each stakeholder will have his/her own motivations and must be educated to understand and appreciate the objectives, motivations, apprehensions, and resources of the others.

Action plan.—The action plan will detail all strategies and tactics within a matrix that assigns responsibility for implementation of the strategy, and the time frame for execution.

Budget.—Every element of the marketing plan must be budgeted in detail and reviewed by each team member. The contacts and networks made available by the team members may lead to complementary funding from other sources.

Step 3: pretest and revise.—This is the step that can save an enormous amount of time, energy and money. It is important to pretest the strategy, materials, and messages. In both commercial and social marketing settings, there are abundant examples of campaigns and messages that have sent the wrong messages because of language problems, different reference points of the sender and the recipient audiences, and religious, cultural, and ethnic differences that no one on the design team expected. This step does take time and requires sharing the storyboard, the message text, or the strategy document with selected members of the intended target audience. How do they react to the communication strategy, materials, and/or message? Are those the desired reactions? Are the target audiences motivated to take on the new behavior? Are they confused? Did they get a different message than was intended? This is the time to find out and to make necessary modifications in the communication/education plan. Even major corporations have had major failures from skipping this step. It is critical, given the limited resources communicators have to address these issues.

Step 4: implement.—Implementation has been long awaited. Much can be learned even through the implementation process as the campaign rolls out if communicators pay close enough attention. Communicators can learn from each step and from the process of actually starting the campaign. Did the campaign start on the right day of the week? Who learned about it first? Did that work well? Keep looking at every dimension of the campaign. What is learned may be surprising.

Because both the environment and people's behavior are dynamic, communicators must make sure that the implementation process is well monitored and flexible. As the context or information changes, so must the content or design of the campaign. Ideally, a campaign will be rolled out in stages. Sometimes these stages overlap, given that different stakeholders may be targeted simultaneously.

If there are enough resources that more than one activity can be launched in close proximity to another, the combination of changes happening in the community can be greater than the sum of the efforts that have been put forth. When exciting things happen, they create their own pull or gravity. People want to be a part of new exciting things. As they see others—they may not be responding to the communication effort, but to the fact that others are making changes. Some people call this synergy, others an organic whole, and in communication this is often called the "heating up process" (AED 2002b).

Step 5: conduct monitoring and evaluation.—The continued success of the social marketing strategy will depend on regular monitoring and periodic evaluation. The quantitative KAP research can be repeated to measure impact, guide the development of new educational and marketing materials, and guide the regular refinement of strategies. Tracking and evaluation research should use the same methodology and questionnaire used in the baseline survey.

The social marketing plan should be compared with the project's success in achieving defined objectives. All team members are encouraged to discuss their satisfaction or frustrations. This input, combined with ongoing market research, can be the basis for a participatory planning process through which the marketing plan will be refined as needed.

When people think about evaluation, they often think about "how did it go" from a subjective perspective. For evaluation to be most useful, there must be some form of comparison, quantitative when possible. This makes it much easier to judge the achievement of real outcomes, satisfy funders, and keep programs going. For longer-range projects, which most environmental projects need to be, evaluation must be ongoing, annually for instance. To do this well, indicators of success must be identified and applied. Progress on achieving aquatic stewardship indicators can be reported through the media, providing reinforcement to the behavior change that has taken place.

Because communicators know that many other variables will change even without the campaign, and hopefully some new directions will take place because of it, communicators should be prepared to innovate. Both human behavior and the aquatic environment are very dynamic, with changes taking place all the time. In the assessment stage, both the qualitative research and the baseline study were extractive—that is, information was collected from the community with no direct information return. During this stage, consider how to report back to that community about what has happened. Results should be shared.

Conclusion

There is no magic bullet for changing behavior. There is no cookie cutter approach that works everywhere. For those engaged in trying to encourage aquatic stewardship, there is a process that many others in related environmental fields and in other social applications have found helpful. It is much more rigorous, requires more time, and often goes well beyond the promotion efforts that people think of when trying to create a communication program. However, if all these elements are truly taken into account, there is an increased opportunity for success. If aquatic resource managers are going to be successful in bringing about aquatic stewardship behavior, they must utilize every communication and education tool available. The steps and methodology outlined here provide overall guidance for communication/education programs seeking to foster increases in aquatic stewardship behaviors through social marketing.

References

AED (Academy for Educational Development). 1998. GreenCOM Project: knowledge, sttitudes, and practices of Egyptian farmers towards water resources: a national survey, October 1998. El-Zanaty & Associates, Cairo. Available: www.greencom.org/greencom/pdf/Egypt1.pdf. (August 2006).

AED (Academy for Educational Development). 1999. GreenCOM Project: knowledge, attitudes, and practices of district irrigation engineers in Egypt: impact survey final report. Cairo: Available: www.greencom.org/greencom/pdf/Egypt1.pdf. (August 2006).

AED (Academy for Educational Development). 2002a. Social marketing lite. Academy for Educational Development, Washington, D.C.

AED (Academy for Educational Development). 2002b. Heating up society to take environmental action: a guide to effective environmental education and communication. Academy for Educational Development, Washington, D.C.

Bandura, A. 1977. Social learning theory. Prentice Hall, Inc., Englewood Cliffs, New Jersey.

Day, B. A., and M. C. Monroe, editors. 2000. Environmental education and communication for a sustainable world: handbook for international practitioners. Academy for Educational Development, Washington, D.C.

Day, B. A., and W. A. Smith. 1996. The applied behavior change (ABC) framework: environmental applications. Advances in Education 2:5–9.

Festinger, L. 1964. Behavioral support for opinion change. Public Opinion Quarterly 28(3):404–417.

Haskins, J. B. 1964. Factual recall as a measure of advertising effectiveness. Journal of Advertising 4(1):2–8.

Hernandez, O. 2000. Formative research. Pages 47–56 *in* B. A. Day and M. C. Monroe, editors. Environmental education and communication for a sustainable world: handbook for international practitioners. Academy for Educational Development, Washington, D.C.

Hough, R., and B. A. Day. 2000. Pages 33–37 *in* B. A. Day and M. C. Monroe, editors. Environmental education and communication for a sustainable world: handbook for international practitioners. Academy for Educational Development, Washington, D.C.

Kotler, P., and G. Zaltman. 1971. Social marketing: an approach to planned social change. Journal of Marketing 35:3–12.

Knuth, B. A., and W. F. Siemer. 2004. Fostering aquatic stewardship: a key for fisheries sustainability. Pages 243–255 *in* E. E. Knudsen, D. D. MacDonald, and Y. K. Muirhead, editors. Sustainable management of North American fisheries. American Fisheries Society, Symposium 43, Bethesda, Maryland.

Krugman, H. E. 1965. The impact of television advertising: learning without involvement. Public Opinion Research Quarterly 29(3):349–356.

Schram, W. 1971. The process and effects of mass media communication. University of Illinois Press, Urbana.

Smith, W. A. 1999. Marketing with no budget. Social Marketing Quarterly 5(2):6–11.

American Fisheries Society Symposium 55:55–72, 2007

Overview of the Recreational Boating Industry's Aquatic Stewardship through Technology, Innovation, and Education

MONITA W. FONTAINE AND MATHEW P. DUNN[1]

National Marine Manufacturers Association
444 North Capitol Street, Suite 645, Washington, D.C. 20001, USA

Abstract.—This study provides an overview of the recreational boating industry's contributions to aquatic stewardship and environmental responsibility. It provides a thorough analysis of the boating industry's efforts to promote responsible recreation through the promotion of education and outreach programs, the development and marketing of new, environmentally friendly products, and the cooperative efforts of the industry to work in conjunction with state and federal government to institute policies that protect the environment.

Introduction

The U.S. recreational marine industry, along with other outdoor recreation interests, has long been faced with the challenge of balancing the need to protect and preserve the environment with the desire to keep outdoor aquatic recreation open and accessible to the American public. Often, these two demands are seen to compete and are sometimes even viewed as mutually exclusive. The National Marine Manufacturers Association (NMMA), however, takes a different view: environmental protection and open access for boating are mutually reinforcing—two goals that can be achieved by similar means and at the same time. NMMA's goal is to make boating the number one choice in outdoor recreation. With that endeavor comes the responsibility to promote proper, environmentally sustainable uses of America's aquatic resources.

NMMA is the nation's largest recreational marine industry association, representing more than 1,600 boat builders, engine manufacturers, and marine accessory manufacturers, as well as more than 800 marina operators and owners through its affiliated Association of Marina Industries (AMI). NMMA members collectively produce more than 80% of all recreational marine products made in the United States, includ-

ing boats, engines, and marine accessories and components.

NMMA and its member companies are well aware of the need to promote responsible boating. It has long been the aim of NMMA and the companies, large and small, comprising it to attain this outcome through a variety of mechanisms that at once serve the environment, the industry and those who depend on it for their economic well-being, and the boating enthusiasts who are closest to the resource. To that end, they have been actively involved in advancing the cause of aquatic stewardship through the development and marketing of new, innovative products and through the support of environmental initiatives and outreach.

Environmentally friendly products are often pursued by companies because there is consumer demand. When companies offer pioneering, state-of-the-art products, they are helping shape consumer preferences. Boaters are increasingly concerned about things like water quality and the protection of important aquatic habitats and ecosystems (see, for example, Lipton 2003). Although innovative products initially come with a higher price tag, boaters are demonstrating their commitment to the environment by electing to purchase them. This is consistent with polling, which indicates that consumers are increasingly drawn

---

[1] E-mail: mdunn@nmma.org

to green marketing campaigns and, given the choice, will opt for environmentally friendly products and companies most of the time. (For a general discussion of environmentalism and its impact on consumer purchasing, see Ketchum, Inc: http://www.ketchum.com/DisplayWebPage/ 0,1003,2870.html.)

The need for these product offerings is abundantly clear. The corporate role in—indeed responsibility for—advancing aquatic stewardship is based centrally on the notion that the making and marketing of advanced, environmentally safe products constitutes an articulation of the need for responsible recreation and offers consumers the widest possible opportunities to do so. Though central, the corporate role in aquatic stewardship is far greater than simply offering environmentally sensitive products. Therefore, we outline the marine industry's larger role in aquatic stewardship by discussing a sampling of past and present environmental initiatives as well as attempting to chart a course for future corporate participation in the important task of preserving the beauty and bounty of the world's oceans, lakes, rivers, and coasts—all of which are essential to a thriving recreational marine industry.[2]

Although 70% of boating occurs in the nation's lakes (Duda et al. 2000), NMMA has taken note of the warnings regarding ocean environmental health issued by the U.S. Commission on Ocean Policy in its 2004 Final Report to the President and the U.S. Congress (U.S. Commission on Ocean Policy 2004). In that report, which rightly acknowledges that "oceans affect and sustain all life on Earth," the commissioners conclude that "our oceans and marine resources are in serious trouble" (U.S. Commission on Ocean Policy, Letter to the President, October 2004). NMMA has expressed its broad support for nearly all of the commission's more than 200 recommendations directly to the Bush administration and to key members of Congress, as well as to the commission itself. Like our oceans, many of our

lakes and rivers are experiencing similar environmental stresses, and users of these resources, federal, state, and local agencies, and the public at large must be aggressive in attempting to improve the conditions of all of America's aquatic resources. In America's nearly 1,800 federal lakes, which host more than 900 million visits each year and generate more than $44 billion in economic impact (National Recreation Lake Study Commission 1999), almost 40% are said to suffer from some source of pollution or habitat degradation, while nearly half of America's 2,000 watersheds are "seriously or moderately deficient" in water quality (USEPA 1998, cited in National Recreation Lake Study Commission 1999).

Boating, A Growth Industry

From the thrills of wakeboarding and waterskiing to fishing to simply enjoying the sunshine and fresh air of cruising along the coast, millions of Americans enjoy boats and related recreation every year. In 2004, recreational boating contributed approximately $33 billion to the nation's economy (NMMA 2004). The more than 33,000 marine businesses in the United States support some 500,000 well-paying American jobs (NMMA 2004). The number of boats in use in 2004 was 17.6 million, an increase of 210,000 over 2003 and a more than 12.5% increase from 1989 (NMMA 2004). There are approximately 69 million boaters in the United States (NMMA 2004). Despite a modest drop in overall boating participation during the past 15 years, it is clear that interest in boating is once again gaining traction among the American public. Certainly, the demographics are ripe for a significant increase in participation, with the baby boomer generation now reaching the age where time and financial resources for boating are no longer constraints but opportunities. NMMA is dedicated to growing boating further and expanding the industry in order to sustain a strong and socially rewarding American enterprise. But as the popularity of recreational boating grows, so too does the responsibility to effectively foster a national ethic of sound environmental stewardship. The boating industry takes this responsibility seriously. The efforts of the boating industry to help foster environmentally appropriate behav-

---

[2] Of necessity, this overview represents merely a sampling of activities, accomplishments, and developments and is not intended to comprise a comprehensive or exhaustive litany of the myriad innovations in products, technologies, or outreach that the industry has inaugurated.

iors among recreational boaters provide the focus for this paper.

The marine industry depends on its users to protect the environment, a behavior that comes naturally to most boaters. On water, especially, every action or sound a boater makes has a potential impact on air and water quality, nearshore and shoreline ecosystems, and the marine life that inhabits them. A responsible, common sense approach to boating will help protect aquatic ecosystems. Clearly, clean water is the foundation for enjoyable boating. At a basic level, it is up to those who appreciate and recognize the privilege of using America's aquatic environments to protect those resources now and for future generations. It is also incumbent upon manufacturers of boats and related products, however, to promote responsible boating practices and manufacture products that help safeguard the environment.

Industry is in a position to be a very positive force in promoting environmental stewardship through the "pursuit of new business opportunities and markets, reduction of operation footprints, development and deployment of new technology, and establishment of effective partnerships. In addition, business can demonstrate leadership in support for and reform of public policy that seeks to raise industry environmental performance standards in order to gain first-mover advantages while improving the reputation of their industry as a whole with important customers and constituencies" (Millennium Ecosystem Assessment Business and Industry Synthesis Team 2005) In the marine industry, through research and development, testing, and employing technology of related industries, propulsion systems are gaining efficiency, waste treatment systems are becoming more effective, and maintenance products are getting greener. Industry workers understand that their livelihood depends on clean water and that they play a critical role in helping to keep waters clean.

Indeed, it has long been the position of the association that a healthy and clean marine environment makes solid business sense. Not only does careful attention to environmental issues stave off cumbersome government regulations that slow business growth, but without clean and healthy waterways, the desire to boat will diminish. This outcome would have a direct and negative impact on the boating industry, shrinking the demand for boats, reducing interest in coastal tourism, and slowing the local economies that depend on these industries. Moreover, the marine industry recognizes that it is in the interest of everyone, from boat, engine and accessory manufacturers to boaters themselves, to promote sound environmental policies, enhance environmental awareness, and develop innovative marine technologies that ensure the long-term sustainability of America's aquatic treasures for current and future generations to enjoy.

Demand for marine products is inextricably tied to the health of marine environments. This linkage affirms the view that businesses in the marine industry are enhanced rather than hindered by adhering to environmental standards and advancing products that protect aquatic resources. This explains why the recreational boating industry has historically been well ahead of the curve in advancing new technologies, meeting new government regulations, and never shying from the apparent challenges associated with maintaining a healthy corporate bottom line as well as a healthy environment. As the entire marine industry embarks on a coordinated, multiyear, multimillion dollar venture to increase interest in boating and create an entirely new crop of boating consumers through the Grow Boating Initiative,[3] it is clear that environmental awareness and corporate environmental responsibility will play a key role in locating new market opportunities, attracting new boaters, and enhancing the overall boating experience.

Environmental Challenges for the Boating Industry

In April 2003, *Environmental Health Perspectives*, a journal on environmental and human health, published an article discussing some of the envi-

---

[3] The Grow Boating Initiative is a cooperative effort by the recreational boating industry leaders to increase participation and ultimately improve sales for any business with a financial interest in the recreational marine industry. Working in collaboration, industry leaders have endorsed a 3-year program with a $50 million budget to pursue national advertising campaigns and other initiatives to raise awareness and improve product quality and services. For more information, see http://www.growboating.org.

ronmental concerns associated with recreational boating. The article, "The Environmental Pain of Pleasure Boating," overly dramatizes and substantially mischaracterizes boating's impact on the environment as "death by a thousand cuts," in which recreational watercrafts "put petroleum products, human and pet waste, trash, and potentially toxic metals into coastal waters, lakes, and rivers," as well as "slice swaths through slow-to-heal marine vegetation" and produce noise that "disturb[s] sea life" (Fields 2003) The article also impugns marinas, which it says "provide a treasure trove of potential ecological disruptors, including slips, mooring pins, launch ramps, gas docks, sewage pumpout stations (if used improperly), boating supply stores, and boatyards where vessels are repaired and maintained" (Fields 2003) But the article also notes the considerable progress made by the marine industry and others to mitigate boating's footprint on the environment, and it concludes optimistically with a quote from Andre Mele, an environmentalist who wrote a now hard-to-find book called *Polluting for Pleasure*. Says Mele, "Boaters can be the best conservationists on the water" (Mele 1993) And increasingly, the recreational marine industry and its manufacturers are providing boaters new products that tap into the innate conservation ethic common to most boaters.

Boating can impact the environment in numerous ways, including air and water pollution, habitat disturbance, fuel and oil spills, trash and other marine debris, and sewage disposal and waste treatment. Recreational boat engines have been identified as a source of air pollution, and older marine engines have an impact on water quality, although that impact is difficult to determine with any precision. While the environmental impacts of petroleum discharges from boats have in many cases been greatly exaggerated, the marine industry has recognized the need to mitigate the risk of fuel spillage, increase the fuel economy of marine engines, and reduce water and air emissions. Manufacturers are promoting new technologies and products to address these challenges in addition to limiting engine pollution; bilge waste, which contains wastewater mixed with oil and fuel; and refueling spills, which leak volatile organic compounds directly into aquatic ecosystems.

The industry is working proactively to promote more effective disposal of maritime trash and sewage, cleaner waste treatments, and the elimination of marine debris, including discarded fishing gear, which can entangle marine wildlife. Marine manufacturers are also developing new products to mitigate the environmental impact of boat cleaners, hull stripping, painting and repair products, and antifouling and bottom paints, which can introduce toxins and heavy metals into ecosystems.

The Revolution in Marine Engines and the Selling of Cleaner Boating

In the mid-1990s, the U.S. Environmental Protection Agency (EPA) initiated a rulemaking that had profound implications for boat engine manufacturers.[4] Because, as some studies allege,[5] conventional carbureted two-stroke outboard marine engines release as much as 20–30% of fuel directly into the air or water, and consequently emit hydrocarbons (HC) and nitrogen oxide (NOx) into the environment, EPA began consultations with the marine industry to begin a process to address this concern. Working closely with NMMA and marine engine manufacturers, EPA developed regulations in 1996 that should result in an unprecedented 75% reduction of hydrocarbon emissions by 2025 from outboard engines, personal

---

[4] A provision was added to the Clean Air Act in 1990 authorizing EPA to regulate "non-road vehicles," which included marine outboard motors and personal watercraft.

[5] It is important to note that NMMA does not concur with the findings of some studies that suggest significant fuel discharges into the water from recreational boat engines. Many of these studies employ faulty methodologies and test in nonrepresentative environments (e.g. enclosed test tanks), the findings of which cannot be verified or replicated in actual marine environments. In fact, several credible scientific studies indicate no substantial or detectable water pollution from boats. These studies include (1) Keuka Lake Water Quality Testing Program. Peter Landre and Amy Barkley, Keuka Lake Association, (Hammondsport, New York: 2000); (2) Water Test: Donner Lake, California, Deloro Water Co./ Donner Lake Division, (1999); (3) Water Test: Anaheim California. Orange County Water District (1997); and (4) Oregon Department of Environmental Quality. Water Quality Status Assessment Report, Section 305(b) Report (2000).

watercraft (PWC) engines, and jet boat engines (USOFR 1996). From 1998 to 2006, the corporate average exhaust emission standards for outboard and PWC marine engine manufacturers become increasingly more stringent, with EPA expecting to achieve the following projected hydrocarbon and NOx reductions nationally: 4% in 2000, 26% in 2005, 52% in 2010, 68% in 2015, 73% in 2020, and 75% in 2025, with the model showing a constant 75% reduction in HC and NOx emissions through 2050 (USEPA 1996).

At the time of the rulemaking, the technology to meet EPA standards did not, on the whole, exist—EPA acknowledged then that its emission standard would "require revolutionary technology that does not currently exist across the product line, the lead time for implementation is short, and the targeted reductions across the phase-in are large" (USOFR 1996). Engine manufacturers responded to the rulemaking by pursuing two key technology advancements: direct fuel injected (DFI) two-stroke engine technology and four-stroke engines. In two-stroke DFI engines, fuel is injected directly into the combustion chamber and burned while the exhaust port is blocked by the piston at the top of its stroke, effectively reducing emissions by preventing unburned fuel from escaping through the exhaust port. Four-stroke engines, like those in a car, are lubricated by circulating multiviscosity oil in the engine. These engines require oil changes after a certain period of time and easily meet EPA's emissions standards. Although four-stroke engines are heavier, more complex, and more expensive than traditional two-stroke engines, they are far quieter, improving the quality of the boating experience and minimizing environmental impacts on sensitive habitats. They are also 40% more fuel efficient, lowering fuel costs and significantly limiting pollution impacts. Despite not having technology at the ready when the EPA regulation was finalized, the marine industry's aggressive pursuit of new technology means the four-stroke and DFI two-stroke marine engines available today already meet the EPA emissions standards for 2006.[6]

The EPA rulemaking is so important because of its reach. According to EPA, more than 10 million marine engines are operated in the United States, contributing to "hydrocarbons (HC) and oxides of nitrogen (NOx) emissions in many areas of the country" (USEPA 2005a) Accelerating the retirement of old-technology two-stroke engines is one environmental challenge that remains. Clearly, it is in the business interests of the marine industry to sell the new engine technologies which it has spent so much time and money developing. In this instance, maintaining a healthy corporate bottom line converges with that which is best for the environment. The boating industry is pursuing rapid fleet turnover—that is, the accelerated transition from traditional two-strokes to four-stoke and DFI two-stroke technology—through a variety of channels, including broad-based public relations and marketing efforts, incentive programs, warranty deals, and others. This change in engine technology and the accompanying educational and marketing efforts to prompt consumers to switch from two-stroke to four-stroke engines demonstrates how industry interests and stewardship interests go hand in hand. The two-stoke marine engine population, as a result of the EPA rulemaking as well as innovative product development and aggressive marketing by engine manufacturers, is rapidly declining. But the accelerated decline in the two-stroke population also is due in large measure to government–industry voluntary, cooperative partnerships in several critical areas of the country.

Although the California Air Resources Board[7] elected to pursue a command-and-control approach, which placed more stringent regulations[8] on the marine industry than had EPA in 1996, several state environmental agencies chose a different tack and implemented cooperative programs with industry that have proved immensely successful. For example, the New Hampshire De-

---

[6] Unlike the auto industry, which had 25 years to comply, outboard and PWC builders were given 10 years to achieve the same standard.

[7] California is the only state in the nation that has the authority to pursue more rigorous clean air regulations than the U.S. Environmental Protection Agency. Such regulations are promulgated through the California Air Resources Board.

[8] California Air Resources Board regulations require marine engine manufacturers to reduce HC emissions by 75% on 2001 models and by 90% on 2008 models.

partment of Environmental Services (DES) in 2000 approached the New Hampshire Marine Trades Association (NHMTA), a local marine trade group that includes marine engine dealers, to form a partnership designed to encourage boating consumers to purchase and use low-pollution two- and four-stroke marine engines through a statewide education and outreach campaign (see the Clean Marine Engine Initiative at the DES Web site: http://www.des.state.nh.us/ard/marine_engines.htm). The New Hampshire boating industry responded enthusiastically—NHMTA signed a Memorandum of Understanding (MOU) with the state environmental agency in February of 2000, and nearly 40 marine retailers in the state had signed onto the agreement by 2002. Through the program, New Hampshire marine dealers agreed to immediately encourage customers to buy low-pollution engines and report sales totals back to DES in order evaluate the success of the program. As a result of the program, participating dealers "met the New Hampshire program's goal for 2001 of having clean engines comprise 75% of all new engine sales, well ahead of the schedule required by EPA regulations. The program has set a goal of 90% for 2002 through 2005," and is well on track (USEPA 2002).

The program in New Hampshire turned out to have a lasting impact beyond the state's borders. In early 2002, NMMA joined EPA and other national partners in celebrating the success of the New Hampshire program and with that backdrop embarked on a program to expand the initiative to the entire New England region. Out of the New Hampshire program was born the New England Clean Marine Engine Initiative (http://www.epa.gov/ne/assistance/cmei/index.html). This cooperative effort, also known as the "Get on Board Initiative," was designed "to accelerate the sale of low-pollution two- and four-stroke marine engines that emit substantially less pollution than conventional marine engines" (USEPA 2005a). The New England agreement, formalized in an MOU among NMMA and other parties, includes Connecticut, Maine, Massachusetts, New Hampshire, New York, Rhode Island, Vermont, and 10 tribal nations. NMMA signed a similar accord with the state of Wisconsin in 2001, an important development since that state is home to both Mercury Marine and Bombardier Recreational Prod-

ucts, two major engine manufacturers. In addition, NMMA signed clean engine MOUs with appropriate state agencies in Oregon and Florida in 2002 and with New Jersey in 2003. In 2000, NMMA's Canadian affiliate, the Canadian Marine Manufacturers Association, signed an MOU with Environment Canada, the federal environmental agency, designed to "fast track the early introduction of cleaner engines" in that nation (Environment Canada 2000).

There is no question that these efforts have hastened the introduction of these new-technology, low-emissions engines into these markets and had a demonstrable impact on consumer purchasing. Indeed, statistics released in July of 2005 by the New England office of the EPA, which runs the Get on Board Initiative, verify the success of that program. "About four-fifths of the outboard motors and watercraft engines sold in New England in the last three years by participating retailers were low pollution models," according to EPA. These cleaner engines "help meet EPA low-pollution requirements by reducing air pollution by 75% or more, lowering gasoline discharges to the water, improving fuel efficiency by 35–50%, and using up to 50% less oil" (USEPA 2005b).

Boat builders are also doing their part to increase fuel efficiency through the design and development of lighter, more technologically advanced hulls. MJM Yachts, a Boston-based company, is manufacturing a 34-ft vessel using pieces of fiberglass cloth injected with a resin to reduce the weight from fiberglass without compromising any additional strength. The 34Z requires only 11 gal of diesel fuel per hour to run at 25 knots, which is up to three to four times less fuel than its comparable counterparts. Duroboats, a fishing boat manufacturer, uses a unique hull contouring system to offer several high performing models that operate with minimum fuel use, including a 16-ft craft that can achieve speeds up to 30 mph when combined with a new 40-Hp four-stroke engine or two-stroke DFI engine. One such product used in making lighter, more fuel-efficient hulls and decks is BALTEK Balsa cores. In addition to conserving fuel, the cores are a renewable resource that is produced without depleting hydrocarbons.

When confronted with the prospect of increased government regulation, the industry engaged rather than obstructed the process. Instead of hiring a team of corporate attorneys and systematically attempting to delay or derail new government mandates on marine engine technology, NMMA and its member companies embraced reform, offering technical expertise, testing data and facilities, and industry-wide cooperation. The boating industry, from manufacturer to dealer, in essence acknowledged its inherent responsibility as an environmental steward. The Get on Board Initiative and similar efforts in other states in effect amount to a specific aquatic stewardship education campaign. In the participating states, boating consumers were educated about the environmental benefits associated with the new generation of marine engines, made aware of the environmental concerns associated with older technology, and directed to retailers offering the cleaner option. These programs have been demonstrably successful in raising awareness as sales data indicate that consumers, in large numbers and well ahead of regulatory deadlines, are actively choosing the environmentally safer product, even though these products come with a higher price tag. Independently, this provides compelling evidence about the efficacy of education and outreach in general, and it validates the view that most boaters have an innate sense of personal responsibility to the environment—a sense that can be further cultivated through targeted and purposeful education campaigns, government–industry cooperation, and dedicated resources.

Boat Sewage: A Three-Pronged Approach

The release of untreated sewage into the water by recreational boaters is an important environmental and human health concern. In lakes, waters surrounding marinas, and other waters with low hydrologic flushing rates, the impact of improper waste disposal can be particularly significant. Untreated sewage discharges result in the increased concentration of fecal coliform bacteria and consequent human health risks (Milliken and Lee 1990[9]). Such discharges contaminate and de-

grade water quality by introducing microbial pathogens and hazardous compounds into the marine environment and reducing dissolved oxygen levels (biological oxygen demand) required to decompose organic matter, therefore negatively impacting local aquatic habitats and fish species. The marine industry has approached the boat sewage issue in three central ways: (1) supporting a federal grant program for the construction and maintenance of pumpout facilities under the Clean Vessel Act, and the legislation that authorizes it; (2) participating in and supporting educational outreach on boat waste; and (3) developing innovative products that effectively treat and/or safely contain waste while mitigating or eliminating pollution concerns.

To address the issue of boat sewage, Congress enacted two central pieces of legislation. The Federal Water Pollution Control Act of 1972 required recreational boats with installed boat toilets to be equipped with marine sanitation devices (MSDs) to treat sewage. Amended in 1977, the Federal Water Pollution Control Act became commonly known as the Clean Water Act (2000; CWA). Under the Clean Water Act, the discharge of untreated sewage from vessels within all navigable waters of the United States, including coastal waters within 3 mi of shore, is prohibited (Clean Water Act 2000). The Clean Water Act also provides for states to petition through a written application for a No Discharge Area (NDA) designation from EPA, which may only be approved if EPA determines that there are adequate and reasonably available facilities for the safe and sanitary removal and treatment of sewage (Clean Water Act 2000:[f][3]). Within No Discharge Areas, neither treated nor untreated waste may be released from a vessel. NMMA has always supported the designation of No Discharge Areas only when an adequate number of open, operable pumpout facilities are available to boaters.

In 1992, Congress passed a second legislative remedy in the Clean Vessel Act (CVA). CVA established a 5-year federal grant program, administered by the U.S. Fish and Wildlife Service (FWS), authorizing $40 million from the Sport Fish Restoration Account of the Wallop-Breaux Aquatic Resources Trust Fund for use by states to establish a network of pumpout stations at marinas throughout the United States. Congress reau-

---

[9] According to Milliken and Lee, "there have been no studies directly linking the discharge of boat sewage to disease incidence."

thorized the program in 1998, providing $50 million to establish additional pumpout stations to serve as alternatives to the overboard disposal of untreated sewage. Under the law, CVA grants provide up to 75% federal matching funds for education programs for recreational boaters regarding the environmental pollution problems associated with untreated sewage discharges from vessels; information on the location of pumpout stations; construction, maintenance, and operation of pumpouts; pumpout boats; and any activity necessary to hold and transport sewage to sewage treatment plants. Grantees are responsible for 25% of the costs under the program.

NMMA helped secure the passage of the Clean Vessel Act in 1992, as well as reauthorization of the program in 1998. NMMA worked closely with the present Congress to secure another round of reauthorization—as well as increased funding—for the act through legislation to reauthorize the Wallop-Breaux Aquatic Resources Trust Fund, which houses the act. Following an aggressive lobbying campaign by NMMA and a coalition of interested parties, President Bush signed into law on August 10, 2005 the Transportation Equity Act: A Legacy for Users, which included language reauthorizing the Wallop-Breaux Aquatic Resources Trust Fund. The language in this bill included a recapture of the entire 18.3 cent gasoline tax attributable to motorboats, which will mean more than $110 million additional dollars each year for boating safety and fish restoration programs.

The Clean Vessel Act also dedicates a portion of its total funding for educational outreach programs regarding the environmental and human health effects of dumping untreated sewage overboard. This outreach campaign is made possible by the support and cooperation of marina owners and operators, many of whom are members of the Association of Marine Industries, as well as North American pumpout manufacturers, all of which voluntarily pledged to affix the national pumpout symbol developed by FWS on every unit they produce. Other outreach efforts conducted through the National Clean Boating Campaign include educational seminars and distribution of promotional materials such as pamphlets and posters that provide tips on how to protect the environment while boating. According to FWS, the overall "awareness campaign has reached thousands of boaters through magazines, newspapers and television" (Division of Federal Assistance, U.S. Fish and Wildlife Service, The Clean Vessel Act: http://federalaid.fws.gov/cva/cva_info.html#CVA). This number does not include the on-the-ground outreach at marinas and other boating facilities and at events such as NMMA-sponsored Clean Boating Week, which have reached additional thousands. The mere availability of pumpout facilities at marinas has likely heightened environmental awareness among boaters and led to proper waste disposal, something which has been anecdotally documented by the service (Division of Federal Assistance, U.S. Fish and Wildlife Service, The Clean Vessel Act: http://federalaid.fws.gov/cva/cva_info.html#CVA). Clearly, the act has had considerable success, much of which was made possible through the cooperative efforts of various segments of the marine industry. From the passage of the act up to 1999, the grant program "resulted in 49 States receiving $47.6 million for 207 grants," and "involve[s] surveys and plans in 33 coastal States, construction of 2,730 pumpout and 1,778 dump stations in 45 States, and education programs in 40 States" (Division of Federal Assistance, U.S. Fish and Wildlife Service, Clean Vessel Act Pumpout Grant Program: http://federalaid.fws.gov/cva/cvajul97.html).

Marine sanitation products

Marine sanitation device manufacturers are also providing consumers new products to protect the marine environment from boat sewage. Manufacturers are working hard to develop and market innovative technologies that treat, store and contain waste more effectively and result in fewer environmental consequences for habitat and fish species.[10] For example, Raritan Engineering Company's *Lectra San*, MSD, treats waste through a process of maceration and electrolytic decontamination. Raritan has also developed the *ManaGerm*, which utilizes an aerobic biological sewage treatment system in which air, water, and naturally occurring bacteria biologically convert waste to water and carbon dioxide. Headhunter

---

[10] It has been argued by some in the environmental community that the chemicals used in marine sanitation devices are unhealthy for marine wildlife.

Inc. produces a new chemical-free MSD, the *TidalWave HMX*, which uses a four-stage system featuring a patented crossflow separation technique to thoroughly destroy biomass and treat waste water. Standard models can treat up to 50,000 U.S. gallons each day.

Manufacturers are also developing environmentally friendly products to limit holding tank odors. Sealand's line of holding tank products eliminates odors without using formaldehyde, glutaraldehyde, quaternary salts, or other harsh chemicals. In these and other instances, marine sanitation device manufacturers are increasingly offering boaters the opportunity to practice stewardship-related behaviors by providing innovative technologies that effectively mitigate the environmental concerns associated with marine waste.

The Sound of Boating: Voluntarily Quieting American Waterways

Manufacturers of boats, engines, and marine accessories are working proactively to limit noise from boats and prevent its potential negative impacts for human and marine populations. The industry's aggressive self-regulation has far outpaced any government mandates. In May 2003, NMMA joined the efforts of the National Association of State Boating Law Administrators (NASBLA) to quiet waterways across the country so that both boaters and nonboaters can enjoy the natural environment. The NMMA Board of Directors, composed of representatives from all aspects of the boating industry, unanimously voted to endorse the NASBLA model Noise Act, sample legislation that restricts boat noise (National Association of State Boating Law Administrators, model Noise Act: http://www.nasbla.org/pdf/model%20Acts/Motorboat%20Noise.pdf; NMMA partners with state boating law administrators to quiet the waters, 2003).

Through the combined effort of NMMA and NASBLA, the model Noise Act has now been adopted by a high percentage of the states where boat noise had become a major source of complaints, mostly from shoreline residents. The act requires all boats with above-water exhaust to employ exhaust silencers (mufflers) to reduce exhaust noise. To demonstrate compliance with this requirement, boats must not produce noise levels in excess of 88 decibels (dBA; 90 dBA in some states) when subjected to a stationary-mode test standard. The act also limits the shoreline sound level to 75 dBA for individual boats. Compliance with these restrictions has been accomplished by industry development of high quality exhaust silencers on boats with above-water exhaust. To date, 32 states have adopted noise regulations equivalent to the standards set forth by the model Noise Act, and NMMA actively lobbies other state legislatures to do so.[11]

The PWC industry has moved rapidly to reduce noise emissions from its watercraft. Personal watercraft manufacturers, in the absence of government regulations, have invested more than $1 billion over the last several years to develop technologies to reduce both noise and hydrocarbon emissions from their vessels. Some of these technologies include baffles, insulation, and resonator-equipped mufflers.[12] Employing these new technologies, personal watercraft manufacturers have reduced noise emissions by some 70% since 1998 (Personal Watercraft Industry Association 2000). In sensitive aquatic environments, the Personal Watercraft Industry Association (PWIA) endorses the use of shoreline sound measurement laws and the establishment of slow- or no-wake zones, as well as the development of educational programs that promote environmentally sensitive PWC use.

Marine Accessories: Marketing Stewardship through Product Innovation

Marine businesses are working to develop environmentally friendly technologies in order to position themselves as innovators and market leaders and meet consumer demand. Such an approach allows companies to keep pace with competitors, improve brand reputation, and, in many ways,

---

[11] These states include Alabama, Arizona, California, Colorado, Connecticut, Florida, Georgia, Idaho, Illinois, Iowa, Maine, Maryland, Missouri, Mississippi, Minnesota, Michigan, Montana, New Hampshire, New Jersey, New York, Nevada, North Carolina, Oklahoma, Ohio, Oregon, Pennsylvania, Tennessee, Texas, Utah, Washington State, Wisconsin, and Vermont.

[12] Personal Watercraft Industry Association. PWIA is an affiliate of NMMA.

determine the direction of the market. As consumers increasingly demand environmentally sensitive products, the boating industry is responding boldly and enthusiastically. Many marine accessories and components manufacturers are demonstrating leadership in support of advancing clean boating technologies and products that improve the overall environmental performance of the industry.

Introducing these products into the marketplace serves two vital functions that contribute to aquatic stewardship. First, these products draw attention to environmental concerns with boating that they claim to mitigate or avert. Second, they empower boating consumers to take personal responsibility for protecting the environment. Purchasing is an affirmative act, and it involves a choice between or among competing products. The act of purchasing a product that is branded as good for the environment signals that a boating consumer is both knowledgeable about the skills and behaviors necessary for being a good aquatic steward and willing to make a personal investment in the environment (Knuth and Siemer 2004). That these products have flourished in a competitive marketplace is a measure of the effectiveness of green marketing initiatives based on environmental branding.

Savvy marketing professionals within the boating industry have long understood the appeal of environmentally sensitive products. In a race-to-the-top style of competition, many industry leaders have sought to establish a reputation for having products that minimize the human impact on the environment. These companies have sought to increase the appeal of their products by communicating their environmental commitment directly to customers, competitors, peers, distributors, and others. The success of this type of marketing is premised on two central foundations: (1) a good product that does not harm the environment, and (2) consumer demand fueled by an ingrained environmental ethic.

NMMA encourages and supports the development of innovative new products through the NMMA Innovation Awards, which are awarded with substantial publicity to companies in the marine industry that have developed interesting new products. NMMA, and its partner in this endeavor, Boating Writers International (BWI), issue the awards at NMMA-owned or -sponsored industry events, such as boat shows and product exhibitions. Many of the products selected represent environmental solutions—accessories designed to address a particular environmental concern, which may be perceived to be tied to boating. NMMA specifically awards an Environmental Innovation Award to recognize what has become a niche market in the boating industry that focuses on manufacturing products that minimize boating's impact on aquatic systems across a broad spectrum of environmental concerns. These awards serve to reward companies that have elected to take an environmentally responsible corporate posture, to encourage other companies in the industry to do so, and to alert consumers about the availability of these products and the companies that make them. Many of the green products listed below have been honored by NMMA as leading examples of the marine industry's commitment to environmental responsibility.

Fuel and petroleum spill and pollution products

Clean Water Solutions, Inc. has developed a line of products that mitigate petroleum pollution by efficiently bioremediating oil and other pollutants; these products target marinas, boat bilges, catch basins, and holding tanks. Immediate Response Spill Technologies' *CI Agent* is another petroleum pollution option that uses revolutionary technology to solidify petroleum-based spills and encapsulate them into a removable mass. Clean Water Solutions, Inc. was awarded the NMMA Environmental Innovation Award at NMMA's Accessories Trade Show Las Vegas in July 2005.[13] Power Service's *Diesel Kleen Performance Improver with Cetane Boost* exceeds industry standards for thermal stability and improves diesel fuel's resistance to thermal and oxidative degradation to improve engine efficiency.

Several manufacturers are developing new, innovative products to prevent spillage. Racor Parker Filtration's Lifeguard line of fuel/air sepa-

---

[13] The company immediately publicized the award, issuing a press release and detailing news on the award on its homepage. See Press Release, Clean Water Solutions, Inc., Breaking News: Clean Water Solutions Wins NMMA Innovation Award and Environmental Innovation Award at MAATS 2005 Trade Show in Las Vegas (2005) at http://www.cleanwatersolutionsinc.com/
.

rators has an automatic shut-off feature that trips to let you know your fuel tank is full. Davis Instruments has patented a fuel-resistant bottle designed for temporary attachment to the hull, over the fuel tank vent, to capture any spillage that would otherwise run into the water. Bocatech Inc. produces a bilge mate switch that does not switch when oil is present in the bilge, which prevents oil from polluting surrounding waters. EMP Industries *SaniSailor BilgeMate Systems* eliminate harmful oily bilge water from entering our waterways by integrating high suction peristaltic vacuum pump with an oil and water separator along with a hydrocarbon accumulator and suction hose to cleanly and conveniently remove oily bilge water from recreational boats.

Another product that is beginning to penetrate the marine market is biodiesel, a fuel made from renewable sources like soybeans and natural fats and oils. Although increasingly common in commercial marine applications, such as charter boats and water taxis, biodiesel fuel is relatively new to the recreational sector, with only a small number of private marinas in the United States making it available to boating consumers. Nevertheless, interest in this ecofriendly product continues to grow, and biodiesel is the fastest growing alternative fuel in the United States (Thurlo Pearson 2005).[14] Pure biodiesel fuel (B100) contains no petroleum and can be used in any diesel engines "with few or no modifications" (Thurlo Pearson 2005). The fuel is good for marine engines, burns efficiently, and significantly reduces soot emissions. The most common formula of biodiesel fuel, B20 (80% regular diesel and 20% biodiesel), biodegrades three times as fast as regular diesel, mitigating the environmental impact of spills. An NMMA-backed federal tax incentive, which went into effect January 2005, should further increase the availability of the fuel.

Antifoulants, paint, and cleaning products

The marine industry has been proactive in other areas as well. When it became clear that phos-phate-based boat soaps degrade water quality and contribute to algal blooms and low dissolved oxygen levels, the industry developed and made available a series of nontoxic, nonphosphate-based, biodegradable boat soaps, which have a minimal impact on the aquatic environment. The marine industry is increasing its reliance on silicon, Teflon, and similar slick-surface, nonfouling agents rather than toxins to keep marine growth off boat bottoms as well. Natural Marine's new *One and Only Spot Remover* is a unique, color safe oxygen release gel that removes spots without the use of bleach or other hazardous materials. Many manufactures are also developing more environmentally friendly paint strippers. Pettit's *Bio-Blast* and Sea Hawk's *Marine Paint Stripper 1280* are biodegradable products that remove antifouling paint without the use of traditional toxic chemicals.

Marine generators and mufflers

Westerbeeke, a prominent manufacturer of generators for the marine market has garnered several honors for developing and marketing revolutionary products that limit carbon monoxide emissions. Carbon monoxide is a colorless, odorless, and extremely poisonous gas that can have fatal consequences when inhaled. Westerbeeke's *Safe-CO* generators use a combination of innovative engineering and electronic fuel injection to reduce carbon monoxide emissions by 99% compared to conventional generators. Westerbeeke, already a recipient of an NMMA Innovation award for its small gasoline-fueled generator in 2003, was honored again last year as the winner of the 2005 Electrical Systems Innovation award from NMMA. Gentek, a manufacturer of marine exhaust mufflers and systems, recently developed the compact *Gen-Kleen*, the first product that protects boating waters by removing hydrocarbon contamination from generator exhaust.

Batteries and horns

Amptronix, Inc. is introducing *ABC-DS12*, an innovative 12V Battery Desulfator that prolongs the life of lead batteries. By utilizing the power

---

[14] Idaho National Laboratory, U.S. Department of Energy. Biodiesel: fastest growing, high-quality American-made fuel." Available: http://www.inl.gov/scienceandtechnology/factsheets/d/biodiesel.pdf (January 2007).

of the battery and returning it as a surge or pulse, the Battery Desulfator actually delays and reduces sulfation within the battery, the primary cause of premature failure. The product can also revive many old batteries to a state of normal functionality. The SeaSense *EcoBlast Refillable Air Horn* is a chemical-free refillable horn that does not introduce CTC toxins into the air when used. The horn is refilled using a bicycle pump and contains no batteries or disposable metal containers.

Mooring and sonar products

In some marine environments, such as marine sanctuaries, coral reefs, and other sensitive or essential habitats, mooring a boat can disturb certain benthic communities and wildlife. New elastic mooring technologies have been designed by companies such as Hazlett-Marine and Seaflex to specifically address the increasingly stringent environmental regulations associated with marina siting and construction.

Marine manufacturers are developing advanced scanning technology to give boaters the ability to prevent injury to marine life. Interphase's line of iScan sonar products provides boaters long-range bottom to surface color sonar up to 1,200 ft, helping to protect manatees, whales, and other aquatic species. These and other products in the accessories marketplace are pursued because there is consumer demand, and when companies offer more pioneering, state-of-the art products, they in turn help shape consumer preferences. Nevertheless, the success of aquatic stewardship education programs will have a direct bearing on consumer purchasing and will ultimately benefit those marine businesses who are marketing a green product.

Advancing Clean Boating through Education, Legislation, and Outreach

In a December 2004 article published by the American Fisheries Society, the authors attempt to define "aquatic stewardship" and outline the components of programs fostering the ethic of personal responsibility that forms the basis for stewardship. The article emphasizes that a successful aquatic stewardship program should con-

vey three fundamental elements: (1) awareness of aquatic systems, (2) personal investment in the environment, and (3) knowledge and skill in the behaviors of a good aquatic steward (Knuth and Siemer 2004). The boating industry, although not in the business of designing or implementing aquatic stewardship education programs, participates, either directly or indirectly, in all three components, particularly in making accessible to boaters certain behavioral options that constitute desirable aquatic stewardship. The businesses that make up the membership of NMMA are already proactively contributing to aquatic stewardship education and outreach, and many have been leading this effort for quite some time. The historical significance of the boating industry's financial and political support in helping to establish and maintain environmental initiatives is significant. This section will outline specific aquatic stewardship education initiatives undertaken by either NMMA and its affiliates or by prominent members of the industry, along with specific legislative proposals that NMMA is working on to help protect the environment.

The NMMA Water Watch Program

In the early 1990s, NMMA secured a one-time $25,000 grant from EPA to develop and distribute educational materials directly to boaters at the point of purchase.[15] This educational brochure, called the Water Watch program,[16] was one of the first comprehensive clean boating brochures to be developed and represented the first time that such materials were systematically distributed to boating consumers. The Water Watch brochure, called "What Boaters Can Do to Be Environmentally Friendly," includes a top 10 list

---

[15] National Marine Manufacturers Association, "Water watch: what boaters can do to be environmentally friendly." The brochure used material prepared by the Chesapeake Bay Foundation in a similar document, "Your boat and the bay," edited by Margaret Podlich, now of BoatU.S., as well as material provided by the Izaak Walton League of America and other outdoor recreation groups.

[16] National Marine Manufacturers Association, "Water watch: what boaters can do to be environmentally friendly."

of ecofriendly boating practices, including adherence to federal marine sanitation rules, use of biodegradable cleaning agents, proper fueling to avoid spills, control of bilge water, and others. The brochure explains in detail the environmental concern at issue and outlines a set of actions that boaters should take to mitigate risks to aquatic systems. Once the brochure was finalized, NMMA, using grant monies as well as its own resources, distributed the brochure to marine dealers nationwide and to every consumer who purchased a new boat that year, a massive undertaking. The dealers were to provide to boating consumers the brochure with the packet of informational materials (owner's manual, warranty documentation, etc.) that comes with the purchase of new boat. Although the program was not extended because the grant expired after 1 year, NMMA continues to make this brochure available upon request. More importantly, as federal and state agencies develop similar educational materials for boaters within their juris- dictions, they have drawn heavily on the expertise and advice contained in the Water Watch brochure, often employing virtually identical language. In that regard, the legacy of this particular outreach initiative has been sustained over the long term, extending beyond its own life and reaching thousands of boaters nationwide.

The Tread Lightly! campaign

Tread Lightly! is a national, nonprofit organization based in Utah dedicated to empowering "generations to enjoy the outdoors responsibly through education and restoration." Although the program began in 1985 in the U.S. Forest Service as an effort to address growing participation in outdoor recreation, Tread Lightly! became a private endeavor in 1990, funded by a variety of "individual members, corporations, dealerships, clubs, retailers and other organizations interested in spreading the message of responsible and ethical use of the outdoors." In 1997, Tread Lightly! expanded from its traditional focus on land issues to include water-based recreation. In addition to its Tread Trainer program designed to produce a network of instructors of the campaign's responsible recreation message, the organization also produces a multitude of educational pieces for outdoor enthusiasts, including a guide to responsible PWC use. Tread Lightly! also develops public service announcements (PSAs) focused on spreading the message of aquatic stewardship. In this way, Tread Lightly! serves as an "ethical and educational force in bringing together and unifying a broad spectrum of stakeholders including agencies, industry, media, conservation and enthusiast groups, and concerned individuals who share a common goal—to find a balance between humans and nature."

Tread Lightly! also seeks to increase dialogue and expand government–industry partnerships regarding environmental stewardship. From 2000 to 2002, NMMA and PWIA sponsored Tread Lightly!'s Convergence Dialogue Series, which was designed to "open lines of communication, build common ground, and discuss pertinent issues and challenges facing the future of responsible outdoor recreation by bringing together representatives from various forms of recreational interests." This series brought together state and federal resource management agencies, conservation organizations, resource users, industry, and other stakeholders, who worked to identify common challenges facing responsible recreation, including stewardship education, and develop an agenda for future cooperation and actions. Water-related recreation was a major focus of the series.

NMMA and PWIA, along with the individual manufacturers of personal watercrafts, have provided significant support and technical expertise to the Tread Lightly! campaign over the years. The campaign has reached 8 million people each year through its print public service announcements in enthusiast magazines and another 8 million through the display of its PSAs as signage on public lands. Since 2003, as a result of boating and water recreation enthusiast magazines donating advertising space to the Tread Lightly! campaign,[17] the initiative has

---

[17] Several enthusiast magazines have donated at least $166,293 of advertising space for Tread Lightly! water-related public service announcements. E-mail from D. Olson, Tread Lightly! Inc., to M. P. Dunn.

communicated its responsible recreation message to at least 3.8 million boaters, anglers, and other water recreationists.[18]

The FishAmerica Foundation

Recreational boating and fishing are closely tied, with approximately 60–70% of boaters claiming to use their boats for angling (Duda et al. 2000). The FishAmerica Foundation, founded and largely financially supported by boating and fishing companies, represents a highly successful conservation grant-giving program, well regarded within the conservation and environmental communities. According to the foundation, FishAmer-ica provides "nearly $1 million in matching grants each year to community partners across the country. Over the last 20 years, FishAmerica has provided more than $6 million for nearly 750 grassroots conservation projects that improve fisheries habitat and fishing opportunities."[19]

Environmental legislation

The NMMA Government Relations team monitors legislation and lobbies policymakers on behalf of the environment in Washington, D.C. and in state capitals.

The Wallop-Breaux Aquatic Resources Trust Fund

In addition to the Water Watch program, NMMA has been and continues to be a major player in the political fights that seem to inevitably accompany the authorization of funds for the Wallop-Breaux Aquatic Resources Trust Fund, a user-pay fund used to enhance the boating and fishing experience. Congress allocates funds generated directly by boaters through taxes on motorboat fuel and fishing tackle, along with other fees. Part of the monies generated by the tax are dedicated to specific environmental restoration and protection projects, including coastal wetlands restoration, a variety of sport fish restoration programs, grant programs for the

construction of pumpout stations under the Clean Vessel Act, and monies for the Recreational Boating and Fishing Foundation (RBFF),[20] which actively researches and promotes conservation among boaters and anglers. Significant dollars go directly toward funding state-based aquatic stewardship education programs. More than $4 billion has been collected and invested in the program since its inception.

The Sport Fish Restoration Account of the Aquatic Resources Trust Fund (1984) has been nothing if not successful. The funds in the account are generated through a 10% excise tax on certain items of sportfishing tackle; a 3% excise tax on fish finders and electric trolling motors; import duties on fishing tackle, yachts, and pleasure craft; interest on the account; and a portion of motorboat fuel tax revenues and small engine fuel taxes authorized under the Internal Revenue Code. Funds for state sport fish restoration and related programs are apportioned on a formula basis (see Buck 2005) and pay up to 75% of the cost for approved programs, including restoration efforts, land acquisition, research on habitat and fish stocks, surveys and inventories of fish populations, and the development and improvement of boating facilities, among others. States are also directed to use up to 10% of the funds for aquatic stewardship education and boating access facilities (U.S. Fish and Wildlife Service, Federal Aid in Sport Fish Restoration Act, Digest of Federal Resource Laws of Interest to the U.S. Fish and Wildlife Service: http://laws.fws.gov/lawsdigest/fasport.html).

Wallop Breaux monies are also used to fund critical education programs. For example, the Fish and Wildlife Research Initiative of the Florida Fish and Wildlife Conservation Commission, a state agency, has developed a series of boating and angling guides to inform boaters and anglers about Florida's coastal and marine ecosystems. The guides, which originally appeared in 1992 and are divided regionally, consist of maps displaying the "distribution of natural marine resources" along with text explaining "the role of the marine habitat in the

---

[18] E-mail from Olson to Dunn.

[19] American Sportfishing Association, Fish America Foundation (2005) at http://www.fishamerica.org/faf/projects/index.html.

[20] The Recreational Boating and Fishing Foundation is a partner in NMMA's Discover Boating Mobile Marketing Tour.

health of the marine ecosystem and how boating and angling behavior can influence the environment" (Florida Fish and Wildlife Institute: http://research.myfwc.com/features/view_article.asp?id=5862). According to the Florida Fish and Wildlife Conservation Commission, more than 1.9 million guides have been printed to date. Monies from Wallop-Breaux are also directed to the RBFF in order to carry out a National Outreach and Communications Program. This program seeks to increase responsible participation in boating and angling through an aquatic resource education initiative that provides for states to be "reimbursed not to exceed 15% of the state's total Sport Fish Restoration apportionment"(Buck 2005)

In order to ensure that the Wallop-Breaux monies are reauthorized and dedicated appropriately, NMMA has worked closely with the American League of Anglers and Boaters (ALAB), which spearheaded the coordinated effort by stakeholders to secure passage of reauthorizing legislation in the 109th Congress. ALAB is composed of 34 member organizations, including NMMA, Association of Marina Industries, American Fisheries Society (AFS), American Sportfishing Association (ASA), Association of Fish and Wildlife Agencies, Trout Unlimited (TU), and Boat Owners Association of the United States (BoatU.S.). In addition to featuring Wallop-Breaux as an issue at NMMA's annual legislative conference, the American Boating Congress, the association's government affairs staff routinely meet with congressional staff in order to advance the consensus legislative objectives of ALAB, which include creating a permanent appropriation of funding, as well as a reallocation of the fuel tax receipts, part of which have heretofore been redirected to the General Fund for deficit reduction rather than to the boating and angling accounts for which they were intended.[21] The recapture of the diverted funds, a major advocacy coup in 2005, now means that an additional $110 million a year will be directed back into the Wallop-Breaux account.

---

[21] Until recently, only 13.5 cents was sent to the Aquatic Resources Trust Fund, which was only a portion of the 18.3 cents that is collected on motorboat and small engine fuels.

Marine debris

Clean water is the foundation for an enjoyable boating experience, which is why protecting the environment is a priority for the recreational boating industry. NMMA testified in support of S. 362, a bill that seeks additional monies for the National Oceanic and Atmospheric Administration and the U.S. Coast Guard to improve enforcement of illegal vessel-based pollution and debris, before a joint committee of the U.S. House Resources Subcommittee on Fisheries and Oceans and the House Transportation Subcommittee on Coast Guard and Maritime Transportation in 2005. The bill proactively deals with marine debris such as discarded rope and line that foul propellers, and plastic bags and sheeting that clog seawater intakes and damage marine ecosystems and human health. This bill has been signed into law.

Invasive species

NMMA is also supporting several pieces of legislation that address the increasing menace of invasive species on America's waterways. NMMA is working with the U.S. Senate to draft a comprehensive bill that would identify aquatic invasive species and how they are transported; set protocols, systems, and standards to monitor the efficiency and efficacy of prevention methods; and establish ballast water and sediment standards for vessels of the armed forces.

The Clean Marina Program: Achieving Sustainable Marina Ecosystems

Over a decade ago, NMMA initiated an effort to recognize leaders in the marina industry who were striving to implement policies and protocols that fostered clean marinas. One such effort, the Recreational Boating Facilities Environmental Responsibility Award, generated considerable national publicity and facilitated efforts to draw attention to clean marina programs. In an attempt to build upon this program, NMMA worked with European marine industry counterparts to develop a program to certify clean marinas, known as the Blue Flag Program (Brazda 1999). After lengthy consultations with administrators of the European program, NMMA and its partners sought out the Marine Environmental Education Foundation to implement and administer a similar education and certification program in the United States. Despite efforts by industry to implement this endeavor, a lack of available federal grant monies hindered, for a time, further progress and led to a series of ad hoc, yet highly successful, efforts by states, in conjunction with the National Clean Boating Program, to implement clean marina programs. To date, Clean Marina programs have been developed in 18 states, the District of Columbia, several federal agencies, and the Tennessee Valley Authority (TVA).[22]

In 2002, the Association of Marina Industries (AMI), then the Marina Operators Association of America (MOAA), worked with other industry partners to conduct a national workshop designed to address the necessity of implementing EPA's national management measures to control nonpoint source pollution from marinas and recreational boating (USEPA 2001). This workshop brought together the National Park Service, U.S. Army Corps of Engineers, TVA, U.S. Fish and Wildlife Service, U.S. Coast Guard, Bureau of Reclamation, numerous state agencies, the marina industry, and the majority of Clean Marina programs in the United States. In total, more than 100 local, state, and federal officials responsible for the development and delivery of Clean Marina programs as well as national and regional marine trade group representatives attended the workshop. For the first time, the nation's leading clean marina practitioners agreed on a set of Clean Marina principles. The results continue to have a significant impact on the development of Clean Marina programs nationwide.

AMI—the new association born out of the January 2005 merger of MOAA and the Institute of Marina Industries (IMI)—has worked closely with states and marina owners and operators to implement clean marina programs based on best practices and educational outreach. For example, AMI offers professional training and program development in furtherance of clean marina objectives. In addition, AMI will continue to advance

the cause of clean marinas through the Certified Marina Manager (CMM) program. The CMM designation, requiring extensive marina management training, signals a marina owner's or operator's commitment to professional standards and environmental stewardship.[23] The CMM designation affords marina managers the opportunity to market their marinas as environmentally responsible and gives them an edge over competitors. Many marina owners are turning to the CMM program to improve their company's bottom line.

As state clean marina programs continue to gain traction across the nation, AMI has pursued a federal track that would establish a national clean marina program, a goal that would significantly raise the profile of clean marinas and possibly offer a stable revenue stream and grant-giving program. The U.S. Commission on Ocean Policy's Final Report and President Bush's response in his U.S. Ocean Action Plan call for a federal clean marina program (U.S. Commission on Ocean Policy 2004). As a result, NMMA initiated an aggressive lobbying campaign with key staff of the Council on Environmental Quality, the president's environmental advisory panel charged with overseeing federal environmental programs, to secure federal dollars for a national program. Unfortunately, the present federal fiscal climate has made securing these funds difficult, although AMI and NMMA will continue to advocate for such a program.

The marina industry is increasingly adhering to strong environmental standards and principles. Indeed, industry has worked with government regulators and nonprofit organizations to systematically promote aquatic stewardship. The resulting norm, which has been developed within the marina industry, is beginning to take hold, and it is clear that the future promises additional, voluntary adherence to environmentally responsible marina management. The 1996 EPA study confirms this view, noting that "clearly, the marina industry has begun to embrace the need to promote clean boating, clean facilities, and clean operations" (USEPA 1996). The 25 marinas explored as case studies in that evaluation were, 10 years ago, already "demonstrating innovation,

---

[22] States include Alabama, California, Connecticut, Delaware, Florida, Georgia, Louisiana, Maryland, Massachusetts, Michigan, New Hampshire, New Jersey, New York, North Carolina, Ohio, South Carolina, Texas, and Virginia.

[23] The CMM program was previously administered by IMI, but has been incorporated into AMI as the result of the recent merger.

determination, and an almost missionary zeal for clean operations" (USEPA 1996). Importantly, the study also determined that the majority of the facilities it evaluated had voluntarily employed clean marina practices in order to "improve their service to boaters and to stay ahead of the regulations" (USEPA 1996).

The Corporate Role in Aquatic Stewardship Education: Future Prospects

The desire to advance aquatic stewardship and create a national stewardship ethic with respect to the boating public is one shared by conservation groups, scientific organizations such as the American Fisheries Society, federal and state agencies, and the marine manufacturing industry. For its part, the boating industry will continue to pursue technological solutions to environmental concerns, adhere to environmental regulations, and utilize the marketplace to encourage boating consumers to act responsibly on the water. NMMA believes strongly that, although unconventional, the advertising of environmentally-sensitive products constitutes a form of aquatic stewardship education. Such an approach raises awareness about environmental risks and provides environmental solutions to the users of America's aquatic resources. Affording boaters the choice to affirm and employ their inherent conservation ethic is at once empowering and effective.

In addition, industry has an important role to play in working with those organizations dedicated to conserving and protecting aquatic environments. Industry's role is derived from its recognized corporate social responsibility, as well as the desire to sell product. As has been noted, clean and healthy waters are the foundation of enjoyable boating. Consumers, too, are increasingly demanding products that serve to remedy environmental concerns, rather than exacerbate them.

The products, innovations, technologies, and educational outreach described herein do not constitute a comprehensive or exhaustive litany of the accomplishments and developments within the recreational boating industry. What is presented is meant to provide an illustrative overview and sampling of some of the significant activities and milestones. An overview of this length and scope could not begin to capture each important development or innovation.

References

Aquatic Resources Trust Fund. 1984. U.S. Code, volume 26, section 9504.

Brazda, R. 1999. The Clean Marina Program: public recognition for environmentally proactive marinas. Marina Dock Age (November 1999). Available: http://www.marinamanagement.com/articles/rs-11_99.html.

Buck, E. H. 2005. CRS Report for Congress: The Aquatic Resources Trust Fund. Congressional Research Service, RS22060, Washington, DC. Available: http://www.ncseonline.org/NLE/CRSreports/05apr/RS22060.pdf.

Clean Water Act. 2000. U.S. Code, volume 33, section 1322.

Duda, M. D., V. L. Wise, W. Testerman, S. J. Bissell, and A. Lanier. 2000. Factors related to recreational boating participation in the United States: a review of the literature. Responsive Management, Harrisonburg, Virginia.

Environment Canada. 2000. Environment Canada and the Canadian Marine Manufacturing Association fast track the introduction of cleaner engines in Canada. Press release. Available: http://www.ec.gc.ca/press/cmma_n_e.htm.

Fields, S. 2003. The environmental pain of pleasure boating. Environmental Health Perspectives 111(4):A216–A223.

Knuth, B. A., and W. F. Siemer. 2004. Fostering aquatic stewardship: a key for fisheries sustainability. Pages 243–255 in E. E. Knudsen, D. D. MacDonald, and Y. K. Muirhead, editors. Sustainable management of North American fisheries. American Fisheries Society, Symposium 43, Bethesda, Maryland.

Lipton, D. 2003. The value of improved water quality to Chesapeake Bay Boaters. University of Maryland, Working Paper, College Park. Available: www.arec.umd.edu/Publications/papers/Working-Papers-PDF-files/03–16.pdf.

Mele, A. 1993. Polluting for pleasure. Norton, New York.

Milliken, A. S., and V. Lee. 1990. Pollution impacts from recreational boating: a bibliography and summary review. Rhode Island Sea Grant Publications, Narragansett.

Millennium Ecosystem Assessment Business and Industry Synthesis Team. 2005. Millennium ecosystem assessment, ecosystems and human well-being: opportunities and challenges for business and industry. World Resources Institute, Washington, D.C.

National Recreation Lake Study Commission. 1999.

Reservoirs of opportunity. National Recreation Lake Study Commission, Washington, D.C.

NMMA (National Marine Manufacturers Association) 2004. Recreational boating statistical abstract. National Marine Manufacturers Association, Chicago.

NMMA partners with state boating law administrators to quiet the waters. 2003. National Marine Manufacturers Association, Press release, Chicago. Available: http://www.nmma.org/news/news.asp?id=1232&sid=3.

Personal Watercraft Industry Association. 2000. Industry achievements in engine exhaust and sound, the environment, safety and boater relations. Personal Watercraft Industry Association, Washington, D.C.

Thurlo Pearson, A. 2005. Biodiesel takes to waters and brings environmental advantages. Boat and Motor Dealer (May 2005):34.

U.S. Commission on Ocean Policy. 2004. An ocean blueprint for the 21st century. U.S. Commission on Ocean Policy, Washington, D.C.

USEPA (United States Environmental Protection Agency). 1996. Regulatory impact analysis: control of air pollution emission standards for new nonroad spark-ignition marine engines. U.S. Environmental Protection Agency, Washington, D.C.

USEPA (U.S. Environmental Protection Agency). 1998. National water quality inventory: 1996 Report to Congress. U.S. Environmental Protection Agency, EPA 841-R-97–008, Washington, D.C.

USEPA (U.S. Environmental Protection Agency). 2001. National management measures to control non-point source pollution from marinas and recreational boating. U.S. Environmental Protection Agency, EPA 841-B-01–005, Washington, D.C.

USEPA (U.S. Environmental Protection Agency). 2002. EPA and national marine industry associations celebrate New Hampshire initiative for cleaner small boat engines. Press release. Available: http://www.epa.gov/ne/pr/2002/mar/020319.html.

USEPA (U.S. Environmental Protection Agency). 2005a. Boating pollution prevention tips. Available: http://www.epa.gov/otaq/boat-fs.htm.

USEPA (U.S. Environmental Protection Agency). 2005b. EPA efforts to promote clean marine engines paying off—most of New England's marine engine sales are lower polluting models. Available: http://www.epa.gov/ne/pr/2005/jul/sr050707.html.

USOFR (U.S. Office of the Federal Register). 1996. Air pollution control; gasoline spark-ignition marine engines; new nonroad compression-ignition and spark ignition engines, exemptions; rule. Code of Federal Regulations, Title 40, Parts 89–91. U.S. Government Printing Office, Washington, D.C.

American Fisheries Society Symposium 55:73–77, 2007

Fostering Boating-Related Aquatic Stewardship: Reaching the Boater

RYCK LYDECKER[1]

Boat Owners Association of The United States (BoatU.S.)
880 South Pickett Street, Alexandria, Virginia 22304, USA

Abstract.—Changing the stewardship behavior of boaters can be accomplished through various traditional and nontraditional communication methods when initiated by boaters and their representative organizations. At national, state, and local levels, the recreational boating community, boating media, engaged government agencies and academic/extension programs, and business entities that serve recreational boaters have developed various ways to accomplish such aims. Methods implemented include providing grants to boating groups to conduct environmental projects, using the boating-oriented media to disseminate messages that promote environmentally sensitive behavior, working directly with marinas and other service providers to improve operation of boats and servicing facilities, and boater-supported government affairs programs that advocate sound environmental policies and adequate funding to meet these objectives. Additionally, due to the high percentage of boats used in fishing activities, communication campaigns that promote ethically sound behavior have successfully reached recreational boaters as well as sport anglers. Specific programs within each of these arenas, conducted by Boat Owners Association of The United States and other organizations, will be discussed in the context of target audience, message content, delivery method, potential measures of success, and future directions.

Introduction

BoatU.S. stands for Boat Owners Association of The United States, a membership organization of recreational boaters that has been representing the interests of boating consumers since 1966. Membership currently stands at 650,000, all of whom receive *BoatU.S. Magazine*, giving this bimonthly publication a circulation larger than that of the three next-largest circulation boating magazines combined. About 68% of BoatU.S. members are self-described as anglers (40% saltwater, 28% freshwater) (Mediamark Research, Inc. 2002). Overall in the United States, 60–70% of boats are purchased with fishing in mind (J. Petru, National Marine Manufacturers Association, personal communication).

The nation's 69 million recreational boaters (NMMA 2004) have an important stake in marine and aquatic resource stewardship, whether they know it or not. The boating community in the United States owns some 17 million boats with 13 million registered under state authorities (NMMA 2004). Ownership breaks down into six categories, by boat type, as shown in Table 1.

Recreational boaters as a group are difficult to categorize since they are found in all age-groups, backgrounds, ethnicities, and income levels. They participate in boating using a wide variety of vessel types and engage in on-the-water activities that range from water skiing to blue water cruising to racing to just "messing about in boats." The one thing held in common by all recreational boaters is the need for clean water to cruise on, ski over, and dive into; clean water is one of the chief appeals of boating.

It has been the experience of BoatU.S. that boaters generally want to protect the aquatic resources that they use; often they just need some direction and modest education in how to do it

[1] E-mail: RLydecker@boatus.com

TABLE 1. Categories of boat ownership within the United States, for boats in use in 2004 (NMMA 2004).

Boat type	Number in use (2004)
Outboard powerboats	8, 480,000
Inboard powerboats	1,750,000
Sterndrive (inboard/outboard)	1,820,000
Personal watercraft	1,480,000
Sailboats	1,580,000
Other (canoes/kayaks, etc.)	2,500,000
Total boats in use	17,610,000

effectively (M. Podlich, BoatU.S. Foundation for Boating Safety and Clean Water, personal communication). Indeed, the process of changing or reinforcing positive aquatic stewardship behaviors on the part of recreational boaters is currently well underway nationwide. This is being accomplished through various channels of communication and activity, as follows.

Boating Media

Magazines and newspapers

The boating media present the most obvious pathway to reach recreational boaters with stewardship messages and information. Nationally, there are about 25 boating magazines, most of which cater to a segment of the market (e.g., sailors) or to a specific boat type (e.g., personal watercraft) or a discrete category of boating activity (e.g., wakeboarding). To that can be added approximately 30 regional publications plus a dozen or more local magazines and newspapers, of which many are distributed free-of-charge. These, it should be noted, often are eager to use public service-type filler articles and advertisements, providing a possible dissemination mechanism for stewardship messages prepared by agencies and educators. These sources are often well read locally, but few of these titles are listed in the standard media databases.

Totaling this print circulation shows that it is theoretically possible to reach approximately 3.7 million recreational boaters with a stewardship message. Factoring in total pass-along readership yields a total, reachable universe that could be three times that number or more, perhaps 9–10 million boaters. The amount of overlap of readers is diffi-cult to assess, although surveys of *BoatU.S. Magazine* readers indicate that readers only read one or two other titles on a regular basis, and these are usually regional or activity-specific publications (www.BoatUS.com/news/media_01.htm). [NOTE: The above refers only to boating publications; the list of fishing magazines is more than 300 titles.]

Daily and weekly newspapers that regularly cover boating on their sports or outdoor pages may be added to the total pool of print media outlets. Given these multiple outlets, more than 2,000 reporter contacts could be expected to write about boating, at least occasionally.

Television

Television is another medium to reach boaters, but there currently is no network programming devoted to boating. Currently, five national cable networks can and do carry boating programs or include boating in fishing and/or outdoor recreation programming. In addition, a cable network start-up in the summer of 2005, "The Water Channel," promises to provide boating and fishing programming, in addition to surfing, scuba diving, and luxury cruising content, to "all those for whom water is the defining element of their lifestyle" (Press release, MCE Television Network, Everett Washington, August 29, 2005). The network, which was to launch in October 2005 and was anticipated to reach 12 million homes, could presumably include stewardship programming once established.

There are a number of regional cable providers that carry local outdoor programs that also may cover boating and or fishing. Mike Waller, president of the public relations and marketing firm, The Walker Agency, which has many clients in the outdoor field, indicated, "I'm sure there are lots [of local outdoor cable tv programs] out there, but they are either brief fishing reports or so small or rinky-dinky that they don't show up on the cable TV listings" (M. Walker, The Walker Agency, personal communication).

Radio

Radio is much the same; M. Walker reports that most stations will carry boating information if it applies to their market. To provide a frame of reference, The Walker Agency distributes material to about 190 stations nationwide (Walker, personal communication), and the Outdoor Writers Association of America lists 245 radio broadcasters/producers among its membership, either staff or freelance (Outdoor Writers Association of America 2005–2006 Directory, Missoula, Montana).

Internet

Internet Web sites devoted to boating and fishing are another vehicle to reach this target audience, but getting conclusive numbers and audience figures is almost impossible. An Internet search engine query for "Boating, Websites" returned 3,870,000 entries, a number that provides no useful indicator; however, a refined query could potentially provide a more realistic universe.

Recreational boaters do utilize the Internet in pursuit of boating information as indicated by activity at www.BoatUS.com. This Web site, which carries stewardship messages and articles regularly, receives 400,000 unique visitors monthly (T. Parrow, BoatU.S., personal communication).

Outreach Programs

One of the most obvious and effective outreach programs currently available to educators and communicators wishing to distribute stewardship messages to recreational boaters is the national Sea Grant College Program Extension network of 30 academic institutions operating in each of the 30 coastal and Great Lakes states.

The Sea Grant network employs 380 extension agents nationwide, 22 of whom conduct recreation-related programming specifically related to boating (J. Murray, NOAA Sea Grant, personal communication). Sea Grant's network of marine education specialists, who currently conduct environmental education at the primary and secondary school levels, could presumably direct effort to boating-specific stewardship education in the classroom as well. Additionally, the BoatU.S. Foundation for Boating Safety and Clean Water conducts education campaigns aimed directly at recreational boaters, often promoting stewardship habits and suggesting "green boating" purchasing options for supplies and gear. The foundation also conducts consumer tests of environmentally friendly boating equipment and maintenance products. The results of such tests

are then disseminated via *BoatU.S. Magazine*, on www.BoatUS.com, and/or via the in-house media relations operation capabilities of the Boat Owners Association of The United States. For example, the foundation conducted controlled tests of the effectiveness of products know as "oil socks" or "bilge booms" that are designed to remove leaked oil or fuel from bilge water, in order to prevent overboard discharge (Anonymous 2001) and products designed to prevent spills during vessel refueling (Turken 2005).

Formal Training

Information on "green boating" is now being incorporated into the boating education classes of training organizations such as the U.S. Power Squadrons (USPS) and many state boating safety education programs. The USPS, which has conducted boating education for 90 years, created a Marine Environment Committee in 2004 to develop "green boating" modules for inclusion in beginner boating courses. The USPS trains 32,000 new boaters annually and reaches 50,000 old hands (their own members) while conducting about 72,000 vessel safety checks, which do or soon will include "green boating" information (J. Hamilton, U.S. Power Squadrons, personal communication).

The U.S. Coast Guard Auxiliary conducts boater safety training for some 70,000 new boaters each year, as well as the same type of courtesy safety inspections of recreational boats. The auxiliary now incorporates stewardship information in both programs, aimed largely at boater compliance with state and federal law and reaches another 50,000–60,000 children through its classes and "Officer Snook" environmental responsibility campaign (R. Clincy, U.S. Coast Guard Auxiliary, personal communication).

In addition, all 50 states have their own boating safety education programs that can and do incorporate environmental messages. In 42 states, some form of safety class now is mandatory, usually as defined by age-group and/or boat type (e.g., under age 14 or power boaters over 10 hp). Many states now incorporate some form of environmental education in their classes, including fuel spill prevention, sewage discharge, and bilge water management. Some states have added information to deal with aquatic nuisance species and engage boaters in helping to prevent their spread.

Partnerships

There are a number of partnerships already providing public education on stewardship aimed at recreational boaters. The Ocean Conservancy's Good Mate program (www.oceanconservancy.org/site/PageServer?pagename = op_goodmate) is one, the Tampa Bay Estuary Program has its Bay Friendly Boater Kit (www.tbep.org/newtoboating.html), and the California Clean Boating Network (www.coastal.ca.gov/ccbn/ccbnhomenew.html) trains "dock walkers" to conduct one-on-one boater education.

BoatU.S. has found that one of the best ways to encourage aquatic resource stewardship on the part of boaters is to bring them into the process; that is, to engage them in an activity or education campaign of their own. The foundation's Grass Roots Grants program for 2005 provided $80,000 in funds donated by BoatU.S. members in the form of grants in support of local boating safety and clean water projects. In the clean water/environmental category, 18 groups (e.g., boat clubs, Boy Scout troops, civic groups) received half that money ($40,000) for projects ranging from instructional videos to billboard public service announcements to brochures. That approach is particularly effective because the local boaters know the opportunities and challenges in their home waters, and they also have the contacts and enthusiasm to address them. The return for the modest investments in such grants, which range from a few hundred dollars to $4,000, is significant (Podlich, personal communication).

West Marine, the nation's largest boating equipment retailer, also makes grants to nonprofit organizations that work toward "the preservation and protection of the marine environment, focusing on such topics as pollution prevention, preserving fisheries, educating the boating public on environmental issues and restoring and protecting coral reefs" (www.westmarine.com/sponsorship). The retailer, which has made donations to some 500 organizations, often commits a portion of receipts at its new store openings to "community groups that promote marine resource stewardship and clean boating as well as youth programs and boating safety education (L. Fried, West Marine, personal communication).

The Boating Market Place

Two avenues for reaching the boating consumer with stewardship messages have opened up in recent years as boaters, along with the general public, have become more concerned with environmental issues: boat shows and retailers. Some 190 consumer boats shows are held in the United States annually, according to the National Marine Manufacturers Association (NMMA; www.nmma.org/calendar). The majority of shows are produced by national, state, or local (often county or market area-based) industry trade associations. Discussion among networks of show promoters indicates a willingness to put more emphasis on stewardship educational offerings as a "natural opportunity to work with those kinds of groups (nongovernmental organizations) to promote a well-rounded picture of the boating lifestyle to the consumer" (B. Wold, NMMA, personal communication).

The NMMA produces 23 consumer shows of its own and incorporates stewardship information in many, either directly, as in show-sponsored seminars, or by providing discounted or gratis exhibit space to nonprofit environmental advocacy organizations and/or natural resource agencies. In both cases, personnel from the organization or agency are encouraged to interact with show attendees and distribute educational materials to the public. Typically, 30% to 35% of NMMA show attendees are new to boating (Wold, personal communication); thus, consumer boat shows can provide an opportunity to reach newcomers to the sport with stewardship information at the outset of their boating experience.

So too, the nation's 10,000 boat dealerships and equipment retailers, and its 12,000 recreational marinas (NMMA 2005), many of which are already key outlets for boating safety information, represent a potential pathway for reaching recreational boaters with stewardship information. According to the Association of Marina Industries (formerly the Marina Owners and Operators Association of America), a trade association, marinas are increasingly inclined to provide space to display or distribute educational materials and "would like to be considered as not only sites for access to the water, but as gateways for education and outreach about responsible angling practices, ANS [aquatic nuisance species] prevention strategies, and general 'clean boating' information" (M. Livingood, Marina Operators Association of America, personal communication).

Recognizing a trend toward environmental sensitivity among its customers, West Marine now runs periodic "Clean and Green" discount coupon campaigns for certain environmentally friendly products. With more than 400 stores in 38 states, the company provides the largest potential direct contact point with recreational boaters. The chain is amenable to displaying and distributing stewardship materials from outside organizations at in-store Community and Environmental Bulletin Boards "in keeping with West Marine's corporate mission statement" (Fried, personal communication).

Summary

There are a variety of ways to reach recreational boaters with stewardship messages, all of which are being employed currently to pass along stewardship or "green boating" messages to some degree. This presentation reviewed many of these, including print, television, radio, Internet, retailing, and various partnerships. To be most effective, however, messages should be tailored to the various target audiences within boating, (e.g., by the type of boater, sailor, or personal watercraft rider; by region). To ensure effective and credible delivery, presenters should be boaters themselves and they should use visuals to which boaters can relate. A message targeted to sailors, in a magazine print public service advertisement or in a race tune-up class, for example, ought to have a picture of a sailboat or sailing props to make its points. Such information packages should be as relevant as possible to the interests of the receiver of the message in order to elicit positive results and thereby gain the support of boaters as important allies for aquatic resource stewardship in the days and years ahead.

Acknowledgments

Many individuals provided invaluable insight and information for this paper: Richard Clincy, U.S. Coast Guard Auxiliary; Laurie Fried, West Marine; Jean Hamilton, U.S. Power Squadrons; Larry Innis, Marine Retailers Association of America; James D. Murray, NOAA/National Sea Grant College Program; Mari Lou Livingood, National Fish and Wildlife Foundation; Terri Parrow, Boat Owners Association of the United States; Jim Petru, National Marine Manufacturers Association; Margaret Podlich, Boat Owners Association of The United States; Mike Walker, The Walker Agency; and Ben Wold, National Marine Manufacturers Association.

References

Anonymous. 2001. Pillow talk: go soak your bilge. Foundation Finding Report #34. Available: www.boatus.com/foundation/findings/oil_removal_products.htm (August 2006).

Mediamark Research, Inc. 2002. Subscriber survey. Mediamark Research, Inc., New York.

NMMA (National Marine Manufacturers Association). 2004. Recreational boating statistical abstract National Marine Manufacturers Association, Chicago.

NMMA (National Marine Manufacturers Association). 2005. Recreational boating statistical abstract. National Marine Manufacturers Association, Chicago.

Turken, J. S. 2005. Spill? What spill? Products to keep fuel where it belongs—in your tank. BoatU.S. Magazine 10(2):32–34.

American Fisheries Society Symposium 55:79–84, 2007

The Trout Unlimited Experience Teaching Aquatic Stewardship to Youth

DUNCAN BLAIR[1]

Trout Unlimited

1300 North 17th Street, Suite 500, Arlington, Virginia 22209, USA

Abstract.—Trout Unlimited (TU) is a private, nonprofit organization with more than 150,000 members dedicated to conserving, protecting, and restoring trout and salmon fisheries and their watersheds in North America. TU staff and volunteer members engage in education programs, restoration projects, advocacy campaigns, and other conservation activities in support of the organization's mission. In 2001, TU launched a new national initiative named First Cast to teach students the principles of coldwater resource stewardship through the skills of fly-fishing. The initiative, delivered by TU's nationwide network of more than 400 volunteer chapters, teaches children from age 7 through 18 in a variety of settings ranging from 1-d casting clinics to 5-d residential camps. These programs have led to demonstrable benefits, including increased angling participation and stewardship behaviors by the participants and strengthened TU chapters. There have also been significant challenges in implementing a rigorous evaluation system and spreading the use of best practices in a decentralized, volunteer organization.

Introduction

Trout Unlimited (TU), a nationwide grassroots conservation organization, has a mission of protecting trout and salmon fisheries and their watersheds. In our society, each generation is increasingly disconnected from the natural environment as a larger percentage of the population grows up in urban environments without any exposure to rivers, streams, ponds, and lakes. Like many organizations dedicated to environmental stewardship, TU is concerned that today's youth has no personal experience and therefore no personal stake in the natural environment. To address this situation, in 2001, TU launched First Cast, a nationwide initiative to introduce youth to coldwater conservation topics through fly-fishing. First Cast is delivered by local TU volunteer chapters across the country in a variety of different formats from single-day casting clinics to week-long residential camps.

In the first 3 years of the First Cast program, TU had many successes, including increasing angling and stewardship behaviors by the participants in addition to strengthening TU chapters. The experience of First Cast also taught TU valuable lessons about the difficulties of conducting rigorous evaluation and spreading best practices in a decentralized, volunteer organization. This paper describes the First Cast program and provides insights and recommendations for other angling and stewardship education programs, based on knowledge gained through 3 years of First Cast program implementation.

Background of Trout Unlimited

The mission of Trout Unlimited is to "conserve, protect and restore North America's coldwater fisheries and their watersheds." TU was founded in 1959 and has grown to over 150,000 members assigned to more than 400 volunteer chapters across the country. Volunteers in these local chapters do stream restoration, local and state-wide advocacy, public outreach, and youth education programs that further TU's mission of coldwater fisheries conservation. In addition, as of 2005,

---

[1] E-mail: dblair@tu.org

TU has a staff of approximately 80 professionals who also coordinate conservation projects, conduct salmonid research, organize and advocate for environmentally sound legislation, and support TU chapters in the work that they do.

TU as an organization has always relied upon the link between stewardship and angling. TU members are typically passionate anglers and passionate conservationists. Often, it is the interest in angling that brings people to TU. For example, the largest single source of new members for TU is direct mail campaigns that offer premiums related to fly-fishing gear (rods, reels, flies, angling books, etc). Another indication of the importance of angling to TU's recruitment is that the most common reason given to attend a chapter meeting for the first time is "to find out where or how to fish" in a given area. Members often join and become active in the organization because of an interest in angling. At some point, the interest in learning about angling is overtaken by an interest in the conservation mission of the organization. Long-time TU volunteers, many of whom move up to be state or national-level volunteer leaders, describe a shift in focus from angling to conservation. Fishing is what gets them in the door, but it is stewardship that keeps them in TU.

Background of the First Cast Youth Education Program

Although local TU chapters have been conducting youth education since TU's founding 45 years ago, there was not a full-time position on the TU staff to support chapter youth education programs until 2001, when TU entered into a cooperative agreement with the Recreational Boating and Fishing Foundation (RBFF) and Cortland Line Company. With the support provided by the agreement, TU launched First Cast (Blair and Genova 2001), a program to teach youth a message of coldwater conservation through fly-fishing. The First Cast program is based on a curriculum (Genova 1999) and a book (Genova 1998) written by the late Phil Genova of the Cortland Line Company that break up the skills of fly-fishing, including casting, fly-tying and angling, into a series of units and lessons (see Table 1). TU chapters find this curriculum to be extremely flexible and useful. In general, TU members are experienced anglers and already know the skills of fly-fishing, but have not taught these skills in an organized program. The First Cast curriculum is useful for TU chapters, therefore, because it provides a ready-made structure for youth education

TABLE 1. Contents of the First Cast curriculum.

Unit 1 – Mentor and apprentice	
Unit 2 – Fly tying: tools and materials	Lesson 1 – Fly tying tools
	Lesson 2 – Fly tying materials
	Lesson 3 – Fly tying hooks
Unit 3 – Fly tying: flies and instruction	Lesson 1 – Fly design and intro to fly tying
	Lesson 2 – Fly tying instruction
	Lesson 3 – Fly tying instruction: additional skills, concepts, and patterns
Unit 4 – Tackle and equipment	Lesson 1 – Intro to fly tackle: rod and reel
	Lesson 2 – Fly tackle: line, backing, and leader
	Lesson 3 – Fly tackle: assembling the outfit
Unit 5 – Fly casting	Lesson 1 – Fly casting instruction
Unit 6 – Skills, rules, and techniques	Lesson 1 – Knot tying
	Lesson 2 – Reading the water
	Lesson 3 – Fly choice and presentation
Unit 7 – Saltwater fly fishing	Lesson 1 – Getting started
	Lesson 2 – Casting and retrieving
	Lesson 3 – Understanding the saltwater environment
Unit 8 – Field trips	
Unit 9 – Exploring the aquatic environment	Lesson 1 – Understanding the aquatic environment
Unit 10 – Community programs	

programs. For example, if a chapter has 1 h of teaching time, they can teach one lesson. If a chapter has a full day of teaching time, they can teach up to four or five lessons. First Cast program types vary, as do the subjects covered (Table 2). TU chapters can tailor the curriculum to a wide range of program settings and student ages.

To support these programs, TU's youth program coordinator has developed a number of other resources beyond the First Cast curriculum. In 2002, TU introduced a Coldwater Conservation Education Guide (Blair and Sherriffs 2002). The guide contains information and activities relating to coldwater conservation topics, including trout biology, stream ecology, water quality, and stewardship behaviors (Table 3). Each section of the guide references particular lessons in the First Cast curriculum, so conservation information and activities can be paired with the angling lessons as appropriate for the time available, venue, and age of participants.

Beyond the First Cast curriculum and Coldwater Conservation Education Guide, the youth program coordinator also provides resources to TU chapters such as discounted youth fly-fishing equipment in addition to technical assistance with program development and delivery. Through the efforts of the youth program coordinator, the number of participants in TU youth education programs has increased steadily from approximately 5,000 youth in 2002 to more than 14,000 in 2005.

Evaluation

When designing First Cast, TU included a range of evaluation measures to determine the effectiveness of these youth education programs and gather feedback to continually improve delivery. These evaluation measures included participant surveys, educator surveys, and anecdotal reports.

Participant surveys

The youth program coordinator provided a standard participant survey to chapter volunteers conducting youth education programs. The volunteer educators were asked to administer the surveys to their students and return the completed surveys to the coordinator. As a volunteer program, though, there was no way to ensure compliance. In the first full year of the program (2002), 947 participant surveys were distributed to a set of randomly selected First Cast programs. This represented approximately one-fifth of the total number of First Cast participants that year. This survey (Table 4) gathered basic information about the participants, including previous angling experience, conservation knowledge and involvement in stewardship behaviors. Three versions of the participant questionnaire were prepared for use in preprogram, postprogram, and follow-up participant surveys. All three versions of the questionnaire include the same core questions, but some questions were changed or omitted based on applicability.

The preprogram survey was given to students by the volunteer educators at the beginning of the program, and the postprogram survey was administered before the students left. Of the 947 surveys distributed, 161 preprogram surveys (17%) and 206 postprogram surveys (22%) were returned to the coordinator. The reasons for the low response rate are discussed in the "Program Challenges" section below. Additionally, the youth program coordinator administered a follow-up survey 6 months later by e-mail to 153

TABLE 2. Examples of First Cast programs and subject coverage.

Program type	Ages	Length	Possible subjects covered
Casting clinic	7 to 18	3 h	Casting, safety, angling
Fly tying class	7 to 18	2 hours (repeatable)	Fly tying, entymology
Conservation and fishing camp (residential)	11 to 14	3 to 5 d	Entymology, ecology, casting, fly tying, angling, safety, ethics
Boy scout merit badge	14 to 18	6 to 12 h	Angling, knots, safety, ethics
School physical education class	7 to 18	1 h (repeatable)	Casting, safety

TABLE 3. Sample topics and activities from the Coldwater Conservation Education Guide.

Topic	Concepts	Activities	Ages	Time
Ecology	Ecosystems	Observing a stream	all	1+ h
	Competition	"Connect the Critters" worksheet	up to 12	30 min
Hydrology	Water cycle	"Water Cycle Fill-in" worksheet	up to 14	30 min
	Watersheds	Create a watershed model	10 and up	30 min
Stream life	Trout food	Stream life collection	12 and up	30 min
	Metamorphosis	"Insect Life Stages Fill-in" worksheet	up to 12	3+ h
	Adaptation	Water quality assessment with macroinvertebrates	12 and up	3+ h
Trout biology and behavior	Trout body	"Trout Fill-in" worksheet	up to 12	30 min
	Basic trout life cycle	"Color a Trout" worksheet	up to 10	30 min
	Fish senses	Lateral line game	up to 12	20 min
	Sea-run life cycle	Salmon farming debate role-play	15 and up	3+ h

participants randomly selected from the group that returned a postprogram survey. Slightly more than half (51%) of the contacted participants responded to the follow-up survey.

Educator surveys

TU hired an outside contractor, Dr. Tony Fedler, to conduct two mail surveys of all TU chapters to evaluate their experiences with youth education programs. The two surveys were done in 2001 and 2002, and each consisted of three waves of mailings to maximize response rate. The 2001 survey resulted in a response rate of 49%, and the 2002 survey resulted in a response rate of 39%. After each mail survey, Dr. Fedler conducted a follow-up phone survey with nonrespondents. The phone surveys indicated there was no meaningful difference between the nonrespondent (telephone) group and mail survey respondents, so we were able to safely extrapolate survey results to all TU chapters. These surveys provided data on the scope of chapter youth education programs, program successes and challenges, and the effect of youth education programs on the TU chapters themselves.

TABLE 4. Questionnaire used in participant surveys (pre-program version).

1. Who brought you to this program? Please give relationship, not name (friend, mother, teacher, by self, etc.)
2. Have you ever fly fished before?
    ____ No → skip to Question 4.
    ____ Yes → go to Question 2 below.
3. How many years have you fly fished? ___ Less than 1 year ___ 1–2 years ___ 3 years or more
4. Who taught you to fly fish? (friend, relative, learned yourself)
5. What are two of your other favorite hobbies or sports?
6. Did you know that there were fishing opportunities near your home?
7. Had you heard of Trout Unlimited prior to this program?
    ___ No → skip to Question 9.
    ___ Yes → go to Question 8 below.
8. Are you a Trout Unlimited member? ____ No ____ Yes
9. If you can, name two threats to trout habitat.
10. If you can, name two actions you or your family can take to help trout.
11. Have you ever done any of the actions you listed in Question 10?
    ___ No ___ Yes ____ "Yes," which actions?
12. Have you ever done an environmental project before?
13. Name two older people who are important influences in your life. Please give relationship, not name (coach, grandmother, teacher, etc.)

Anecdotal reports

The youth program coordinator, as the central point of contact and resource for TU youth education programs nationwide, was able to gather extensive anecdotal information about the successes and challenges of these programs. The coordinator communicated with educators by phone, by e-mail, by program visits and by facilitating workshops and trainings in the field.

Program Successes

The ultimate goal of TU youth education programs is to change participants' behavior. Desirable behaviors include going fishing again, demonstrating stewardship behaviors to protect trout and salmon habitat, and joining and staying active in TU. Based on the follow-up participant surveys, TU youth education programs had significant success in changing some of these behaviors.

For example, one question on the follow-up survey asked participants to list (if they could) up to two "activities that help trout." Common answers included "use less water," "don't pollute," and "catch-and-release." The next question asked participants if they had engaged in one or more of these activities. In the preprogram surveys, 68% of participants said that they had engaged in an activity that helps trout. In the follow-up survey (conducted 6 months later), 78% of participants said that they had engaged in such an activity.

TU youth education programs had even better success with encouraging angling. In the preprogram surveys, 53% of participants stated that they had fished before. In the follow-up survey, 80% of participants stated that they had been fishing again in the 6 months since the program.

Beyond the successes of changing participant behavior, these youth education programs brought significant benefits to the chapters that delivered them. In the chapter surveys, chapter leaders reported that their chapters received greater press attention, funding, and active volunteers due to youth education programs that they conducted.

Program Challenges

Most of the challenges that TU experienced with the First Cast youth education program were because the program is delivered by a decentralized network of volunteers. One of the areas that suffered because of this structure was evaluation, in particular the participant surveys. The coordinator had to rely on the volunteer educators to distribute, collect, and return the participant questionnaires before and after each program. There were many reasons that could have contributed to the low response rates described above, including lack of student cooperation and a lack of educator follow-through. The participant surveys also had the possibility of built-in biases. Some possible biases include the following:

- Participants are likely to overreport conservation or angling behaviors because that is what they are "supposed to be doing";
- Because not all participants returned a questionnaire, the data may include a response bias toward greater fishing participation or stewardship behavior; and
- Participants in TU programs are often children or friends of TU members and are therefore predisposed to angling and having a conservation ethic.

Another challenge is conducting follow-up surveys. It was difficult to track down participants after 6 months, again resulting in a low response rate with the possibilities of the biases described above. Additionally, it would have been useful to conduct another follow-up survey a year later to see if the trends continued.

Beyond the issue of evaluation, it is generally difficult to get a decentralized network of volunteer educators to follow best practices. The coordinator had access to the Best Practices in Aquatic Education materials developed and promulgated by the Recreational Boating and Fishing Foundation (Fedler 2001), but it was difficult to get chapters to absorb and implement the recommendations. For example, the research shows that large, single-day "fishing derbies" are not as effective as longer-term programs that involve a mentorship component in changing participant behavior. TU's own experience with First Cast supported the greater effectiveness of longer programs. Despite this knowledge, it is hard to convince volunteers to change what they have done for years to undertake a more sophisticated and resource-intensive program.

Addressing Challenges

The challenge of adequately evaluating the success of youth education programs requires significant resources in both staff time and expenses. This should be included in the original design and budget for any program. Evaluation is a time-intensive exercise, so if program coordinators will not have time to adequately complete evaluation tasks themselves, then they should use an outside resource.

The other significant lesson that TU learned over the first 3 years of the First Cast program is how to encourage volunteers to use best practices. TU found two strategies to be most effective. The first strategy was to tie incentives to the use of best practices. For example, the coordinator had some resources that could be distributed in a discretionary manner, such as donated education equipment. That equipment was made available to chapters that had developed programs in accordance with best practices (e.g., longer term programs that effectively conducted evaluation). In a decentralized, volunteer organization, incentives work where top-down requirements and penalties do not.

The other effective strategy for spreading best practices through an organization is to have peers share their positive experiences. In TU's case, the coordinator facilitated workshops on the design and delivery of youth education programs. Whenever possible, the "lessons learned" portions of the workshops would be led by volunteers sharing their experiences. Their message would be the same as the "Best Practices" document, but the examples drawn from fellow TU chapters resonated with other workshop participants.

Acknowledgments

Trout Unlimited thanks the Recreational Boating and Fishing Foundation and Cortland Line Company whose initial support made possible the launch of First Cast, the first nationwide youth education initiative in TU's 45 year history. In particular, First Cast is the result of the inspirational vision and passion of the late Phil Genova.

References

Blair, D., and P. Genova. 2001. TU First Cast manual, 1st edition. Trout Unlimited, Arlington, Virginia. Available: www.tu.org/atf/cf/{0D18ECB7–7347-445B-A38E-65B282BBBD8A}/First_Cast_Manual_1st_Ed.pdf (August 2006).

Blair, D., and M. Sherriffs. 2002. TU coldwater conservation education guide, 1st edition. Trout Unlimited, Arlington, Virginia. Available: www.tu.org/site/pp.asp?c=7dJEKTNuFmG&b=404659 (August 2006).

Fedler, A. J. 2001. Defining best practices in boating, fishing, and stewardship education. Report to the Recreational Boating and Fishing Foundation, Alexandria, Virginia.

Genova, P. 1998. First Cast: teaching kids to fly-fish. Stackpole Books, Mechanicsburg, Pennsylvania

Genova, P. 1999. First Cast - fly fishing education curriculum. Trout Unlimited, Arlington, Virginia. Available: www.tu.org/atf/cf/{0D18ECB7–7347-445B-A38E-65B282BBBD8A}/curriculum.pdf. (August 2006).

American Fisheries Society Symposium 55:85–91, 2007

Government, Nongovernmental Organizations, and Industry: Programs that Foster Aquatic Stewardship

ANNETTE L. GLICK[1]

Florida Fish and Wildlife Conservation Commission
620 South Meridian Street, Tallahassee, Florida 32399, USA

Abstract.— In 1950, Congressman John Dingell (Michigan) and Senator Edwin Johnson cosponsored a piece of legislation that changed the face of fisheries conservation. The Federal Aid in Sport Fish Restoration Act (Public Law 81-681), also known as the Dingell-Johnson Act, allowed excise taxes collected on rods, reels, creels, and artificial baits to be placed into a special account for apportionment to the states. In 1984, the Sport Fish Restoration Act was further strengthened by additional legislation that increased available funds and formed the new Aquatic Resources trust fund. The Wallop-Breaux Amendment, in addition to increasing funds for conservation programs and boating access, allowed states to use up to 10% of the states' annual apportionment on Aquatic Resources Education. Since 1984, states, nongovernmental organizations and industry have developed numerous programs that engage and educate the public on sound conservation issues that protect and enhance the environment for the next generation. This chapter provides an overview of successful, research-based conservation education programs that augment the overall effort to sustain the fisheries of the United States.

Introduction

Adapting from a model for environmental education, Knuth and Siemer (2004) proposed that aquatic stewardship education programs should foster growth in three sequential areas: (1) they should provide the learner with entry-level knowledge (awareness and knowledge of aquatic systems); (2) they should create a personal investment and a knowledge of the consequences, both positive and negative, a specific behavior will have on the aquatic system; and (3) programs should provide the learner with the knowledge and skills necessary to implement specific stewardship behaviors. In this chapter, I argue that entry-, ownership-, and empowerment-level variables are best achieved through programs that consider the learner's life stage, starting with the learner's immediate environment and later expanding to include broader issues and the global environment. A young learner, for example, who is in the beginning stages of developing stewardship behavior, cannot be expected to understand and actively modify an environment beyond his scope of perception and observation. Therefore, a program that provides this young learner with knowledge and skills, and empowers him to modify his immediate environment, is a critical step in producing the same behaviors beyond his immediate scope of reference. I further propose as a learner expands his frame of reference, if given an opportunity, or called into action, he will take the ultimate step of educating others and seek to produce a positive change in the environment, by becoming an advocate. This chapter will describe several programs that aquatic educators are using to engage learners at all levels and to provide vehicles for adults to become activists for sustainable sport fishing.

Stewardship Education Programs

Green schools

Green schools programs are interventions intended to encourage students and staff of a school to take actions that make the school environment

____

[1] E-mail: anne.glick@myFWC.com

more environmentally friendly. Green schools programs take a variety of forms. The specific program requirements vary according to the state; for example, the Maryland Department of Natural Resources requires a 2-year application process for the school to document the changes made in the school environment (additional program information about the Green schools Award program is available from the Maryland Department of Natural Resources). Oregon Green Schools is a nonprofit organization that was formed in 1997. More than 200 schools participated in the program in 2006. A statewide network of Oregon Green Schools regional coordinators help participating schools conduct waste audits, implement waste reduction and efficiency programs, and identify related curriculum materials and grant opportunities (more information about Oregon Green Schools is available at www.oregongreenschools.org/about.cfm). All Green Schools have in common two main goals: to help students and staff change their personal environment, and to recognize schools that achieve success.

Green schools programs are designed to make staff, students, and families aware of the need for change and initiate a desire to change behavior for the sake of their personal environment. These are crucial beginning stages before an individual may move on to making changes in the broader environment and, ultimately, convincing others to make changes as well.

Kentucky's Big River poster project

The *Big River* poster is part of a series of posters created and distributed by the Kentucky Department of Fish and Wildlife Resources (other titles in the poster series include *Stream, Small Stream, Upland Reservoir, Wetland Sloughs,* and *Freshwater Mussel*). Each poster is the focal point for classroom studies of a specific ecosystem found in Kentucky. The posters are accompanied by teacher's guides that describe the aquatic ecosystems of Kentucky and how human actions may change those ecosystems. Teachers are encouraged to follow classroom study with opportunities for their students to visit local aquatic ecosystems, where students can collect and study aquatic organisms and make first-hand observations about human impacts on their local environment.

This type of study within the classroom, linked to an outside experience, is intended to help students move from an awareness of the need for aquatic stewardship to taking ownership of their immediate environment. The goal is to enable these students first to change their feelings about the need for aquatic stewardship, and then move towards making a positive change in the environment around them.

Storm drain painting projects

Storm drain painting projects have been conducted nationwide for more than 25 years. The North Carolina Storm Drain Stenciling Project has been in effect since 1994, and Chesapeake Bay Foundation has been highlighting Chesapeake Bay drainage projects since the mid-1980s. As a regional outreach, the Ocean Conservancy has a Storm Drain Sentries program that clearly marks storm drains acting as conduits for potential marine pollution. Program volunteers use stencils to paint storm drains near the ocean with messages such as *Keep Clean* in North Carolina, *Chesapeake Bay Drainage*—Don't Dump in Maryland, and *Don't Dump! Protect Your Water.* The goal of these projects is to create public awareness of the results of pouring foreign materials, such as anti-freeze, oil, or even solid trash, down storm drains.

A secondary goal for these storm drain painting projects is to initiate an advocacy role among volunteers. These projects engage the participants in the long-term process: contacting local government for appropriate permits, publicizing the project through interviews with local media sources, contacting the businesses and residential homes affected by the project, and organizing additional volunteers. During the painting process, volunteers often have the opportunity to discuss the need for the project with interested observers, further emphasizing the advocacy role.

"In the classroom" projects

"In-classroom" projects are a vehicle that teachers use to help their students become environmental stewards in their local community. In-classroom projects often focus on raising a specific type of aquatic animal in the classroom and then releasing that animal into the appropriate environment. The species vary by region (e.g., horseshoe crabs

Limulus polyphemus in Maryland, salmon in Washington, trout in New York). Program participants typically begin with eggs or small fry and raise animals to a stage of early development in their immediate environment. Lessons are designed to help students understand the organism as a keystone species in a locally important ecosystem. For example, one of the main goals for the *Raising Horseshoe Crabs* project sponsored by the Maryland Department of Natural Resources is to enable students to understand the ecological connection between horseshoe crabs and shorebirds.

This type of project helps students move through entry-, ownership-, and empowerment-level variables for one species in a locally important ecosystem. While growing the organism in the classroom, students are changing their feelings and emotions towards an animal they may have originally seen as a "yucky fish" to a salmon holding a special place in the local ecosystem. Second, in all of these projects, the organism is released into the environment by the students. In Maryland, for example, all participating schools assemble during a single-day event to release horseshoe crabs. Program developers hope that these release events, coupled with other outside activities (e.g., stream monitoring) will stimulate students to make positive changes in their personal environment.

Third, students have the opportunity to impact a larger environment going beyond simply raising salmon, trout, or horseshoe crabs and mapping local watersheds or constructing streamside nature trails. This important step in development of aquatic stewardship is intended to assist students in seeing beyond the organism raised in the classroom to the environment at large.

In-classroom projects can include elements that make students aware that they can influence the opinions of others. Some students using this project have written articles for school and local newspapers, started environmental resource libraries, created information panels, produced videos on salmon-related projects, and participated in community environmental fairs. It is an important lesson to teach children they have the ability to lead others to make positive changes in their local environment.

In addition to providing youth education opportunities, in-classroom projects provide opportunities to engage adults in a community for aquatic

stewardship. *Trout in the Classroom*, for example, has an adult trout coordinator assist the teacher in raising the trout and planning fieldtrips. This trout coordinator may be a member of Trout Unlimited or simply a knowledgeable and interested adult. The goal is to create an opportunity for a member of the community to not only engage in aquatic stewardship on a committed level, but also to engage in the stewardship education of youth.

Canon Envirothon

The Canon Envirothon, sponsored by Canon USA, Inc., is an annual competition testing the knowledge and problem-solving skills of state teams in five main areas of environmental science: soils, forestry, wildlife, aquatics, and one current issue. The primary mission is to develop knowledgeable, skilled, and dedicated citizens who are willing and prepared to work towards achieving and maintaining a natural balance between the quality of life and the quality of the environment.

Teams of interested students and a volunteer advisor are formed at the local community level and spend up to 1 year learning about environmental science, often by conducting research and literature searches, taking appropriate fieldtrips, and inviting pertinent speakers. Each team practices questions concerning all aspects of environmental science, including a current topic. Each student involved is supposed to utilize problem-solving skills and research techniques to solve environmental problems. These local teams compete on a state or provincial level and ultimately on a national level.

Many states host statewide Envirothon challenges, including Utah, Pennsylvania, and Maryland. The organizations that deliver these programs hope that as students and adult volunteers participate in envirothons, they will become empowered to change their personal environment, acquire the skills needed to change their extended environment, and ultimately, become leaders of change in their local communities.

Future Fisherman Foundation

Arguably, the main goal of the Future Fisherman Foundation (F3) is to create new anglers and boaters through on-the-ground education programs.

However, sustaining the quality of fishing and boating opportunities that attracts participation will not be possible in the future unless the boaters and anglers of today become wise resource stewards. Thus, F3 has developed two education programs—Hooked On Fishing – Not On Drugs and the National PE Grants Initiative—that include an aquatic stewardship dimension. Both programs are intended to lead interested children through the processes of changing their feelings about the environment, changing their personal environment, changing their extended environment, and ultimately, leading other youth and adults to change their behavior.

Hooked On Fishing – Not On Drugs (HOFNOD) is an educational program intended to assist youth in becoming ethical anglers who will act as environmental stewards while making positive life skills decisions, such as goal-setting, communicating meaningfully with others, and choosing to remain drug-free for life. HOFNOD is used by schools, after-school clubs, Scouts, 4-H, Boys and Girls Clubs, YMCAs, religious organizations, state natural resource agencies, and anti-drug organizations, such as the National Guard. HOFNOD is customized in a variety of ways, such as a vehicle for teaching fly fishing in the Northeast, ice fishing in North Dakota, saltwater fishing in South Carolina, or spin casting nationwide. Each HOFNOD program has certain requirements: youth will learn to fish, become involved in their personal aquatic environment, and practice positive life skills.

HOFNOD may be used to help children change their feelings about the aquatic environment. Simply going fishing allows a child to witness the need for learning about and taking care of the environment. It is impossible to become a good angler without studying the aquatic organisms serving as food for the fish. Children are given the opportunity to change their personal aquatic environment by coordinating clean-ups, creating submerged habitat, and doing other environmental projects. Other HOFNOD activities encourage students to write to their local politicians and newspapers with their environmental concerns. HOFNOD uses angling with the intention of stimulating interest in the environment and helping youth make positive life decisions. The program aims to promote environmentally responsible behavior (Siemer and Knuth 2001).

The National PE Grants Initiative offers grants of up to $5,000 to certified physical education (P.E.) teachers in public or private schools to include fishing and/or boating in their P.E. classes. These grants have been used to teach spin casting, fly-fishing, kayaking, canoeing or any combination of these activities. While the goal of this grant initiative is to teach students the skills necessary to continue these activities for a lifetime, they may be coupled with environmental activities by the P.E. teacher working with a content teacher, such as a science teacher. Grant recipients are encouraged to use the equipment purchased outside of P.E. class, such as in clubs or grade-wide field days. It is often in these types of activities students are given the opportunity to learn about their personal aquatic environment and humans' effect on this environment.

FishAmerica Foundation

The FishAmerica Foundation (FAF) unites the sport fishing industry with conservation groups, government natural resource agencies, corporations, and charitable foundations to invest in fish and habitat conservation and research across the country. FAF supports fisheries conservation and research by providing matching grants to empower citizen conservationists in their own communities. These grants combine with broader efforts to conserve the outdoors for the future.

FAF provides funding for hands-on projects at the local level that enhance fish populations, restore fish habitat, improve water quality, or advance fisheries research. FAF provides an opportunity for interested individuals to make a meaningful change in their extended environment. FAF hopes that, by gathering matching funds and publicizing the project, program participants may lead others to change their views and actions regarding the aquatic environment.

FAF offers grants in four main categories. General Conservation Project grants fund freshwater projects and nonhabitat restoration projects for marine and anadromous fish. FishAmerica/Chesapeake Bay Trust Projects fund projects benefiting sport fish and/or sport fish within the Chesapeake Bay in Maryland habitat. General Research Projects directly address national/regional concerns regarding sport fish and/or sport fish habitat. FishAmerica/National Oceanic and

Atmospheric Administration (NOAA) Community-Based Marine and Anadromous Fish Habitat Restoration Projects fund marine and anadromous fish habitat enhancement efforts.

FAF's grants range from under $1,000 to well over $50,000. This range of grants allows communities to improve their aquatic habitat and take personal ownership of either their personal or a regional extended environment. In addition to obtaining funding, each grant applicant is responsible for obtaining the necessary permits and is encouraged to publicize the project. As an individual or group moves through the grant application and project implementation process, the intent is that they are becoming environmental stewards capable of changing their extended environment and, possibly, leading others in the community to change as well.

Line Recycling

Discarded fishing line creates a significant environmental problem. Birds, fish, and mammals become trapped in fishing line or ingest line and eventually die. One means of reducing this problem is to recycle the line. Line recycling is done by both industry, such as Pure Fishing's Berkley division, and other organizations, such as the Florida Fish and Wildlife Conservation Commission.

Making anglers aware of the need to recycle line is accomplished through publicity, including line recycling bins. The publicity associated with line recycling is aimed at persuading anglers to make a personal choice to recycle. This change in attitude leading to a conscious decision to change the local angling environment is the first crucial step in becoming an environmental steward.

Berkley takes recycling fishing line one step further to assist the angler in improving the local environment by offering a recycled line fish habitat. The Fish Hab is an artificial, underwater habitat structure constructed of recycled monofilament line and other postconsumer plastic products, such as a used gallon milk jug. The Fish Hab is available to any person or organization that wishes to place some cover to help in creating a healthy fish population. For 75 universal product codes from Berkley line products, an individual or group may obtain the Fish Hab at no cost. This is another way for individuals to make a positive change in their personal environment.

The Florida Fish and Wildlife Conservation Commission makes the individual angler aware of the need for recycling and offers an opportunity for the angler to recycle used line, either in recycling receptacles near fishing spots or at tackle shops that contain Berkley line recycling receptacles. The program has three main goals: heighten awareness about the negative impacts that fishing line debris has on human welfare, marine life, and water quality; decrease the amount of fishing line entering and remaining in the natural environment; and increase the amount of fishing line being recycled. These goals all work toward assisting the angler in recognizing the need for recycling and making a conscious decision to recycle line.

Tournament Fishing

Tournament fishing and tournament anglers are a venue for industry to promote aquatic stewardship. Although at first glance this partnership between industry and aquatic stewardship seems strained, in reality, tournament anglers have become leaders for many anglers, and potential anglers, nationwide. As leaders, these professional anglers have the opportunity to promote sport fishing and the need for conservation and aquatic stewardship. B.A.S.S., the sponsor of the B.A.S.S. tournament circuit, supports aquatic stewardship on the national level by supporting appropriate legislation. Additionally, B.A.S.S. functions on the local level, by funding and participating in stewardship projects, such as planting habitat and participating in clean-up and awareness projects in local waters. Industry sponsors are not only supporting the tournament angler, but also supporting the stewardship projects the tournament angler embraces.

The change over the last 25 years from fishing being viewed as primarily a male sport to a family sport has increased the opportunities for aquatic stewardship to become a more integral part of enjoying the sport. Tournament fishing, instead of being viewed negatively as solely a user of the resource, can be an opportunity to publicize the need to conserve and manage aquatic resources for everyone to enjoy their use in the future. Michael Iaconelli, the 2003 Bassmaster Classic world champion, is a 23-year-old enthusiastic sportfishing role model for many youth and young adults. Michael break dances on his bass boat and connects with today's youth, with the potential to help make them aware of the need for stewardship of our aquatic resources. As a part of the B.A.S.S. organization, Michael also participates in aquatic conservation on both the local and national levels.

The overall change in tournament fishing from the realm of bearded "Bubba Bassers" to include women and younger adults on the pro tour promotes fishing as a sport for everyone to enjoy. Making fishing more inclusive may result in a wider view by the public on the need for aquatic stewardship. This recognized need for aquatic stewardship may then result in more aquatic stewardship projects and programs being supported by B.A.S.S. and other tournament organizations.

Northwestern Sportfishing Industry Association

The Northwestern Sportfishing Industry Association's (NSIA) mission clearly states the organization's commitment to aquatic stewardship: NSIA is dedicated to the preservation, restoration and enhancement of sport fisheries and the businesses dependent upon them. This commitment has resulted in NSIA being the voice of sport fishing industry business leaders, with the goal of achieving positive changes at the local, state, regional, and federal levels.

NSIA has catalyzed the public and local decision makers around specific local actions resulting in more and healthier fish. For example, NSIA was instrumental in achieving additional spill-over dams on the Columbia River to assist in the out-migration of salmon and steelhead *Oncorhynchus mykiss*. For members of the public who are ready to assist in stewardship behaviors on a regional level, NSIA may be a good way to become involved.

Conclusion

The process of encouraging aquatic stewardship behaviors may seem complex and daunting on the surface, but in fact is attainable if government, nongovernmental organizations, and industry work together to provide integrated, complementary stewardship education experiences. To instill a sense of aquatic stewardship,

an individual needs to be engaged on four distinct and equally important levels, all of which move the learner from a specific environment into global action:

1. The individual will be made aware of the aquatic environment and develop a feeling the situation should be changed.
2. The individual will make an effort to change their personal environment, such as their home routine or their school environment.
3. The individual will change their extended environment, such as a pond in their local community.
4. Last, the individual will begin to influence others in the community to change their behavior.

It is important for a community to have opportunities for people to experience all four levels of this process. This may be accomplished in one all-inclusive program, such as "In-Classroom" programs when fully implemented. However, this may be more likely to be accomplished with a variety of programs, offered by a diverse array of sponsors, and specializing at different levels of the process. It is important to note that one program may address various levels of stewardship development depending on one's type of participation in that program. A student participant may just be embarking on the awareness and understanding role, while an adult volunteer most likely has achieved the advocacy role, influencing other participants.

Across the country, many good aquatic stewardship programs exist that can be implemented for minimum cost. The key to success will be to provide access to aquatic stewardship programs that address all levels of the continuum and address the needs of the specific community and to conduct evaluations of different types of programs to determine which models are most likely to achieve their goals or to help individuals move along the aquatic stewardship spectrum from entry-level concern to empowerment-level action skills.

References

Knuth, B. A., and W. F. Siemer. 2004. Fostering aquatic stewardship: a key for fisheries sustainability. Pages 243–255 *in* E. E. Knudsen, D. D. Mac-

Donald, and Y. K. Muirhead, editors. Sustainable management of North American fisheries. American Fisheries Society, Symposium 43, Bethesda, Maryland.

Siemer, W. F., and B. A. Knuth. 2001. Effects of fishing education programs on antecedents of responsible environmental behavior. Journal of Environmental Education 32(4):23–29.

American Fisheries Society Symposium 55:93–101, 2007

Citizen Science: Stewardship Education in Washington State

MARGARET TUDOR[1] AND MICHAEL O'MALLEY

Washington Department of Fish and Wildlife, Olympia, Washington 98501, USA

Abstract.—Washington State has used education reform best practices to redesign stewardship education. The directors of state natural resource agencies, education associations, businesses, and nonprofits who created the Pacific Education Institute (PEI) provide the leadership. PEI represents a systematic effort to work in the formal education sector using environmental education (EE) standards that align with subject area standards and provide a framework for integrated learning. PEI undertakes education research based on those EE standards to understand student achievement and its relationship to environment-based experiential education. PEI has refined the description of science inquiry to include three types of field investigation with rigorous protocols that will be included in the state's science tests beginning in 2007. Finally, PEI has fostered a citizen science initiative with NatureMapping to connect the research undertaken by students through field investigation to questions asked by scientists. In partnership, the Washington Department of Fish and Wildlife expects citizen science to contribute to the statewide biodiversity index now being designed. Integral to delivering these opportunities to K–12 is the university teacher preparation faculty and their work to prepare preservice teachers with these opportunities. The result is school districts now foster stewardship education, contributing to community sustainability.

Introduction

The Washington Department of Fish and Wildlife (WDFW) has demonstrated a longstanding commitment to enhancing environmental education (EE) opportunities for the youth of Washington State. Over time, the nature of that commitment has evolved into a commitment to integrate the principles and practice of citizen science into the agency's approach to natural resource management and into formal EE experiences in K–12 classrooms. Citizen science relies on scientists to develop research designs with a citizen component, to design protocols for field studies, to give citizens access to agency or local technical guidance, and to provide meaningful feedback to the citizens who participate in research projects. In this chapter, we describe how citizen science is now becoming the means to educate for stewardship in Washington State.

What led stewardship education to this point was the need for natural resource management agencies and others to work with schools on their own terms, or be sidelined by the education system as it underwent education reform. Education reform advocates determined through research[2] that student learning increases after the use of an inquiry-based science curriculum. The studies also indicated that this benefit extends to other subjects like reading, writing, language development, and math.

Education reform brought about change in the expectations of what students should know, how they should be taught, and how teachers

---

[2] In 1995, The National Science Foundation created the Local Systemic Change (LSC) program. The purpose of LSC was to improve science and math teaching and learning, by applying insights from a series of large-scale research initiatives designed to improve teacher training and student learning. Education reform in Washington State was especially influenced by the results from the Imperial Valley LSC project in El Centro, California.

---

[1] E-mail:mtudor@wfpa.org

should be trained. State standards tests were instituted at each grade level as a measure of teacher accountability. Teachers are now expected to complete rigorous professional development activities. They receive continuous professional development to prepare curriculum plans with an assessment component that connect students with meaningful learning opportunities. K–12 education reformers systematically developed research based best practices for school administration, teacher training, student learning, and assessment. These best practices now inform how stewardship education can effectively work in schools.

The Role of the Pacific Education Institute

In order to meet the demands of education reform, WDFW's Project WILD Education programs joined with Project WET and Project Learning Tree to form a consortium to understand how to work with schools in a way that added value both for schools and for natural resource management agencies. We reviewed the research undertaken by the State Education and Environment Roundtable (SEER) and reported in *Closing the Achievement Gap* (Lieberman and Hoody 1998). The SEER research examined teacher perceptions of student change as a result of integrated learning using the "environment as an integrating context" or EIC (a term coined by Lieberman). Teachers reported better standardized test performance, reduced discipline problems, increased levels of engagement, and greater ownership in accomplishments. Encouraged by these findings, the consortium used EPA grant funding to create a not-for-profit, academically based research group called the Pacific Education Institute (PEI). PEI strives to advance environmental stewardship by maximizing the student learning impact of stewardship education providers in the formal school system. The experiential programs developed by PEI foster decision-making abilities about the environment while deepening critical thinking and problem-solving skills, which are evaluated through direct student assessments designed to measure environmental literacy (Taylor et al. 2005). The In-

stitute supports K–12 teachers and school districts, providing integrated, subject-based environmental education. The PEI board of directors represents a coalition of public and private stakeholders consisting of leaders of education associations, education and natural resource agencies, business and industry, and nonprofit organizations.

PEI has been involved in a number of projects that strengthen the public school curriculum through environmental education. It has developed environmental education frameworks that describe environmental literacy in terms of specific performances (Taylor et al. 2004). The frameworks include

- Systems analysis, in which students examine how natural and human systems interrelate by identifying problems, understanding stakeholder interests, evaluating tradeoffs, and generating alternative solutions;
- Research-based inquiry, in which students analyze research, develop research questions, design and conduct an investigation, and recommend an action;
- Language, visual, and performing arts, in which students investigate how creative expression communicates ideas and values through different media and reveals cultural values and varying societal perspectives; and
- Civic participation, in which leadership skills are expanded and tested as students collaborate to develop plans that contribute to the resolution of a local, regional, or international issue.

Citizen Science and Stewardship

Citizen science in Washington was first described by the University of Washington NatureMapping Program, developed jointly with WDFW in 1992. The NatureMapping Program defined its citizen science role as going beyond volunteer data collection involving participants in the design of the research and the analysis of the data (Dvornich et al. 1995; Tudor and Dvornich 2001). Citizen scientists are encouraged to develop further questions for research.

Citizen science creates an opportunity for

agencies to educate about their mandate through their role as researchers and managers of the resource. For example, in the work of Project CAT (Cougars and Teachers) in the Cle Elum-Roslyn School District, agency scientists involve students and community members in cougar captures, collaring, and releases. Scientists regularly report back their findings, whereupon the school and community work together to interpret the results to develop, revise, and implement an appropriate community action plan to conserve the resource by learning to live with cougars.

Scientists can design research with a citizen science component that complements the scientists' expert role. For example, wildlife scientists with WDFW developed a project that involves students from a rural school district in research on burrowing owls and ground squirrels. Scientists developed ecological models (e.g., to predict species presence or absence) and provided guidance on how students and their families could make descriptive and behavioral observations and report their observations to populate the models.

Part of the challenge of developing citizen science projects that contribute to science education goals is finding ways to provide feedback to participants and involve them in data analysis. The drawback is that agencies need an infrastructure that can handle this type of training and coordination for citizen science.

Natural resources agencies can use citizen science as a means to guide the public to undertake responsible stewardship activities that contribute to their agency's mission. In order to work with K–12 schools, agencies need to examine how national education reform that started in the early 1990s has changed expectations for delivery of education programs to schools. Stewardship educators need to examine how they can collectively contribute to school systems in ways that advance the education reform movement within those school systems. Education reform efforts in Washington State, for example, aim to improve the quality of education by raising the expectations of what students should know, how they are taught, and how teachers are prepared.

Natural resource-based conservation educators can apply the same scrutiny to stewardship education. As part of their needs assessment, stew-

ardship educators who work within schools should determine whether they are a factor in improving student learning. PEI members believe that the main contribution of in-school stewardship educators can be made through the sciences, particularly field science. Given that premise, PEI found it imperative to understand the specific value of field science to the science discipline generally and to help stewardship educators capitalize on extensive experience gained in the 1990s on conducting quality, rigorous stewardship education.

Studying the Value of Rigorous EE to Student Learning

In Washington, we reframed environmental education or stewardship education by studying the value of rigorous EE to student learning. We started by examining what movements like "Environment as the Integrating Context" for learning (Lieberman and Hoody 1998) were finding through research. Lieberman and Hoody's (1998) study for the State Education and Environment Roundtable (SEER) found that this integrated approach to learning resulted in motivated students who tended to perform better on state tests.

Among the members of the PEI consortium were education associations with the expertise needed to assess student progress and design research on best practices in stewardship education. In 2001, the consortium received an EPA Environmental Education and Training Partnership (EETAP) grant for 4 years, which enabled PEI to engage faculty from most of the colleges and university schools of education in the state to investigate what rigorous EE looks like. Faculty worked with PEI in curriculum inquiry, to understand the role of field studies in science inquiry and to define that process for the state department of education. PEI also connected faculty to classrooms practicing rigorous EE, providing placements for their preservice candidates to practice teach.

Schools are interested in working with the PEI consortium because it brings resources, expertise, and tools to assess student progress on subject areas and environmental education through practice tests. The PEI assessment project helped consortium members understand whether programs like Project WILD, Project WET, or Project Learning Tree (PLT) were a factor in improving student learning of the environment and whether stewardship educators were a factor in improving subject area learning.

PEI began by defining the student outcomes the consortium expected from stewardship education. In other words, what did conservation or stewardship educators want students to know and be able to do? In Washington State, PEI expects students to develop an understanding of how natural and human systems interrelate. PEI members expect students to gain skills in conducting natural and social science research within those systems and, with that background, develop and implement a plan to improve a component of the system. Members also expect students to gain skills in communicating what they had learned through persuasion or cultural expression.

PEI then developed tests modeled after state standards tests to examine student performance on the stewardship education expectations and piloted them with more than 3,000 students to establish reliability and validity of the tests. With these tests, PEI can now undertake long-term research to understand student environmental literacy and examine whether it improves with changes in program content or delivery (Taylor et al. 2005).

As a next step, PEI compared 77 schools that conduct environmental education with similar schools that offered little or no environmental education programming (Bartosh 2004). The study paired schools with similar demographic characteristics and compared the schools based on percentage of students who achieved passing scores on state standards assessments.

Figure 1 presents the comparison of average percentages of students who meet or exceed standards on WASL (Washington Assessment of

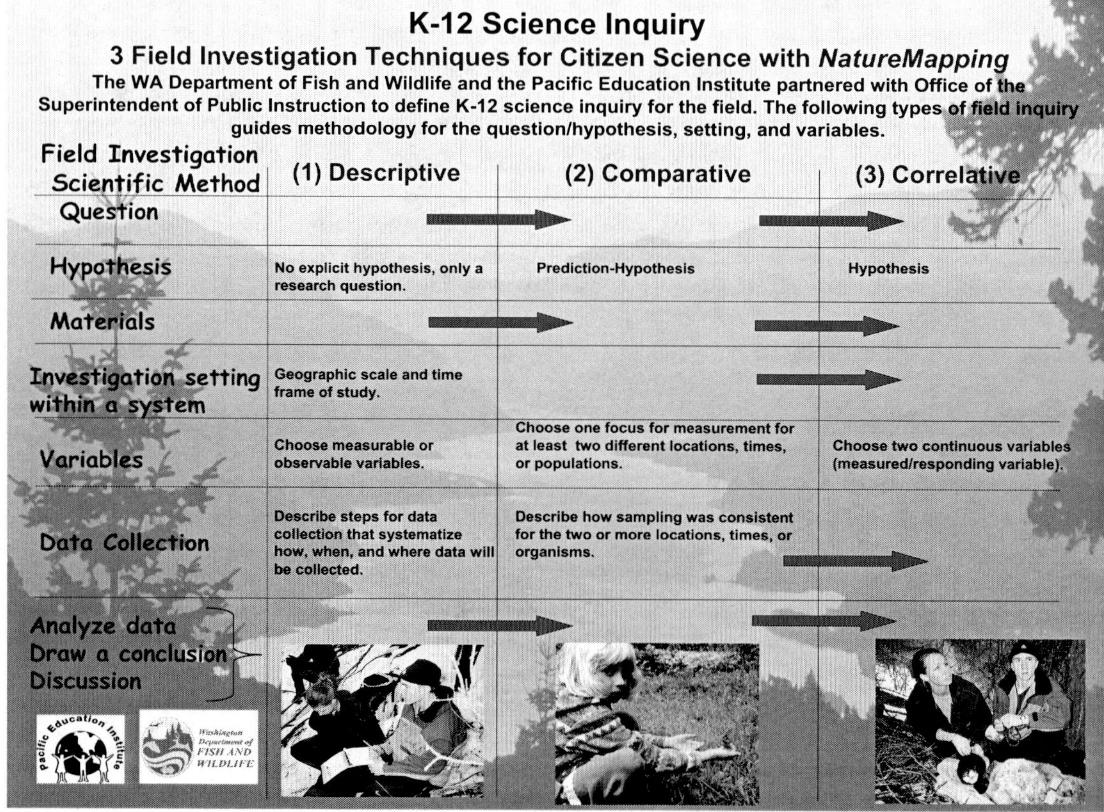

Field Investigation Scientific Method	(1) Descriptive	(2) Comparative	(3) Correlative
Question			
Hypothesis	No explicit hypothesis, only a research question.	Prediction-Hypothesis	Hypothesis
Materials			
Investigation setting within a system	Geographic scale and time frame of study.		
Variables	Choose measurable or observable variables.	Choose one focus for measurement for at least two different locations, times, or populations.	Choose two continuous variables (measured/responding variable).
Data Collection	Describe steps for data collection that systematize how, when, and where data will be collected.	Describe how sampling was consistent for the two or more locations, times, or organisms.	
Analyze data Draw a conclusion Discussion			

FIGURE 1. Contrasts and similarities between research designs of descriptive, comparative, and correlative field investigations.

Student Learning) tests for students in schools with EE programs and for students in comparison groups. As indicated on the chart, the average percentages of students who meet standards on the standardized tests are higher (statistically significant at $p < 0.05$) for EE schools on all four variables. This study indicates a trend that suggests EE schools do better. Results of this study served as the basis for research that examines student learning by direct measurement, to understand the relationship between EE and how well students achieve in school.

PEI engaged national assessment expert Dr. Catherine Taylor from the University of Washington to design research that would answer the question about the relationship between EE and student learning. PEI used the validated tests they had created and, with permission of school districts, tested a cohort of nearly 200 students to understand their learning in the three EE content areas of systems, inquiry, and civic participation. PEI also wanted to understand if EE performance was related to performance in subject area learning (Taylor et al. 2005).

The scores for each student on inquiry, systems, civics, and the total EE score now serves as a baseline against which PEI can compare each year for each grade level, to analyze for improvement in EE. PEI compared those scores for each student with their scores on math, reading, and writing (no science scores were available at the time). Analysis of the data showed a positive relationship between integrated stewardship types of education and student performance on state tests. It is important to note that this project is working with school districts that are in the process of implementing rigorous integration of subject areas around environment themes and field studies using inquiry-based learning.

Quality Stewardship Education

The field of conservation education needs to reflect on what quality stewardship education could look like. In Washington, PEI studied how teachers can integrate subject areas with natural resource themes, what field research the state can make available to students, and how agencies and organizations can provide appropriate restoration opportunities.

Public and private sector K–12 natural resource educators now depend on PEI to provide the appropriate in-depth program. PEI contracts with retired curriculum directors and teachers to work at school districts and, through outdoor learning centers, to provide ongoing professional development through workshops. At these workshops, the national program resources (Project WILD, WET, and Learning Tree) are modeled and used as a launching point to go into deep curriculum planning. Teachers create units or include activities from these resources.

PEI partners (public and private organizations and their educators) work through regional centers to support model school districts. PEI links university schools of education to these core districts—where preservice teachers can gain experience in classrooms that practice integrated learning through the environment. PEI consultants support school district leadership teams who work on developing curriculum plans with environmental themes, developing the capacity to use technology that includes GIS, bringing in focused community support as needed, and assessing student learning through the practice EE tests.

Science Inquiry for Stewardship Education

A set of environmental literacy expectations, devised by the consortium of public private education stakeholders represented by PEI, provided guidance for stewardship education and helped WDFW examine its role in education. WDFW primarily undertakes research on fish, wildlife, and habitat and develops and implements management plans. WDFW educators asked what research K–12 students can undertake and how they can then get involved with natural resource management, both through restoration projects and policy analysis.

WDFW staff found that there was not a close fit between the agency's research program and K–12 science education programs. Fish and wildlife agencies rarely use classic experimental designs to conduct field research because controlled experimentation is technically or ethically difficult to achieve in natural environments. However, schools in Washington currently emphasize experimental design for science inquiry and did not seem to value natural resource agency science as a rigorous form of science inquiry.

In order to address this challenge, PEI worked with the state department of education (Office of the Superintendent of Public Instruction) to expand the K–12 understanding of science inquiry beyond experimental design. With an expert panel of field scientists, teacher preparation faculty, and teachers, PEI developed a model for field investigation (Windschitl et al., in press) describing three protocols for field investigation: (1) descriptive, (2) comparative, and (3) correlative. Variables are handled differently within each protocol (Table 1). Describing the geographical and physical setting is fundamental to field studies and can be the most challenging aspect of study design for learners.

The new protocols for field investigation give stewardship education organizations an opportunity to establish a supporting role in science inquiry that is valued by schools. Washington State students will be tested for science inquiry understanding through field science inquiry items on the state standards tests beginning in 2007, so teachers are seeking those field experiences through stewardship education. Stewardship education can build science inquiry programs using the citizen science approach.

Case Studies Demonstrating Citizen Science and Stewardship

Washington State has about 10 years of experience developing citizen science programs for stewardship. Four case studies are provided here to demonstrate how citizen science and stewardship programs are being delivered. The first case illustrates work within K–12 schools with English language learner populations in remote areas. The second case focuses on work in a high school outdoor academy. The third case illustrates work with a community group. The final case focuses on a program for college students.

TABLE 1. Science inquiry field investigation model for stewardship education.

	Descriptive	Comparative	Correlative
Inquiry	Question to guide observation	Prediction-hypothesis	hypothesis
Identify setting within a system	Identify geographic scale of investigation. Identify time frame of the investigation.		
Identify variables of interest	Choose measurable or observable variables.	Choose one focus variable to be measured/observed in at least two different locations, times or populations.	Choose two continuous variables to be measured together and tested for a relationship.
Collect data (systematize how, when, and where data will be collected)	Multiple measurements over time or location in order to improve system representation (model). Individual measurement is repeated if necessary to improve data accuracy.	Describe how sampling was consistent for the two or more locations, times or organisms (controls) Identify and account for extraneous factors that might have an effect on the focal variable(s).	
Analyze data	Means, medians, ranges, percentages, calculated when appropriate. Organize results in graphic and/or written forms and maps using statistics where appropriate		
Use evidence to support an explanation	Use data to support an explanation. Limit conclusion to the specific study site.	Compare data to standards. Identify factors that may have affected the validity of the findings. Compare data to other similar systems/models. Discuss how results help answer the system's question and add to our understanding of the model/system.	

Sunnyside School District in rural Eastern Washington

PEI, WDFW, and the Yakima Basin Environmental Education Program work in partnership to provide fifth grade classrooms (80% Latin American) the following services and activities:

- State agency and volunteer instruction on science inquiry field investigation;
- Systematic training through NatureMapping on how to observe habitat, report location, and describe wildlife for identification;
- Beginning and advanced courses each last ing 8 weeks for a total of 16 weeks, one period per week during class;
- Opportunity for students to practice skills `during the week at the school site; and
- Funding for four field trips to agency wildlife areas for students to conduct research.

The fish and wildlife science agenda is being addressed by students reporting their observations of local wildlife to the public NatureMapping database. Students also examine the challenges for fish and wildlife in their area (due to a concentration of agriculture), and students work with scientists to develop best practices for stewardship on the land they impact.

Tahoma High School, Semirural Western Washington

Tahoma High School is evaluating an outdoor academy for tenth grade students. These students are developing writing and science inquiry skills through outdoor experiences that include fishing, biking, and hiking. Embedded in these activities are analyses of wetlands and other habitats to describe watershed health.

PEI has sponsored an outcome evaluation of the outdoor academy program. That study will be completed in 2007. The hypothesis of the study is that the participating outdoor academy students will do as well as or better than students in the traditional high school setting on state standards tests. The results of this research will help the participating natural resource agencies understand the impact stewardship education is having on student learning (quantitative results) and student environmental stewardship outlook and aspirations (qualitative results).

NatureMapping for Water and Streams

WDFW's experience with stewardship education broadened in 1999 when the University of Washington and WDFW NatureMapping educators formed a partnership with the Department of Ecology to develop a citizen science opportunity for water and stream studies. Research questions provided by agency scientists guided the design. WDFW used Americorps members to train volunteer groups and teachers around the state to collect and report the data during the first year. Groups reported their data by creating their own web page through NatureMapping, describing their project and entering the data (Figure 2).

WDFW analyzed where the data were collected and by whom (Galloway and Tudor 2000). In the first 10 months, almost half of the state watersheds had at least one monitoring site reporting data. In the first year, 91 groups were reporting data, and most groups providing data reported working with schools. NatureMapping established levels reflecting the quality of data reporting and found that nearly half of the groups reported at the novice level (no significant training) (level 1), and more than 40% reported at level 2 (reflecting some training with better performing equipment), with less than 10% reporting at level 3 (the technical level). Level 2 data and above can be used by state agencies that have included a citizen science component in their research design.

The NatureMapping program data analysis demonstrated that citizens have the capacity to learn methods of field science inquiry and are willing to be guided to gather field data (Galloway and Tudor 2000). Agencies have learned that volunteers can meet standards through training and that volunteer contributions can be built into a study design. The data analysis demonstrated that volunteer data have limits, but scientists can build and design projects around these limits without reducing the quality of the data. However, the limits to citizen science primarily lie in the current infrastructure or lack of it. Infrastructure for citizen science needs to be examined in order for public/private entities to work together to answer research questions.

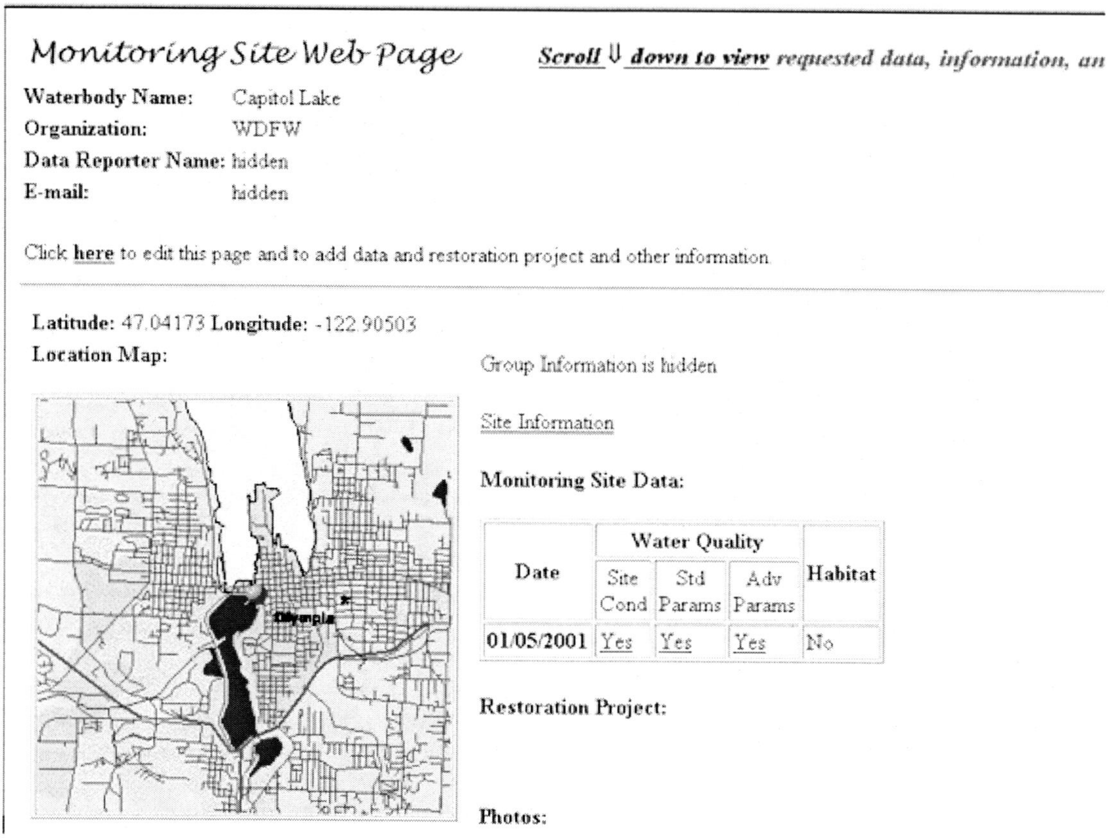

Monitoring Site Web Page   **Scroll ⇓ _down to view_** *requested data, information, an*

Waterbody Name: Capitol Lake
Organization: WDFW
Data Reporter Name: hidden
E-mail: hidden

Click **here** to edit this page and to add data and restoration project and other information.

Latitude: 47.04173 **Longitude:** -122.90503
Location Map:

Group Information is hidden

Site Information

Monitoring Site Data:

| Date | Water Quality | | | Habitat |
	Site Cond	Std Params	Adv Params	
01/05/2001	Yes	Yes	Yes	No

Restoration Project:

Photos:

FIGURE 2. The NatureMapping Program homepage for volunteers reporting water and stream data.

Tacoma Community College Students (Western Washington)

A class of students from Tacoma Community College participated as volunteers with the encouragement of their instructor. WDFW conducted a study to test quality of stream habitat data collection, following an in-depth training, and compared the student data to expert data. No significant difference was found for most variables except reporting qualities of habitat and vegetation (Klotz and Tudor 2003). More or better training may improve the quality of the data. There are limits and more research is needed to understand the cost/benefit of citizen science.

Conclusion

In the experience of the Washington Department of Fish and Wildlife, citizen science is undoubtedly a stewardship opportunity that contributes to the resource agency mission by benefiting agency research, and can be used to educate both students at K–12 schools and the volunteering adult community.

However it is clear that natural resource agencies should understand the needs of the formal education system before designing programs and opportunities that provide a benefit to both schools and to agency missions. The experience of PEI working with formal education institutions has taught stewardship educators in Washington State to develop their programs keeping in mind their contribution to understanding disciplines. Washington State found a conservation education/stewardship education path by expanding the K–12 portrayal of science inquiry to include field inquiry and including this learning expectation in the state standards tests.

However beyond testing, experiential learning in the field through real world opportunities is good basic education practice that engages and motivates students. Through research conducted by consortiums like the Pacific Education Institute in Washington State, the formal education system is starting to recognize the value stewardship education can bring to their bottom line of improved student learning.

References

Bartosh, O. 2004. Pacific Education Institute Technical Report Number 6: environmental education: improving student achievement. A report on systemic use of EE in schools and WASL scores. 2004. Master's thesis. The Evergreen State College, Pacific Education Institute, Olympia, Washington.

Dvornich, K. M., M. Tudor, and C. E. Grue. 1995. *NatureMapping:* assisting management of natural resources through public education and public participation. Wildlife Society Bulletin 23(4):609–614.

Galloway, A., and M. Tudor. 2000. The NatureMapping Program Technical Report Number 1: report on data analysis of the NatureMapping water module. Washington Department of Fish and Wildlife, Olympia.

Klotz, M., and M. Tudor. 2003. The NatureMapping Program Technical Report Number 2: report on NatureMapping for stream habitat (SSHEAR). 2003. Washington Department of Fish and Wildlife, Olympia.

Lieberman, G. S., and L. L. Hoody. 1998. Closing the achievement gap. Using the environment as an integrating context for learning. State Education and Environment Roundtable, Poway, California.

Taylor, C., L. Ferguson, M. Tudor, K. Smith, P. Otto, and K. Pritchard. 2004. Pacific Education Institute Technical Report Number 5: developing WASL-like assessments in environmental education. Pacific Education Institute, Olympia, Washington.

Taylor, C., K. Smith, M. Tudor, L. Ferguson, and O. Bartosh. 2005. Pacific Education Institute Technical Report Number 7: evidence for the validity and reliability of environment based classroom assessments as measures of the Washington State Essential Academic Learning Requirements. Pacific Education Institute, Olympia, Washington.

Tudor, M. T., and K. M. Dvornich. 2001. The *NatureMapping* Program: resource agency environmental education reform. Journal of Environmental Education 32(2):8–14.

Windschitl, M., A. Ryken, M. Tudor, G. Koehler, and K. Dvornich. In press. A comparative model of field investigations: aligning standards for school science inquiry with the practices of contemporary science. School Science and Mathematics Journal 207(1).

American Fisheries Society Symposium 55:103–116, 2007

Revisiting the Stewardship Concept: Faith-Based Opportunities to Bridge from Principles to Practice

WILLIAM F. SIEMER[1] AND GREGORY E. HITZHUSEN[2]

Department of Natural Resources, Cornell University, Ithaca, New York 14853, USA

Abstract.—Contemporary definitions of aquatic resource stewardship are a specific expression of ethical themes that humankind has wrestled with for millennia. The foundations for a stewardship ethic can be secular or spiritual. Other chapter contributors discuss a range of the secular foundations (e.g., fishing, boating); we discuss the implications of stewardship ethics rooted in religious traditions. Some fisheries professionals recognize religious–cultural influences on aquatic stewardship, such as those seen in Native American or Asian immigrant communities. But fisheries professionals have commonly ignored mainline Judeo-Christian faith traditions as an ethical basis for aquatic stewardship behavior, despite the fact that those traditions inform ethical development for large numbers of people in North America and that denominations within those traditions have increasingly engaged in stewardship-based environmental education and advocacy. The proposition that religious values often form the basis for a stewardship ethic presents several challenges for fisheries professionals striving to foster stewardship behavior. However, a basic understanding of these religious foundations could contribute to an improved practice of stewardship education, through outreach to a new constituency—faith communities. To illustrate this point, we briefly summarize some of the sources for stewardship found in the biblical corpus. We offer three examples of how Christian stewardship principles are manifest in aquatic stewardship programs delivered by faith communities. Models of partnership between natural resource managers and local faith communities are emerging across North America. In revisiting the ethical bases of stewardship and identifying new opportunities for stewardship education partnerships, we hope to demonstrate one more means by which fisheries professionals can bridge from stewardship education in principle to an effective practice of stewardship education.

Introduction

A 2001 document on best practices in boating, fishing, and stewardship education defined aquatic stewardship as "the moral obligation to care for aquatic environments, and the actions undertaken to provide that care" (Siemer 2001). By 2003, the Recreational Boating and Fishing Foundation's Stewardship Team had offered a slightly revised definition of aquatic resources stewardship (RBFF 2003). Fisheries professionals will undoubtedly develop new definition statements as they struggle to craft a short phrase that

communicates well to lay and professional audiences. These efforts to coin a new stewardship definition can be aided by considering a broader historical context. Stewardship is a centuries-old concept that has been explored by environmentalists, theologians, and economists, among others. Times change. Definitions change, cultural perceptions, and social contexts change. But through it all, the underlying themes of a stewardship ethic have endured.

Dixon et al. (1995) and Hockett et al. (2004) reviewed literature in several fields to identify themes embedded in most current definitions of natural resources stewardship. Those themes are (1) an ethic of personal responsibility, (2) behavior based on reverence for the earth, (3) an obliga-

[1] E-mail: wfs1@cornell.edu
[2] E-mail: geh23@cornell.edu

tion to future generations, (4) a need for personal action and participation, and (5) a commitment to use resources wisely and efficiently. These common themes identify important categories for reflection and assessment regarding stewardship ethics, but they do not imply that the attempt to understand the foundations of stewardship ethics is restricted to only these themes. As Hockett et al. (2004:11) suggest, definitions of stewardship "are grounded in very different value systems (e.g., religious, economic, anthropocentric, biocentric)." But while the bases for a stewardship ethic can vary widely, drawing from diverse sources both secular and spiritual, most of the literature on natural resource stewardship does not attend to spiritual or religious themes.[3] One way to expand the reach of aquatic stewardship efforts is to explore this broader range of sources.

Designing education programs that build upon the spiritual foundations for a stewardship ethic could be a formidable challenge for fisheries professionals. However, we think this is a challenge that fisheries professionals will want to accept because the potential rewards for doing so are large. Educational programming that works in concert with the learner's underlying ethical framework may contribute to an improved practice of aquatic stewardship education. Other chapter authors outline how fisheries professionals are addressing the challenges through fishing, boating, and in-school education programs. In this chapter, we focus on how fisheries managers might meet the challenge by partnering with faith communities.

Recognizing that religious teachings play an important role in shaping ethics, we discuss faith-based roots of an environmental stewardship ethic. Our discussion and examples are drawn from Judeo-Christian faith traditions, but similar examples exist in other traditions. Given the grassroots emergence of stewardship programs within faith communities across North America, we believe that abundant opportunities now exist for fisheries professionals to encourage stew-

ardship behaviors by forming such partnerships. To support our assertion, we describe the emergence of ecotheology in North America and we offer examples of successful partnerships between natural resource professionals and local faith communities. In revisiting these concepts and discussing their implications, our goal is to provide a foundation for reflection on means by which fisheries professionals can bridge from stewardship education in principle to an effective practice of stewardship education.

Part I: Bases for a Stewardship Ethic in the Judeo-Christian Tradition

In 2004, the American Fisheries Society published the proceedings from a symposium on sustainable management of North American fisheries (Knudsen et al. 2004). In that document, Paul Pajak (2004) comes to the conclusion that the ecological crisis is ultimately a moral problem, not a technical one. He reminds fisheries professionals that the world's major religions have been dealing with spiritual aspects of sustainability for thousands of years. He then asks, "... Why then should fisheries professionals, or human dimensions specialists, be trying to 'reinvent the wheel' of human ethics and morality?...Instead, would our energies not be better invested in trying to understand and work within the ancient and enduring religious frameworks that already exist?" He states, "As a practical example, I can easily envision fisheries scientists and educators collaborating with well established religious institutions on 'caring for creation' curricula addressing fisheries resource conservation and sustainability issues" (Pajak 2004:261).

The religious bases for a stewardship ethic are vast and diverse. This point is made clear by a body of scholarship on religion and environment, including a series of 10 international conferences held between 1997 and 2004 at the Harvard Divinity School, Center for the Study of World Religions. The conference series examined each of the world's major religious traditions and ecology (for more information on these conferences, see http://environment.harvard.edu/religion/information/index.html). Series editors Mary Evelyn Tucker and John Grim produced thick volumes drawing from authorities and scholars

---

[3] One notable exception is Driver et al. 1997. Readers should also note that for the purposes of this discussion, we use the terms spiritual and religious similarly, even though an explicit distinction can be made between these terms (Schneiders 2003; Hitzhusen 2005).

in each tradition, including Buddhism, Christianity, Confucianism, Daoism, Hinduism and Jainism, Judaism, Islam, Indigenous traditions, and Shinto (Tucker and Williams 1997; Tucker and Berthrong 1998; Chapple and Tucker 2000; Hessel and Radford-Ruether 2000; Girardot et al. 2001; Grim 2001; Chapple 2002; Tirosh-Samuelson 2002; Foltz et al. 2003). One overwhelming conclusion from the conference series was that every major tradition has a wealth of resources to offer on the subject of environmental ethics. Any of these traditions might provide the bases for a personal stewardship ethic. In this chapter, we provide a brief overview and discussion of foundations for a stewardship ethic embedded in Judeo-Christian traditions. More in depth discussion of these topics is available elsewhere (several ecotheology bibliographies can suggest a range of sources, e.g., Sheldon 1992; Cobb 1996; Wildman 2006), but a few basic concepts can suggest points of connection.

We focus on the Judeo-Christian tradition for practical reasons: that tradition informs ethical development for a large proportion of people living in North America, where most aquatic stewardship education efforts are delivered. For example, in the United States, various surveys (American Religious Identity Survey, Gallup, General Social Survey, or U.S. Census) estimate that between 78% and 90% of citizens identify themselves with a Judeo-Christian faith tradition. The higher numbers come from polls of voters, which suggests that the voting citizenry is more Judeo-Christian than the nonvoting citizenry. But regardless of the metric, surveys consistently reveal that a strong majority of U.S. citizens self-identify with biblical traditions. Figures for Canadian and Mexican citizens are similar. For instance, Encyclopedia Britannica figures for North America estimate that in 1995, 85% of citizens were Christians (9% identified themselves as atheists or nonreligious; the remainder identified other religious traditions). Proportions of citizens who self-identified with a Christian faith tradition were even higher in 1995 in Latin America (Mexico, Central and South America), with estimates over 90%. Doctrinal preferences and religious devotion obviously vary within these broad categories of denominational identity, but the prevalence of these traditions suggests their obvious significance to stewardship ethics. For instance, Kempton et al. (1995:91) concluded that the influence of biblical traditions explains why the most salient foundation for environmental concern among Americans may be the belief, "because God created the natural world, it is wrong to abuse it." And beyond the potential of religious sources to influence individuals' values, the critical role religious communities have played in social movements in North America (e.g., civil rights) also underscores the potential of faith traditions to contribute to stewardship efforts.

Taking stewardship literally

Religious sources for a stewardship ethic range from the general to the specific. Many relevant moral guidelines can be drawn from broader ethical concepts, such as the call to love one's neighbor, to live humbly and justly, to honor God's good intentions for creation, or just the simple idea that humans are morally beholden to God and to one another. There are also many biblical injunctions that deal specifically with the ethical obligations of humans to God's creation, some of which are discussed below. The theological literature on environmental stewardship is vast[4] (see for instance the bibliographies cited above). In fact, "stewardship" has emerged alongside "environmental justice" and "creation spirituality" as one of the distinct approaches evident in the growing religious environmental movement in the United States (Kearns 1996). To clarify the meaning of these developments, it is useful to consider the origins of "stewardship" as a concept unto itself, one that has been interpreted religiously since antiquity.

Reviewing the religious origins of the stewardship concept is where we will start our examination of how biblical themes resonate with contemporary concerns about aquatic stewardship within faith communities. Biblical references to

---

[4] Some helpful general resources include Nash's (1989) overview of the greening of theology (see also Fowler 1995), environmental philosopher Max Oelschlaeger's (1994) overview of religious environmental approaches, general overviews such as Gottlieb (2004, 2006), or particular theological or ethical examinations such as Nash (1991) or Santmire (2000).

stewardship suggest several connections between issues of ecology, economics, and natural resource management (see Wilkinson 1991). "Economics" comes from the Greek *oikos*, house, and *nomos*, order. *Oikonomos* is thus the ordering of a household—the principles by which it is managed. *Oikonomos* is an ancient word, occurring frequently in the Christian New Testament. Its most common translation there is "steward," and *oikonomia* is usually translated as "stewardship." Even more ancient is the notion of the steward in the Hebrew Bible/Old Testament—Abraham sent his "steward" (*ebed*, or servant, same root as *abad*, or serve/till, from Gen. 2:15[5]), the one who ruled (had dominion) over all he had, to find a wife for his son Isaac (Gen. 24:2). "Ecology" comes from *oikos*, house, and *logos*, knowledge/study of. *Oikologos* is thus the study of the household. *Oikologos* is a new word, invented by 19th century biologists. The "household" under study infers the natural world—humanity's extended household.

Thus, when looking for biblical or Judeo-Christian roots for "stewardship," roots that predate the recent invention of the study of ecology or of modern scientific ecological concern as such, it is important to understand the context of relevant biblical insights and avoid anachronistic interpretations. Most of the direct or literal biblical commentary and narrative regarding the human role of "stewardship" is made in the context of the management of a household, or of a master's property, and addresses the faithful application of oversight in managing the property of the steward's master. And yet, these contexts relate to the faithful observance of care for God's creation entrusted to humans, whom God charged to "till and keep"—serve and protect—the garden (Gen. 2:15). The biblical perspective is that the Earth is the Lord's (Ps. 24:1), and human treatment of the master's creation therefore is connected with the concept of stewardship. Various stewardship parables (e.g., Luke 16:1–2ff; Matt. 18:21–35, 21:43, 25:14ff) suggest that rather than be exploitative, stewards should be skillful, consider-

ate, and fruitful in their management of the master's property. They should leave it better than they found it, maintain its prosperity, and return it with interest earned. Obviously degrading or destroying the master's property for your own quick gain would not please the master, and bad stewards can expect punishment for their irresponsibility (Matt. 24:45–51]; Luke 12:41–48; see Bruggeman 2002). In a variety of ways, the environmental policy statements of most mainline denominations in the United States extend and develop a model of responsible human stewardship of creation (Ellingsen 1993; Keenan 2002; Harvard Forum on Religion and Ecology, Statements: http://environment.harvard.edu/religion/publications/statements/index.html) and of course draw from a host of scriptural resources beyond these particular literal stewardship (household/property management) commentaries. It would be impossible to discuss the full range of biblical stewardship sources here, but a variety of biblical stories and parables provide moral guidance for the human task of stewardship, some of which are described below.

Some biblical stewardship sources

Describing religious bases for environmental stewardship is complex and subject to interpretive complexities, but several common points can be noted. Biblical foundations have been sufficient to inspire significant environmental work within religious communities and generate the diverse range of religious environmental stewardship resources noted above (the emergence of The National Religious Partnership for the Environment [www.nrpe.org] is also a noteworthy indication of these developments). The moral obligation to care for the environment, aquatic or otherwise, is only voiced *directly* in a few biblical passages. And the commonsense idea that mistreatment of the natural world is bad for humans and requires action—especially in the context of contemporary global resource uses—is unsurprisingly not a prominent theme of the biblical corpus. But specific moral prescriptions for the treatment of natural resources do exist and contribute to a biblical stewardship ethic. Sabbath laws, prophetic warnings, and the concept of earthkeeping are noteworthy examples.

---

[5] All scripture citations in this chapter are taken from the Holy Bible, New International Version, © 1973, 1978, 1984 by International Bible Society. Used by permission of Zondervan Publishing House. All rights reserved.

Sabbath laws.—In the biblical narrative, prior to the creation of the law or the Ten Commandments, God establishes the Sabbath as a day of rest at the creation of the world (Gen. 2:2–3)—thus, the very order of creation entails observing rest and restricting productive human work (Bruggeman 2002; Hiebert 1996). Later commentary in Leviticus on the Sabbath laws makes clear that the rest is for land and animals as well as for humans: "…the land is mine and you are but aliens and my tenants. Throughout the country that you hold as a possession, you must provide for the redemption of the land," says God (Lev. 25:23–24). Beyond just one day's rest in seven, Sabbath rest is intended in agricultural land one year of every seven—and after seven sevens, each 50th year is to be a jubilee. These prescriptions are an important part of God's covenant with the people—they prescribe a just and fruitful land economy—and if humans obey these restrictions, they will prosper, as will the land (see Lev. 26:2–5). But if they disobey, their soil will not yield crops, nor trees fruit (Lev. 26:20), and if the people continue to ignore God's commands, they will be exiled and the land will be laid waste (Lev. 26:33). Perhaps to enhance the point and underscore the moral consideration that land deserves, the text concludes, "then the land will enjoy its Sabbath years all the time that it lies desolate and you are in the country of your enemies; then the land will rest and enjoy its Sabbaths. . . . The land will have the rest it did not have during the Sabbaths you lived in it." (Lev. 26:34–35) (In addition to Lev. 25–26, other Sabbath passages include Exod. 16:5, 3; 20:8–11; 23:10–12; 34:21; 35:1–3; see also Heschel [1951] and Bruggeman [2002]). These restrictions apply at two levels. As indicated above, Sabbath laws are a significant part of God's law for the people, and they provide directly for the redemption of the land. Care of the land itself is therefore of vital concern in the Mosaic law beyond its import as a matter of obedience (Habel 1995; Bruggeman 2002). But they are also part of the larger covenant with God, violations of which, warn the prophets, lead to the undoing of creation.

Prophetic warnings addressing materialism and injustice.—Old Testament texts make clear that land, people, and God are bound in a covenantal relation, and human respect for this "symbiotic" relation is critical to the fate of humans on the land (Habel 1995; Bruggeman 2002). In this context, human misbehavior can lead to the undoing of creation. In many places, the Hebrew prophets warn the people of the consequences of being unfaithful to God, of disobeying God's commands, of accumulating wealth irresponsibly, of ignoring the poor, the sick, and the vulnerable, of being greedy, and/or of living in conspicuous luxury (Johnston 1997). These things lead to desolation of the land:

> There is no faithfulness, no love, no acknowledgment of God in the land. There is only cursing, lying and murder, stealing and adultery; they break all bounds, and bloodshed follows bloodshed. Because of this the land mourns, and all who live in it waste away; the beasts of the field and the birds of the air and the fish of the sea are dying (Hosea 4:1–3; see also Jer. 9:12–14, 12:4; Ezek. 33:29, 31; Zech. 7:8–14).

These prophetic warnings reinforce what has earlier been set forth: keep the covenant or the land will be laid waste (see Deut. 29:19–29); immorality defiles land (Num. 35:33–34), and the land then spews out its inhabitants (Lev. 18:24–28; 20:22).

Except in the case of the Sabbath laws (i.e., Lev. 25–26), these warnings about covenant and justice are not aimed at human treatment of land per se, but more broadly at the basic character and faithfulness of the people. The prophets exclaim that forgetting God is a path to decline. Corruption and injustice foster exploitation and destroy the good life on the land. But if the people are faithful, they and their land and their crops and livestock will flourish (Deut. 7:13–14; 11:13–15). Similarly, Jesus rewards the obedient fishermen with an astounding catch of fish (Luke 5), while the book of Revelation warns of the time "for destroying those who destroy the earth" (Rev. 11:18). These prophetic writings declare that degradation of creation is connected to human failings and levy fair warning to discourage unfaithful human ways—both in regard to land regulations and to morality more generally—setting boundaries intended to contain destructive human behavior while encouraging faithfulness.

Earthkeeping.—Beyond prohibitions against breaking the Sabbath and other disobedience, the Hebrew scriptures also provide formative positive charges to care for creation. The creation narrative of Genesis 1 contains God's original blessing to humans: to be fruitful and multiply, to "replenish the earth and subdue it" (King James Version), and to have dominion over the creatures. In Genesis 2, God places the earthling (Adam, who is made from the *Adamah* or earth/soil [see Trible 1978 and Hiebert 1996]) in the garden he has created, and the first thing God charges the earthling to do is to "till it and keep it" (cultivate/serve—*abad*—and care for it). Thus human dominion is a task of stewardship or earthkeeping. An enduring tradition of environmental critique has disagreed with this positive interpretation of dominion, seeing instead in the Genesis texts a sanction for human exploitation of creation (this critique was made most clearly by White 1967). But theological and biblical scholarship has made clear that these texts cannot be coherently interpreted to sanction environmental despoliation (Lohfink 1982, 1994; Hiers 1984; Limburg 1991; Rogerson 1991; Steffen 1992), and decades of social science findings (Shaiko 1987; Kanagy and Willits 1993; Kanagy and Nelsen 1995; Wolkomir et al. 1997a, 1997b; Woodrum and Wolkomir 1997) seriously undermine the claim that biblical beliefs are the cause of environmental disregard (Hitzhusen 2006b). The failure of the anti-nature critique (White 1967) of Judeo-Christian scriptures to hold up under scrutiny has generated a greater openness to the positive environmental messages in these texts.

The genesis story also tells readers that God has brought forth an abundantly fruitful creation—life is literally swarming over the planet. Humans as well as other creatures are blessed to "be fruitful and multiply," and humans are instructed to steward this fruitful creation, which God declares *very* good (Gen. 1:31). Notably, foreshadowing the concern of the prophets, the humans in the story (Gen. 3–6) are disobedient and foster violence instead of fruitfulness, so God wipes the slate clean and starts again with Noah (Gen. 6–9). (Note that in Gen. 1, human dominion over creatures does not involve eating them; meat eating was only granted to humans after the flood). In re-blessing humanity through Noah (Gen. 9), God does not directly recharge humans

with having dominion or subduing the earth (Bouma-Prediger 2001), but does make a covenant with all flesh—with all creatures—never to destroy them again (Gen. 8:21–22). God too must remember the blessing of fruitfulness given to all creatures, and sets the bow in the clouds as a reminder of this covenant (see Johnston 1997).

Thus humans are to be good stewards of God's good creation, which God intends to protect from destruction. Humans should assume that destroying or impairing the blessing of fruitfulness God has given to all creatures is not what God desires. These concepts are the basis for much ecotheology and imply the human vocation as being articulate caretakers of creation. "Earthkeeping" is a popular term among Christian environmentalists that connotes this role. But as Oelschlaeger points out, "every faith across the spectrum of religious belief can either find or has already found its way to an environmental ethic through a metaphor of caring for creation" (Oelschlaeger 1994; cited by Pajak 2004).

The above are not literally "stewardship" references, but these themes provide some of the more obvious biblical sources for a stewardship ethic. The vast and growing ecotheology literature noted above can provide additional themes, but perhaps the bigger challenge is putting such principles into practice.

Part II: Challenges and Opportunities to Bridge from Principles to Practice

The very nature of ethical development presents some challenges for fisheries professionals striving to foster a stewardship ethic and promote stewardship behavior. First, stewardship ethics develop in places that are difficult for us to access as scientists, managers, and educators. Stewardship ethics are rooted in values and moral traditions; they are strengthened (but not created) by scientific understanding of aquatic ecosystems.

A second challenge is that a stewardship ethic develops over time. Life is among other things an ethical journey. Most of that journey will take place in a free choice learning environment (Ballantyne and Packer 2005; Kola-Olusanya 2005) outside one's formal education. Many fisheries managers and aquatic educators concentrate their efforts on developing formal education programs. That is important and useful work. Nevertheless, educators recognize that the contexts of and constraints surrounding in-school education programs make them ill-suited as a venue for ethics education programs (Fortner 2001). Ethics, including stewardship ethics, are transmitted in the context of one's family and community life (Matthews and Riley 1995). If we consider learners as whole persons, it follows that in-school education programs are only one component of any ethics education process. To be effective, aquatic educators also need to deliver education programs in nonformal settings to gain entry to the pathways of ethical development (Fedler et al. 2001). When we think about the importance of reaching people in free choice learning environments, the potential benefits of working with people through voluntary organizations takes on strategic importance. Churches are collectively the number one voluntary membership organization in the United States (Wolkomir et al. 1997a).

Opportunities to create a stewardship ethic

Fortunately, the foundations for a stewardship ethic are not just a challenge. They also represent an opportunity. The knowledge that religious traditions may be the basis of a stewardship ethic for many people could empower fisheries professionals to improve the practice of stewardship education. For instance, the potential opportunities for partnerships with faith communities first became apparent to one of the authors while developing and delivering a National Wildlife Federation program called NatureLink (Riley and Hitzhuzen 1993), which included attention to faith perspectives.

The American Fisheries Society (AFS) strategic plan (www.fisheries.org) identifies AFS' intent to foster fisheries sustainability by improving outreach and enhancing aquatic resource stewardship. Knuth and Siemer (2004) suggest that AFS and other organizations can make progress on their education and outreach objectives by working in partnership with other organizations and by delivering programs that consider community needs and the social context of the learner. It seems to us that an unrealized potential exists for fisheries professionals and aquatic resources educators to foster an aquatic steward-

ship ethic through community partnerships with faith communities.

There are several incentives for fisheries professionals to engage in partnerships with faith communities. First, partnership could be mutually beneficial, so it has instrumental value to both parties. Professionals get an opportunity to deliver an aquatic stewardship message to a new constituency, and churches and synagogues can gain new programming and service possibilities. Such a win–win opportunity also has good potential for success because both partners are already capable of taking such steps—in many ways, it is a ready-made partnership.

Also, since clergy are beginning to learn more environmental stewardship theology in their seminary training[6], they can offer new leadership in stewardship efforts. One way to both reinforce stewardship messages within communities and to bring a more diverse discussion of stewardship into conventional aquatic education programming would be to invite a local pastor to give a presentation of religious and spiritual bases for stewardship. Calling on a pastor (rabbi, imam, minister, shaman, priest, elder, deacon, etc.) to provide moral leadership in this way can add to the perspectives that aquatic educators provide to students, foster wider engagement with aquatic stewardship, and empower new leaders in the work of aquatic stewardship.

Outreach to religious leaders can provide them with additional sermon material and might even encourage them to involve their congregation in aquatic stewardship activities. Such a multiplier effect also helps develop community capacity (Goodman et al. 1998). There could be powerful opportunities for integration if people of faith interact with a science or education partner as part of their ministries. Partnering with faith communities allows space for dialogue that might

---

[6] Courses of environmental study have been promoted in religious educational institutions, such as the AuSable Institute's work within the Council for Christian Colleges and Universities and the efforts of Theological Education to Meet the Environmental Challenge (TEMEC) in seminaries. The study of religious and environmental perspectives has also been encouraged by programs such as the Center for Theology and the Natural Sciences' Science and Religion Course Program.

help people integrate their moral/ethical concerns with ecological understanding.

Finally, outreach to faith communities affords an opportunity to reach people from the perspective of their personal values and concerns. Partnering allows professionals into settings that they would not normally access, and it allows them to approach people from the perspective of core values. As George Bernard Shaw said, "Religion is a great force: the only real motive force in the world; but what you fellows don't understand is that you must get at a man through his own religion and not through yours" (Shaw 1911:290). Fisheries professionals and others interested in stewardship education can address religious teachings to broaden the base of values available to support stewardship behaviors—not by attempting to convert constituents to a new environmental belief system, but by empowering citizens to develop their environmental values within whatever preexisting value system they already occupy (Hitzhusen 2006a).

Part III. Aquatic Stewardship Ethics Manifest in Faith Communities: A Few Examples

In this part of the chapter, we provide a few examples to illustrate how faith communities exhibit stewardship ethics and how researchers and educators are partnering with those communities. Environmental partnerships with faith communities are emerging across the United States. We describe just a few examples here[7] to illustrate the point that successful models of partnerships with local faith communities are available.

The following examples are not offered as model programs with regard to aquatic stewardship behavior change. Since the examples we cite have not been subjected to rigorous outcome evaluation, we cannot offer statements about the long-term effects of these experiences on stewardship behavior (though it bears noting that the same criticism could be levied against

most stewardship programs currently offered in North America). We selected the following examples to illustrate the potential for partnerships with faith communities when programs are founded on the ethical bases for stewardship that already exist and are held dear by a particular audience that the stewardship educator hopes to reach. Once that door is opened, the stewardship education professional has the opportunity to lend her expertise in fostering effective program development.

Protestant dioceses organized around watersheds

Several years ago, the Episcopal diocese in the state of Massachusetts renamed themselves for the distinct watersheds in which they resided. Then each diocese sponsored intercongregational canoe trips on the river for which their diocese was named. Organizers claimed these events were the most successful that they had ever hosted in terms of bringing together both urban and rural parishes and multiple generations. The canoe trips were recreational and fun, but also included some discussion and instruction about the value and importance of water, both ecologically and spiritually. Watershed awareness and appreciation of ritual and sacred functions of water (e.g., baptism—the mikvah would be a Jewish parallel) were popular topics for reflection. These events built community, allowed churches to expand and diversify their Christian education curriculum, and created an opportunity for watershed stewardship education. In most cases, the organizers invited a local aquatic professional or educator to help provide the aquatic education component. This Massachusetts case illustrates how faith communities might include fisheries professionals to support their environmental program as technical speakers (it illustrates the potential role that fisheries professionals could serve as technical speakers or technical advisors to a given program). University faculty members often have opportunities to conduct this kind of outreach. For example, one of the authors observed an environmental scientist and faculty member from Cornell University give a presentation to a congregation interested in environmental justice. The faculty member did not talk about faith, spirituality, or

---

[7] Additional examples are noted by the National Religious Partnership for the Environment (http://www.nrpe.org/statements/index.html) and the Harvard Forum on Religion and Ecology (http://environment.Harvard.edu/religion/publications/projects/index.html).

justice. He spoke to the congregation about forest ecology, but messages he delivered resonated with the group's preexisting dialogue on environmental justice.

Stewardship among Tangier Island watermen

In the Chesapeake Bay, Tangier Island watermen (who had previously battled environmental regulations) became more enthusiastic observers of fisheries regulations after two local churches invited Susan Drake, a researcher who had been working in the community, to deliver a sermon about environmental stewardship themes in the Bible. After the service, 58 watermen signed a covenant to be better stewards of the Bay, committing themselves to refrain from dumping trash and pollutants into the Bay and to observe regulations such as size and catch limits.

This story has become well known.[8] The Chesapeake Bay Foundation had been attempting to encourage a stewardship ethic among residents of Tangier Island for two decades. Drake was able to instigate change by working with a faith community. She did so by doing sustained educational work in the community and delivering a guest sermon at a joint service of two churches whose memberships included many of the local fishermen. She also worked with the wives of the fishermen. She found that the wives made many of the moral decisions in the fishermen's families. Working with this group as a faith community led to visible behavior change by the fishermen. They began demonstrating pro-stewardship behavior as a direct expression of their faith and formed two ongoing organizations to support their stewardship efforts. The Tangier islanders have reportedly gone on to implement clean-up, recycling, and waste-reduction efforts; political advocacy campaigns around fishery legislation; environmental education programs; an experimental oyster aquaculture program; and a Coastal America Project for shoreline

and wetland restoration.[9] Time will tell whether this effort contributed toward long-term behavior change. However, it does offer a well-described example of the opportunities for stewardship education created when the interventionist approaches a community with a deep understanding of their values.

Columbia River pastoral letter

The catholic dioceses of Washington, Oregon, Idaho, Montana, and British Columbia issued a pastoral letter (Columbia River Pastoral Letter Project Web site: www.columbiariver.org) that defines the church's relationship to the Columbia River. This pastoral letter is an indication that a community of faith in an entire continental region found this issue important enough to address through a letter of support. This action has been characterized as the first pastoral letter in history to address an ecosystem as its primary topic. It recognizes the Columbia River system as integral to the cultural and spiritual life of the region. This statement was created after 3 years of study and reflection, including significant collaboration with environmental scientists working in the region. More information about the letter is available at www.columbiariver.org. This sort of action creates an opportunity for fisheries professionals to address a faith community with environmental science information to help them understand the underlying causes or potential solutions to a stewardship issue that is central to their lives. Similar efforts are occurring in other faith communities. The National Council of Churches of Christ recently published an ecumenical statement on water that reflects their aquatic stewardship ethic (NCC, Eco-justice Programs).

The emergence of ecotheology

Though we offer just three examples here, one could offer many more examples of faith-based stewardship programs all across the United States. Hitzhusen (G. E. Hitzhusen, unpublished data)

---

[8] Documentary film producer Jeffrey Pohorski released a film to communicate this story in 2001 ("Between Heaven and Earth: The Plight of the Chesapeake Watermen," Skunkfilms, Inc.). The case also has been described in religious and secular print media (Drake Emmerich 2000a, 2000b; Unger 2000; Horton and Borne 2005).

[9] Activities associated with project are described at length one a Web site sponsored by the Forum on Religion and Ecology (see Christian Engaged Projects: Tangier Watermen's Stewardship for the Chesapeake [TWSC], http://environment.harvard.edu/religion/religion/christianity/projects/tangier.html).

catalogued environmentally active congregations involved in the National Religious Partnership for the Environment in 1998. At that time, there were more than 1,800 active congregations. The biggest concentration of active congregations at that time was in the eastern seaboard cities, but there also were many active congregations in the Great Lakes region and near metropolitan areas of the West Coast.

These churches were engaged in activities that any aquatic educator would find familiar. Examples include church youth groups involved in a storm drain stenciling project, recycling programs, water quality monitoring in local waterways, and stream clean-up days. Some congregations are involved in short-term events, like an earth day program. Others are involved in more extensive and multifaceted programming, such as the development of a creation care awareness center or promoting energy-efficient church facilities. The people who organize these activities commonly look to natural resources professionals for ideas, which explains why their efforts often look like programming that might be offered by a local nature center.

As important as the emergence of environmentally active congregations is the emergence of an ecotheology literature that supports those programs. In addition to the bibliographies previously mentioned, the American Theological Library Association maintains a database of theological literature, including books and journals. A word search reveals that the percentage of theological publications containing the words "ecology" or "environment" has increased over the time interval 1960–2001 (Figure 1). A spike in publications concerned with ecology and environment can be seen right after the first earth day in 1970. Another noteworthy period of increase occurred in the 1990s. These data have not been the topic of much scholarly review, but we know that the growth in the environmental references in the 1990s occurred after the National Religious Partnership for the Environment[10] and the American Academy of

Religion's Religion and Ecology committee were formed, and respectively promoted programmatic development and opportunities to publish theological materials with an environmental theme. Theological libraries are now well stocked with books on earth keeping, and journal articles discussing theology and ecology are common. In addition to that kind of literature, most religious denominations now have an official policy statement, creed, or resolution regarding how their community members should relate to the environment[11] (often, specifically referring to aquatic environments). While such statements still represent the beginnings of environmental advocacy in faith communities, such tenets of ecotheology are clearly being expressed in cases like the stewardship initiative on Tangier Island.

Closing Thoughts

We hope the examples offered in this chapter demonstrate that fisheries professionals really do not have to reinvent the wheel called a stewardship ethic. All across North America, aquatic resource professionals are tapping into an existing ethic and forming partnerships to encourage people to live out those ethics in their daily lives. Likewise, faith-based organizations are taking tangible steps to encourage stewardship partnerships with natural resource professionals. Experience and interest in such partnerships has matured to a degree that an organization called the Biodiversity Project (Lowery and Swartz 2001) has published an outreach guide outlining the practical steps involved in forming working collaborations between government and nongovernmental organizations and faith communities. The National Council of Churches released a similar guide in fall 2005 (NCC 2005) that focuses on the Tangier Island experience and targets congregations interested in watershed stewardship. That guide is called "Stewards of the Bay: A Guide for Congregations in the Chesapeake Bay Watershed." Professionals and educators with concerns about dealing with religious communities can refer to the excellent suggestions found in these outreach manuals. Both

---

[10] The partnership was formed in 1993 by four major religious organizations: the U.S. Conference of Catholic Bishops, the National Council of Churches of Christ, the Coalition on Environment and Jewish Life, and the Evangelical Environmental Network.

[11] Hitzhusen (unpublished data) compiled a set of some 257 creeds and environmental policy statements that have been created since the 1970s, many of which are available online as noted above.

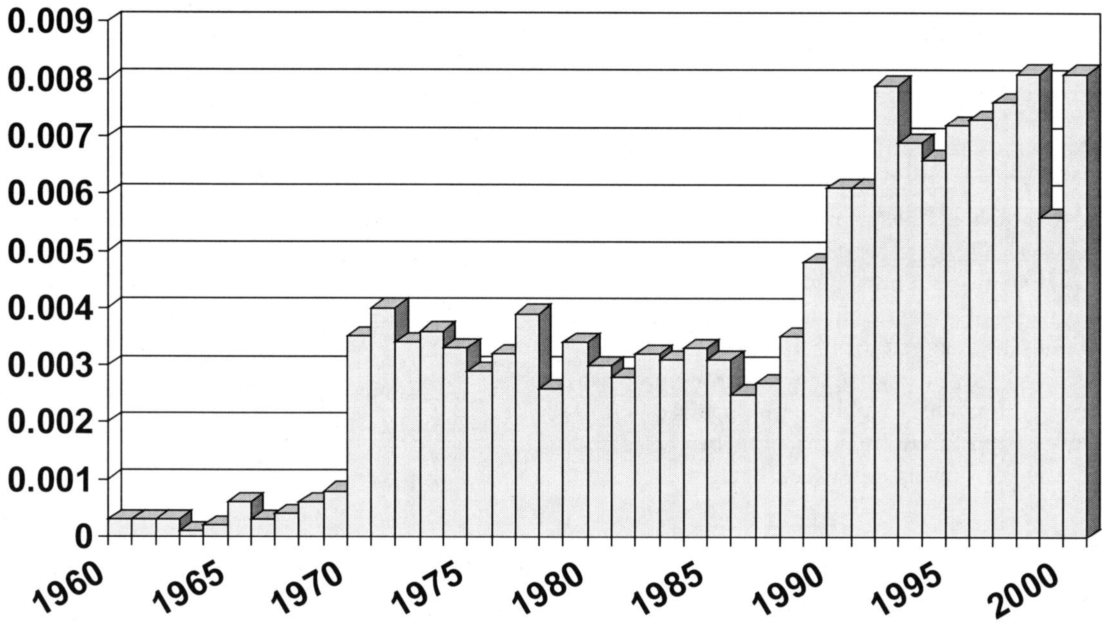

FIGURE 1. Percentage of references containing the key word ecology or environment, in literature maintained by the American Theological Library Association, 1960–2001.

identify ways to overcome potential problems and assure a fruitful partnership.

It has been said that it is unwise to discuss religion or politics in polite conversation. We recognize that the themes of our discussion have the potential to create controversy or raise tensions between people with differing religious views. But controversy and tension is not what we are inviting. Rather, we are encouraging engagement with the hopeful and positive opportunities represented by faith community stewardship concerns. There is no shortage of opportunities for partnerships and outreach, and there are multiple pathways on which to proceed—practitioners are really only limited by their creativity in forming working relationships between fisheries professionals and faith-based organizations. Though we offered examples from Judeo-Christian faith traditions, other faith traditions can offer partnerships too, and many models are emerging within various traditions.[12]

At an individual level, any fisheries professional who belongs to a faith community might explore the possibilities for partnership within their own church, synagogue, or temple. Larger endeavors may build from such modest origins. Again, the possibilities are only limited by our creativity. At a collective level, we can encourage our professional societies to support individual professionals with resources and the capacity to reach out to local communities.

In his article on fisheries sustainability, Paul Pajak offers several provocative statements and questions about engendering the societal change that will be necessary to sustain aquatic resources.

> …most fisheries professionals know that about one out of five adults in the United States is an angler . . . meaning that four out of five are *not*. What is it then, if not fish, that the other four out of five Americans care about with respect to our surface waters? Or more importantly, what is it that might motivate *both* nonanglers and anglers to care enough about fish and fisheries to sustain the watersheds,

---

[12] Example partnerships from other traditions can be found at the Alliance of Religions and Conservation Web site (http://www.arcworld.org/).

rivers, and oceans upon which they depend? [Pajak 2004:258]

He answers his own question by concluding that spiritual values may be the thing that will help people transition toward a more sustainable society. We have argued that linking stewardship education to people's spiritual and religious values is *one* means to encourage a transition toward sustainability. We hope that in revisiting the ethical bases of stewardship, and pointing out new opportunities for stewardship education partnerships, we have demonstrated one more tool fisheries professionals can use to build a bridge from stewardship education in principle to an effective practice of stewardship education.

References

Ballantyne, R., and J. Packer. 2005. Promoting environmentally sustainable attitudes and behavior through free-choice learning experiences: what is the state of the game? Environmental Education Research 11(3):281–295.

Bouma-Prediger, S. 2001. For the beauty of the Earth: a Christian vision for creation care. Baker Academic, Grand Rapids, Michigan.

Bruggeman, W. 2002. The land: place as gift, promise, and challenge in biblical faith (2nd edition). Fortress Press, Minneapolis, Minnesota.

Chapple, C. K., editor. 2002. Jainism and ecology: nonviolence in the web of life. Harvard University Press, Cambridge, Massachusetts.

Chapple, C. K., and M. E. Tucker, editors. 2000. Hinduism and ecology: the intersection of earth, sky, and water. Harvard University Press, Cambridge, Massachusetts.

Cobb, J. 1996. Ecotheology book list. Available: http://www.cep.unt.edu/ecotheo.html (October 2005).

Dixon, D. O., W. F. Siemer, and B. A. Knuth. 1995. Stewardship of the Great Lakes environment: a review of literature. Cornell University, Department of Natural Resources, HDRU Publication 95–5, Ithaca, New York.

Drake Emmerich, S. 2000a. Praxis of the kingdom: Bible-grounded environmental stewardship as a ministry of reconciliation. Creation Care Magazine 11(3):4–9, 15.

Drake Emmerich, S. 2000b. The declaration in practice: missionary Earth-keeping. Pages 147–154 *in* R. J. Berry, editor. The care of creation: focusing concern and action. Inter-Varsity Press, Leicester, England.

Driver, B. L., D. Dustin, T. Baltic, G. Elsner, and G. Peterson. 1997. Nature and the human spirit: toward an expanded land management ethic. Venture Publishing, State College, Pennsylvania.

Ellingsen, M. 1993. The cutting edge: how churches speak on social issues. WCC Publications, Geneva, Switzerland.

Fedler, A. J., W. F. Siemer, B. A. Knuth, and B. E. Matthews. 2001. Developing aquatic stewards. Taproot 12(4):9–15.

Foltz, R. C., F. M. Denny, and A. Baharuddin, editors. 2003. Islam and ecology: a bestowed trust. Harvard University Press, Cambridge, Massachusetts.

Fortner, R. W. 2001. The right tools for the job: how can aquatic resource education succeed in the classroom? Pages 49–60 *in* Fedler A. J., editor. Defining best practices in boating, fishing, and stewardship education. Recreational Boating and Fishing Foundation, Alexandria, Virginia.

Fowler, R. B. 1995. The greening of Protestant thought. University of North Carolina Press, Chapel Hill.

Girardot, N. J., J. Miller, and L. Xiaogan, editors. 2001. Daoism and ecology: ways within a cosmic landscape. Harvard University Press, Cambridge, Massachusetts.

Goodman, R. M., M. A. Speers, K. McLeroy, S. Fawcett, M. Kegler, and E. Parker, S. Rathgeb Smith, T. D. Sterling, and N. Wallerstein. 1998. Identifying and defining the dimensions of community capacity. Health Education and Behavior 25(3):258–278.

Gottlieb, R. S., editor. 2004. This sacred earth: religion, nature, environment, 2nd edition. Routledge, New York.

Gottlieb, R. 2006. A greener faith: religious environmentalism and our planet's future. Oxford University Press, New York.

Grim, J. A., editor. 2001. Indigenous traditions and ecology: the interbeing of cosmology and community. Harvard University Press, Cambridge, Massachusetts.

Habel, N. C. 1995. The land is mine: six biblical land ideologies. Fortress Press, Minneapolis, Minnesota.

Heschel, A. J. 1951. The Sabbath: its meaning for modern man. Farrar, Straus and Giroux, New York.

Hessel, D. T., and R. Radford-Ruether, editors. 2000. Christianity and ecology: seeking the well-being of earth and humans. Harvard University Press, Cambridge, Massachusetts.

Hiebert, T. 1996. The Yahwist's landscape: nature and religion in early Israel. Oxford University Press, New York.

Hiers, R. H. 1984. Ecology, biblical theology, and methodology: biblical perspectives on the environment. Zygon 19(1):43–59.

Hitzhusen, G. E. 2005. Understanding the role of spirituality and theology in outdoor environmental education: a mixed-method characterization of 12 Christian and Jewish outdoor programs. Research in Outdoor Education 7:39–56.

Hitzhusen, G. E. 2006a. Religion and environmental education: building on common ground. Canadian Journal of Environmental Education 11:9–25.

Hitzhusen, G. E. 2006b. Religion and the environment: the contributions of Christianity and Judaism to environmental ethics and education. Doctoral dissertation. Cornell University, Ithaca, New York.

Hockett, K. S., J. A. McClafferty, and S. L. McMullin. 2004. Environmental concern, resource stewardship, and recreational participation: a review of the literature. Recreational Boating and Fishing Foundation, CM1-HDD-04–01, Alexandria, Virginia.

Horton, T., and J. K. Borne, Jr. 2005. Saving the Chesapeake. National Geographic 207(6):22–45.

Johnston, C. 1997. And the leaves of the trees are for the healing of the nations: biblical and theological foundations for eco-justice. Presbyterian Church (USA) Office of Environmental Justice, Louisville, Kentucky.

Kanagy, C., and H. M. Nelsen. 1995. Religion and environmental concern: challenging the dominant assumptions. Review of Religious Research 37(1):33–45.

Kanagy, C. L., and F. K. Willits. 1993. A "greening" of religion? Some evidence from a Pennsylvania sample. Social Science Quarterly 74(3):674–683.

Kearns, L. 1996. Saving the creation: Christian environmentalism in the United States. Sociology of Religion 57(1):55–70.

Keenan, M. 2002. From Stockholm to Johannesburg: an historical overview of the concern of the Holy See for the environment 1972–2002. Pontifical Council for Justice and Peace, Vatican Press, Vatican City.

Kempton, W., J. S. Boster, and J. A.Hartley. 1995. Environmental values in American culture. The MIT Press, Cambridge, Massachusetts.

Kola-Olusanya, A. 2005. Free-choice environmental education: understanding where children learn outside of school. Environmental Education Research 11(3):297–307.

Knudsen, E. E., D. D. MacDonald, and Y. K. Muirhead, editors. 2004. Sustainable management of North American fisheries. American Fisheries Society, Symposium 43, Bethesda, Maryland.

Knuth, B. A., and W. F. Siemer. 2004. Fostering aquatic stewardship: a key for fisheries sustainability. Pages 243–255 in E. E. Knudsen, D. D. MacDonald, and Y. K. Muirhead, editors. Sustainable management of North American fisheries. American Fisheries Society, Symposium 43, Bethesda, Maryland.

Limburg, J. 1991. The responsibility of royalty: Genesis 1–11 and the care of the earth. Word & World 11(2):124–130.

Lohfink, N. 1982. Great themes from the old testament (R. Walls, Trans.). Franciscan Herald Press, Chicago.

Lohfink, N. 1994. "Subdue the earth?" Genesis 1:28. In theology of the Pentateuch: themes of the priestly narrative and Deuteronomy. Fortress Press, Minneapolis, Minnesota.

Lowery, S., and D. Swartz. 2001. Building partnerships with the faith community: a resource guide for environmental groups. The Biodiversity Project, Madison, Wisconsin.

Matthews, B. E., and C. K. Riley. 1995. Teaching and evaluating outdoor ethics education programs. National Wildlife Federation, Vienna, Virginia.

Nash, J. A. 1991. Loving nature: ecological integrity and Christian responsibility. Abingdon, Nashville, Tennessee.

Nash, R. F. 1989. The rights of nature: a history of environmental ethics. The University of Wisconsin Press, Madison.

NCC (National Council of Churches of Christ). 2005. Stewards of the bay: a toolkit for congregations in the Chesapeake Bay watershed. National Council of Churches USA, Washington, D.C.

NCC (National Council of Churches of Christ), Ecojustice Programs. Water: the key to sustaining life (an open statement to governing bodies and concerned citizens). Available: http://www.nccecojustice.org/ecustate.html#water (August 2006).

Oelschlaeger, M. 1994. Caring for creation—an ecumenical approach to the environmental crisis. Yale University Press, New Haven, Connecticut.

Pajak, P. 2004. Elevating social concern for sustainability in fisheries and aquatic resource management. Pages 257–270 in E. E. Knudsen, D. D. MacDonald, and Y. K. Muirhead, editors. Sustainable management of North American fisheries. American Fisheries Society, Symposium 43, Bethesda, Maryland.

RBFF (Recreational Boating and Fishing Foundation). 2003. Request for proposals. Recreational Boating and Fishing Foundation, RBFF-03-C-007, Alexandria, Virginia.

Riley, C., and G. Hitzhuzen. 1993. Facilitator's guide to hosting a NatureLink weekend. National Wildlife Federation, Outdoor Ethics Division, Vienna, Virginia.

Rogerson, J. W. 1991. Genesis 1–11. JSOT Press for the Society for Old Testament Study, Sheffield, England.

Santmire, H. P. 2000. Nature reborn: the ecological and cosmic promise of Christian theology. Fortress Press, Minneapolis, Minnesota.

Schneiders, S. M. 2003. Religion vs. spirituality: a contemporary conundrum. Spiritus 3(2):163–185.

Shaiko, R. G. 1987. Religion, politics, and environmental concern: a powerful mix of passions. Social Science Quarterly 68(1–2):244–262.

Shaw, G. B. 1911. The doctor's dilemma, getting married, & the shewing-up of Blanco Posnet. Constable and Company, London.

Sheldon, J. 1992. Rediscovery of creation: a bibliographical study of the church's response to the environmental crisis. The American Theological Library Association, ATLA Bibliography Series, 29, Metuchen, New Jersey.

Siemer, W. F. 2001. Best practices for curriculum, teaching, and evaluation components of aquatic stewardship education. Pages 18–36 in A. J. Fedler, editor. Defining best practices in boating, fishing, and stewardship education. Recreational Boating and Fishing Foundation, Alexandria, Virginia.

Steffen, L. H. 1992. In defense of dominion. Environmental Ethics 14(1):63–80.

Tirosh-Samuelson, H., editor. 2002. Judaism and ecology: created world and revealed word. Harvard University Press, Cambridge, Massachusetts.

Trible, P. 1978. God and the rhetoric of sexuality. Fortress Press, Philadelphia.

Tucker, M. E., and J. Berthrong, editors. 1998. Confucianism and ecology: the interrelation of heaven, earth, and humans. Harvard University Press, Cambridge, Massachusetts.

Tucker, M. E., and D. R. Williams, editors. 1997. Buddhism and ecology: the interconnection of dharma and deeds. Harvard University Press, Cambridge, Massachusetts.

Unger, K. 2000. Fishing in living waters. Creation Care Magazine 11(3):14, 16–17.

White, L. 1967. The historical roots of our ecologic crisis. Science 155:1203–1207.

Wildman, W. 2006. Bibliography in ecological ethics and eco-theology. Available: http://people.bu.edu/wwildman/WeirdWildWeb/proj_bibs_ecoethics_00.htm (October 2005).

Wilkinson, L. 1991. Earthkeeping in the nineties: stewardship of creation. William B. Eerdmans Publishing Company, Grand Rapids, Michigan.

Wolkomir, M., M. Futreal, E. Woodrum, and T. Hoban. 1997a. Substantive religious belief and environmentalism. Social Science Quarterly 78(1):96–108.

Wolkomir, M., M. Futreal, E. Woodrum, and T. Hoban. 1997b. Denominational subcultures of environmentalism. Review of Religious Research 38(4):325–343.

Woodrum, E., and M. Wolkomir. 1997. Religious effects on environmentalism. Sociological Spectrum 17:223–234.

American Fisheries Society Symposium 55:117–123, 2007

The Role of the American Fisheries Society in Fostering Aquatic Resource Stewardship: Past Successes, Future Opportunities

CARL V. BURGER[1, 2]

United States Fish and Wildlife Service, Marine Fisheries Program Complex
306 Hatchery Road, East Orland, Maine 04431, USA

MICHAEL E. BARNES[3]

South Dakota Department of Game, Fish and Parks
19619 Trout Loop, Spearfish, South Dakota 57783, USA

Abstract.—The American Fisheries Society (AFS) is the oldest professional organization for fisheries scientists in the world. Through its evolution from a fish culture organization to a multifaceted association of diverse specialists, AFS began to implement strategic planning by the early 1990s. Its 2004 Strategic Plan establishes priorities for aquatic stewardship, with three core goals: policy leadership, public education, and resource conservation advocacy. Without leadership and advocacy for local and global stewardship, aquatic resource goals are unattainable. What role should AFS play in fostering future stewardship efforts? With whom should AFS partner and for what goals? To gain insights to answer these questions, several AFS parent society and unit leaders were canvassed to identify examples of stewardship successes at all society levels. The resulting examples were organized into seven major areas encompassing one or more of the stewardship focus areas: (1) scientific communication, (2) resource policy advocacy, (3) global outreach, (4) education, (5) youth activities, (6) habitat restoration and assessments, and (7) leadership development. Responses provided many suggestions for advancing AFS stewardship goals, such as involvement in State Wildlife Grant programs, the National Fish Habitat Initiative, more leadership development/mentor programs, and global partnerships. A major conclusion is that novel opportunities abound and that AFS should seek to cultivate relationships with nontraditional partners such as watershed coalitions, land trust organizations, and community-based service groups. AFS has had many stewardship successes. However, future successes will depend on how AFS leverages its expertise, synergizes innovative partnerships, and creates new connections to promote tangible accomplishments in aquatic resource stewardship. The AFS strategic plan, if fully embraced by all AFS units and creatively leveraged with partners, is the launch pad for catalyzing future strategies that build on past successes.

Introduction

Stewardship involves the moral obligation to use aquatic resources wisely and efficiently (Dixon et

al. 1995). Although the popular writings of Aldo Leopold (1989) and Rachel Carson (1962) captivated the general public with stewardship ideas beginning in the late 1940s, these ethics have been a focus of professional organizations such as the American Fisheries Society (AFS) for a much longer time.

In 1870, the American Fish Culturist's Association was formed when a group of lay profes-

---

[1] E-mail: cvburger@smith-root.com
[2] Present address: Smith-Root, Inc., 14014 NE Salmon Creek Avenue, Vancouver, Washington 98686, USA
[3] E-mail: mike.barnes@state.sd.us

sionals from the United States and Canada convened in New York City (Moffitt 2001). This new professional society initially concentrated on artificial propagation and fish introductions, which (at that time) were the fisheries activities most associated with stewardship. However, the association quickly began to expand its understanding of aquatic resource stewardship and to address problems with barriers to migration, overharvest of fish stocks, and water pollution. To accentuate the realization that stewardship was much more than just fish culture, the name of the association was changed to the American Fisheries Society in 1885 (Moffitt 2001). With the advent of strategic planning in the last decade of the 20th century, AFS formalized the application of stewardship into its lexicon and overall mission.

The current AFS strategic plan (Bireley et al. 2004) lists aquatic stewardship first, among three major focus areas. The plan lists three goals for the society's aquatic stewardship efforts: (1) local and global policy leadership, (2) public education about the plight of aquatic resources, and (3) advocacy for stewardship and resource conservation. What has AFS and its units done in pursuit of these goals? Are there novel ideas, innovative concepts, or pertinent new partnerships that the society could explore to fulfill its mission in "…the conservation and sustainability of fisheries resources and aquatic ecosystems…?" Given that most fisheries stocks are fully exploited worldwide (Burger 2002) and that responsible aquatic stewardship actions are essential to achieve sustainable aquatic resources and maintain their ecosystems (Knuth and Siemer 2004), the answers to these questions are extremely important to the future fate of AFS and the aquatic stewardship activities of its members.

The objective of this paper is to summarize examples of past AFS successes and to describe a framework of strategies and new ideas for the future roles of AFS and its units in promoting aquatic resource stewardship. By reviewing past successes, effective stewardship activities can be shared among the chapters, divisions, and sections (i.e., units) of AFS and with other natural resource partners. By canvassing current officers and unit leaders, novel ideas for AFS stewardship efforts may emerge, along with opportunities to assess and leverage their potential for forging new partnerships with additional successful outcomes. This information is essential if the stewardship goals of the AFS strategic plan are to be fully embraced and met by AFS units and creatively leveraged with diverse natural resource partners.

Approach

A cross section of AFS leaders was queried to determine past and current stewardship efforts at all levels of the society. Past society-level officers, unit officers, and other leaders within AFS were asked to submit examples of stewardship activities directed at achieving aquatic stewardship goals. Those who responded included eight society officers (one who served in the mid-1980s; seven who served from 1997 through current time), the society's executive director, the presidents (and two vice-presidents) of the four AFS divisions, and the presidents of 16 AFS chapters. In addition, the leaders of 13 AFS sections responded, representing perspectives from fishery administrators, managers, international scientists, equal opportunity specialists, educators, and students and disciplines that ranged from endangered and introduced fishes, water quality, marine resources, fish culture, early life history, fish health, and genetics. These respondents were encouraged to provide ideas and suggestions on how AFS could best fulfill the stewardship component of its mission. Although not a systematic survey, the responses received were reviewed within the context of the 2004 AFS Strategic Plan (Bireley et al. 2004) and its aquatic stewardship goals. Some of the actions that typify successful stewardship activities are presented in this paper (however, they are by no means exhaustive of everything AFS and its units are doing in aquatic resource stewardship). Innovative ideas and suggestions for future focus areas emerged from these canvassing efforts.

Stewardship Activities

We identified seven major areas of stewardship actions conducted by AFS and its units: (1) scientific communication, (2) resource policy advocacy, (3) global outreach, (4) education, (5) youth activities, (6) habitat restoration and assessments, and (7) leadership development. These areas are all encompassed within one or more of the stewardship goals outlined in the 2004 AFS Strategic Plan (Bireley et al. 2004).

Scientific communication

The traditional strength of AFS has been its science. Publication of peer-reviewed journals, books, manuals, and resource policy statements has been crucial to the success of aquatic resource stewardship efforts. Although most AFS publications are a direct result of society-level interactions, units (particularly AFS sections) are also involved. An excellent summary of the society's extensive involvement in scientific publications, meetings, and symposia can be found in *Reflections: A Photographic History of Fisheries and the American Fisheries Society in North America* (Moffitt 2001). Recent topical symposia have also contributed greatly to AFS aquatic resource stewardship, as illustrated by several examples: a Sea-Grant-sponsored symposium on climate change at the society's 2001 annual meeting in Phoenix, a freshwater mussel symposium sponsored by the Oregon Chapter, an eel status symposium sponsored by the Canadian Aquatic Resources Section, and a genotyping symposium sponsored by the AFS Genetics Section. These symposia, particularly those emphasizing new technologies, are critical to developing a better understanding of the ecological relationships of the aquatic resources that AFS seeks to conserve. In addition, conferences, workshops, and meetings to exchange information and enhance or leverage working relationships are particularly important in meeting stewardship goals at all AFS levels.

Resource policy advocacy

Leadership in conservation policy development is also crucial to the society and its units. Examples from the AFS parent society regarding conservation education and advocacy include annual trips to Capitol Hill in Washington, D.C. by society officers, the AFS Governing Board, and Potomac Chapter hosts. Although there is ample early evidence of historic communications with Congress (Moffitt 2001), the society began to organize actual Congressional briefings in Washington, D.C. in 1995, then lapsed, but began to reorganize such trips in 2001. These briefings now occur regularly on at least an annual basis. As evidenced by the communications received at AFS headquarters, these informative, educational meetings with Congressional delegations and committees have become extremely successful. The development of the North American Fisheries Action Agenda, Farm Bill white paper, Pew Commission testimony, Marine Stocks at Risk Policy, and Sea Grant Partnerships in Climate Change are just a few examples of the successful parent society-level stewardship activities involving AFS sections and units. As a new outreach tool to promote science-based information about marine and freshwater issues to all stakeholders, the recently created AFS Fisheries Conservation Foundation has tremendous potential for funding new science, resource conservation, and stewardship advocacy.

Divisions, sections and chapters are also involved in local or regional resource advocacy. The Southern Division drafted a white paper to guide brook trout management in the southeastern United States. The Canadian Aquatic Resources, Estuaries, and Marine Fisheries sections have all worked to initiate and guide aquatic resource policy development. The Minnesota Chapter belongs to the Minnesota Legislative Alliance, providing a direct avenue for fisheries policy development. The North Carolina Chapter has been a strong advocate in addressing local mining issues. The Western Division has been historically active in mining law reform, riparian habitat and grazing issues, dam removal debates, and water allocation conflicts. In addition to routinely meeting with their state legislature on aquatic resource policies, the Oregon Chapter has some impressive achievements with legislators, including their role as host of a "Science in the Public Arena" workshop.

Global outreach

The parent society and its International Fisheries Section promote global aquatic stewardship. Examples include initiation, development, and involvement in all World Fisheries Congresses to date. For the first time in North America, AFS hosted a World Fisheries Congress (the fourth) in Vancouver, B.C. (2004). The program included participation and presentations from preeminent scientists from all corners of the globe, state-of-the art science forums, and more than 1,500 attendees from 89 nationalities. This Congress was so successful that the section's goal for an international endowment fund was easily met from Congress proceeds. Other examples include the establishment of a Mexico unit and new inroads with China, Russia, Japan, India, Pakistan, Australia, Great Britain, and other nations to strengthen the World Council of Fisheries Societies and its envisioned stewardship successes at the international level.

Education

Education and outreach with the general public are areas where AFS chapters often take a lead in stewardship activities. AFS examples include a 10-year effort by the Alaska Chapter to produce the comprehensive *Fishes of Alaska* book, hosting of salmon festivals by the California/Nevada Chapter, and the 45,000 posters on invasive species risks created and distributed by the North Carolina Chapter. In addition to the "Fishes of the Dakotas" poster, the Dakota Chapter produced trading cards containing pictures and natural history information for both game and nongame fish species. The Missouri Chapter was instrumental in supporting development of the "Wonders of Wildlife Museum," the Ohio Chapter published its 4-year effort "A Guide to Ohio Streams," and the Montana Chapter hosted a symposium on "Conserving Native Fishes of the West." By partnering with the Seafood Choices Movement, the University of Georgia unit is helping to educate the public about consumer choices and sustainable fish stocks. AFS units, including the Education Section and its Student Subsection, have excelled in coordinating a host of outreach activities and efforts over many years.

Youth activities

Although not regularly involved with hands-on activities to create a sense of stewardship in youth, the AFS parent society has had a major impact with its Hutton Junior Fisheries Biologist Program. More than 60 highly motivated high school students each year have received mentoring, exposure to a new career path in fisheries, and a stipend to work hands-on with fisheries professionals every summer since 2000. Even if these students do not pursue a fisheries career, the society (through this program) is able to foster and ingrain stewardship ideals and ethics that will likely spread to families, communities, and the ultimate chosen professions of the students involved.

Several AFS units are involved in fishing events for children or disabled individuals. For example, the University of Georgia unit partners with the United Way and local businesses in the private sector to host an annual "Fishin' with the United Way" event. This undertaking has proven to be a very effective way to expose young anglers to conservation and stewardship ethics. The Dakota Chapter helps sponsor a "Kids Fishing Day" event that involves almost 2 h of stewardship-related education. The highly innovative Disabled Angler Committee established by the Missouri Chapter has created a novel stewardship program with sportfishing opportunities for handicapped people. Clearly, there are numerous examples of success stories at many levels!

These society and unit activities targeted toward youth are essential to developing adults and future community leaders with the conservation values and environmental sensitivity necessary to promote aquatic resource stewardship ethics. Fishing and other outdoor experiences during childhood are associated with stewardship actions later in life (Tanner 1980), likely by developing a deeply personal connection with the aquatic resource (Knuth and Siemer 2004) and by creating a sense of ownership, critical for responsible stewardship behavior (Hungerford and Volk 1990).

Habitat restoration and assessments

By "rolling up sleeves and getting collective hands dirty," AFS chapters have been leaders in on-the-ground achievements that directly enhance AFS stewardship goals. Atlantic International Chapter members have been active on fish passage restoration projects, the Virginia Chapter has conducted actual instream rehabilitation work, and the North Carolina State unit has been active in planting trees and vegetation to improve riparian corridors. The Fayetteville unit of the Arkansas Chapter secured a conservation easement for a small stream and then had the where-with-all to share this accomplishment with television news media. In addition to hosting watershed-restoration continuing education courses, the Oregon Chapter has worked with ranchers and other partners to improve riparian habitats in western streams. The Wisconsin Chapter and several others have conducted impressive research and fisheries assessments to increase the knowledge base about factors that limit fisheries. Thus, there seems to be a clearly emerging role for ecosystem-level monitoring by AFS and its units.

Leadership development

The Southern Division and Fisheries Administration Section are probably the most aggressive AFS units in advocating and promoting leadership training. Division officers recognize the all-important need to groom and mentor young professionals for future aquatic stewardship roles and successes. The Southern Division hosts a top-notch Mid-Year Mentor Lunch and mixer each year. In addition, it may be the only unit to have a permanent Leadership Development Committee. Student mentorship is also practiced by the Alaska Chapter, the Arizona/New Mexico Chapter (via job fairs), and other AFS units. At the parent society level, training in leadership principles is offered to unit officers annually. However, the Hutton Junior Fisheries Biologist Program, mentioned earlier, is the premier activity for cultivating future aquatic resource stewardship leaders.

Untapped Stewardship Opportunities: Recommendations for Action

AFS has enjoyed numerous stewardship successes. In fact, the above examples merely scratch the surface! However, future successes will depend on how AFS leverages its efforts and how it synergizes with a variety of partners. Those leaders responding to our initial canvassing provided many suggestions for advancing AFS stewardship goals, and they suggested some yet-untapped opportunities (as do this paper's authors) for partnerships that AFS may want to cultivate for further stewardship gains. Possibilities include the following.

State wildlife grants programs

These programs were created by the U.S. Congress in 2001 primarily to support conservation actions to help prevent the listing of threatened and endangered species. The grants require the development of a strategy containing a list of "species of greatest need" along with their status, distribution, and threats. Only a few strategies have been submitted for funding to date. There would appear to be many possible partnerships between state resource agencies and AFS units that could be developed and implemented with this granting program, directly leading to working partnerships and aquatic resource stewardship successes.

National Fish Habitat Initiative

AFS has helped develop this initiative through strong leadership, lots of vision, and a huge amount of networking and partnering. The National Fish Habitat Initiative (www.fishhabitat.org) has gained much momentum in recent time. The parent society has had a prominent role thus far, but there are many upcoming avenues for AFS unit involvement and participation. Units can become bonafide partners in producing the science and/or the on-the-ground activities for this process. Units can also play essential roles in helping to implement this initiative at local and regional levels. This is an opportunity that should not be missed.

Global stewardship

There are additional opportunities for AFS to expand and grow the World Council of Fisheries Societies. Now is the time to bring global resource issues to the table, achieve international buy-in, and begin the process of addressing some of the world's most pressing global resource problems. Large-scale stewardship issues will require more international partnerships. AFS must maintain its relevance and its international leadership in global aquatic resource stewardship.

Leadership development

Identifying and nurturing future AFS leaders is essential for the continuity and long-term success of stewardship actions. Current leadership development has been confined, for the most-part, to just a few AFS units. Although the parent society hosts leadership development workshops at its annual meetings, AFS units should create permanent leadership committees and establish formal mentoring opportunities. Without capable leadership, stewardship goals will likely not be met, and opportunities for future AFS stewardship successes will not be pursued.

New partners

Because AFS has neither the financial resources nor the personnel for meaningful increases in stewardship activities, it is imperative that the society and its units leverage their actions. Several new partnership possibilities were identified during the canvassing of AFS officers and leaders. These include the following.

Watershed coalitions.—Despite their obvious focus on aquatic resource issues, these regional entities have been largely ignored by AFS and its units. Almost every community or county has some form of watershed council. These would seem to be natural partners, particularly for units involved in local or regional water quality monitoring, nonpoint source pollution threats, or aquatic habitat issues.

Land trust organizations.—These land-based, nontraditional partners have a keen interest in stewardship activities. Often their actions involve the purchase of riparian, wetland, or coastal land (or easements) with direct aquatic resource connections. Groups such as the Columbia Land Trust, the Vermont Land Trust, the Sonoma Land Trust, or the Maine Coast Heritage Trust are examples of potential partners to help further the conservation stewardship goals of AFS. With a land trust providing the means to acquire the habitat, AFS could provide the science to help manage the resources and understand the ecosystem interactions.

Community-based service groups.—AFS officers and leaders should not restrict their thinking to partnerships with fishing clubs and other organizations traditionally associated with resource use or conservation. There is a cadre of community-based service groups in existence who may embrace new paradigms and underwrite approaches for involving and motivating citizens or youth for good causes. In a previously mentioned example about the AFS University of Georgia unit partnering with the United Way, achievements were leveraged by bringing private sector businesses into the process (e.g., the Publix Supermarket Chain; Williams Natural Gas) for sponsorship and funding roles. Other community service groups also represent untapped opportunities. For example, the Kiwanas Club is typically focused on youth activities and would appear to be an ideal partner for kids fishing programs. Zonta, a service club organized for women, might be a great partner for Hutton-type activities that would increase the percentage of underrepresented groups in the fisheries profession (a goal of the AFS Equal Opportunities Section). Other groups, such as the Lions Club, Rotary, Masons, Optimists, or local Chambers of Commerce, should also be considered when looking for opportunities to leverage stewardship actions. After all, members of these clubs are typically leaders in the local business community. They present and offer the potential for ideal opportunities to connect possible human and financial resources to help AFS accomplish its aquatic stewardship goals. Have we fully explored such partnership opportunities? There is work to be done in this area!

Summary

What is the role of AFS in fostering aquatic resource stewardship? Despite the society's past stewardship success stories, AFS cannot do this work alone if meaningful change and achievements are the desired outcomes. AFS already provides a global source of credible science, and the society must assure its continued use in addressing the world's critical fisheries issues and problems. AFS must not be afraid to innovate, to "think out of the box," and to try creative partnerships. With the right people, priorities, partners, and passion, AFS can creatively leverage its strategic plan and catalyze new, innovative approaches for stewardship successes. This is the envisioned role of AFS in fostering its ongoing aquatic resource stewardship goals and in maintaining its global leadership in the fisheries profession. It must be embraced and fully imple- mented by all AFS units to achieve the society's full potential in resource conservation and stewardship.

Acknowledgments

We thank Jim Martin for his valuable insights on AFS stewardship roles. We also thank the many past and present AFS officers, AFS unit leaders, and members who have contributed their time, energy, and knowledge in helping us promote the stewardship work of AFS and its units for this paper. The authors wish to reiterate that the examples of unit successes cited here are but a small token of the actual accomplishments completed by AFS divisions, sections, and chapters in recent time from which a virtual compendium could be prepared.

References

Bireley, L. E., J. Claussen, B. A. Costa-Pierce, W. J. Delay, J. Jolley, B. A. Knuth, B. G. M. Parsons, and C. Stevens. 2004. The strategic plan of the American Fisheries Society, 2005–2009. American Fisheries Society, Bethesda, Maryland.

Burger, C. 2002. A global perspective on sustaining fisheries in the 21st century: transitioning beyond existing paradigms to an integrated ecosystem approach. Fisheries Science (Supplement 1) 68:14–19.

Carson, R. 1962. Silent Spring. Houghton Mifflin, Boston.

Dixon, D. O., W. F. Siemer, and B. A. Knuth. 1995. Stewardship of the Great Lakes environment: a review of the literature. Cornell University, Department of Natural Resources, HDRU Series Number 95–5, Ithaca, New York.

Hungerford, H. R., and T. L. Volk. 1990. Changing learner behavior through environmental education. Journal of Environmental Education 21(3):8–21.

Knuth, B. A., and W. F. Siemer. 2004. Fostering aquatic stewardship: a key for fisheries sustainability. Pages 243–255 in E. E. Knudsen, D. D. MacDonald, and Y. K. Muirhead, editors. Sustainable management of North American fisheries. American Fisheries Society, Symposium 43, Bethesda, Maryland.

Leopold, A. 1989. A Sand County almanac: and sketches here and there. Special commemorative issue. Oxford University Press, New York.

Moffitt, C. M. 2001. Reflections: a photographic history of fisheries and the American Fisheries Society in North America. American Fisheries Society, Bethesda, Maryland.

Tanner, T. 1980. Significant life experiences: a new research area in environmental education. Journal of Environmental Education 11(4):20–24.

PART III   Measuring Stewardship: Indicators and Outcomes

American Fisheries Society Symposium 55:127–135, 2007

Measures of Aquatic Stewardship Behavior from the Boating Perspective

ANDREW J. LOFTUS[1]

Loftus Consulting

3116 Munz Drive, Suite A, Annapolis, Maryland 21403, USA

Abstract.—In 2003, more than 69 million people participated in recreational boating in the United States. The tenet that boating activity leads to higher aquatic stewardship ethics is often assumed since heightened environmental sensitivity has been correlated with significant positive contact with the outdoors. However, a direct link between boating and stewardship has not been substantiated. A review of current outreach efforts suggests that measures of boating-related stewardship could include preventing petroleum-based pollution, reducing marine debris, reducing sewage discharges, reducing air pollution, reducing habitat disturbance and physical destruction, and utilizing less harmful chemicals for boating activities. Measures of positive stewardship could also include boater's involvement in, and support of, government programs and funding that promote these on-the-water behaviors. While these behaviors could be considered outward signs of good stewardship ethics, the motivation behind them would be more difficult to assess, thereby complicating the distinction between actual stewardship and behavior motivated by other forces. However, to the natural resources manager, motivation may not be as important as the resulting behavior, as long as the desired behaviors are sustained over time. A review of behaviors being promoted by the boating community (and applied examples), their utility as measures of aquatic stewardship, and the role of motivations are discussed.

Introduction

Recreational boating is one of the most popular water-based forms of recreation. In the United States, more than 69 million people participated in recreational boating in 2003 (NMMA 2003) spending more than 1 billion days on the water (Strategic Research Group 2003).

With this degree of on-the-water activity, the potential impact of boaters' behaviors on the natural resources can be significant. Water quality, aquatic habitat, and air quality can all be affected negatively by the decisions that individual boaters make while pursuing their sport.

A positive linkage between a heightened stewardship ethic and participation in natural resource-based recreation such as boating is often assumed (Fedler et al. 2001). The common belief that outdoor recreation places individuals in direct contact with nature, thereby increasing environmental awareness and concern, has helped to foster this concept (Geisler et al. 1977).

Additionally, the majority of boaters use their vessels for recreational fishing (51% according to Strategic Research Group 2003; 65% according to R. Lydecker, BoatU.S., personal communication), another outdoor activity that is presumed to foster a heightened sense of stewardship for the resources among its participants. However, there has been no definitive demonstration of a positive link between boating activity and increased stewardship ethic (Fedler et al. 2001), although there are numerous anecdotal indications that such a relationship may exist.

Possible measurements of stewardship behavior can be discerned by observing various facets of boating that are presumed to be associated with reducing, or negating, potential negative impacts

---

[1] E-mail: ALoftus@andrewloftus.com

on the natural environment in addition to actions that actually enhance environmental conditions. Some of these behaviors are discussed, with examples, in the context of their potential to be measures of environmental stewardship. In addition, the role of motivations will be explored in the context of implications for the natural resources manager.

Stewardship Behaviors and Common Behaviors Promoted by Boating Organizations

For the purposes of this paper, the definition of aquatic stewardship presented by Knuth and Siemer (2004) is being applied. This definition holds that stewardship is a "moral obligation to care for aquatic environments and the actions undertaken to provide that care." Thus, stewardship is a combination not only of the behaviors, but also of the motivations that spur those behaviors.

Stewardship behavior in general can be identified by several actions and motivations. As outlined by Knuth and Siemer (2004), stewardship involves a measure of personal responsibility by the individuals, personal investment (including self sacrifice), and awareness of the importance of aquatic system health (concern for the environment). Additionally, compromising immediate interests for the sake of future generations is often viewed as one indicator of stewardship. Comparing these traits to those that are commonly promoted within the boating community can help to identify potential measurements of stewardship behavior. Measuring the motivations behind presumed stewardship behavior would necessitate in-depth motivational studies that are beyond the scope of this paper.

A review of the publications and materials directed to the boaters themselves can provide an understanding of the potential stewardship traits being promoted within the recreational boating community. There are approximately 55 national and regional publications in the United States devoted to recreational boating and myriad local publications (Lydecker, personal communication). Additionally, organizations such as the American Boating Association and others heavily promote environmental responsibility to their members (see www.americanboating.org/clean.asp as an ex-

ample). A review of the messages contained in these publications and the behaviors being promoted by organizations provides an indication of the most common "environmental behaviors" from the boating community's perspective. Most often, these behaviors fall within six categories:

- preventing petroleum-based pollution;
- reducing marine debris;
- reducing sewage discharges;
- reducing air pollution, habitat disturbance, and physical destruction;
- utilizing less harmful chemicals for boating activities; and
- various actions to reduce the impacts on the biological community (e.g., prevention of invasive species introduction, reducing boater's interactions with marine mammals, etc.).

Are these behaviors for boaters consistent with the behaviors that have been defined as good stewardship traits? A comparison of the behaviors promoted by the boating community to generic stewardship traits suggests that they are consistent.

For example, preventing petroleum-based pollution incorporates, to some degree, facets of good stewardship outlined by Knuth and Siemer (2004): a boater must take some personal responsibility in deciding to avoid pollution; a degree of personal investment is often required (e.g., purchase of special equipment necessary to avert spillage of gasoline while refueling); the individual is likely reacting to concern for the environment in deciding to take this action; and the individual is compromising some personal interest for the sake of future generations since it would likely be more expedient and less costly for him or her to refuel in a manner that was more likely to result in spillage.

Similarly, the traits common to good stewardship can be applied to the other behaviors being promoted by the boating community to arrive at the conclusion that these behaviors are consistent with good stewardship (Table 1). Thus, by measuring the degree of adoption of these behaviors by boaters, a measure of the degree of environmental stewardship behavior may be possible.

Although stewardship *behavior* can potentially be measured, what about the second part of the stewardship equation, *motivation*? Although

TABLE 1. Overlap of behaviors being promoted by the boating community and stewardship traits outlined by Knuth and Siemer (2004).

Stewardship traits	Boating behaviors					
	Reduce impact on biological communities	Prevent petroleum pollution	Reduce marine debris	Reduce discharges	Reduce air pollution	Use less harmful chemical
Personal responsibility	X	X	X	X	X	X
Personal investment	X	X	X	X	X	X
Environmental concern	X	X	X	X	X	X
Compromise interests for the future	X	X	X	X	X	X

the boating community seemingly is promoting behaviors associated with good stewardship, the motivation behind those behaviors would indicate whether it is true environmental stewardship or perhaps motivated by some other (perhaps self-serving) factor. Activities alone do not necessarily reveal motivations. The following question must be posed: if the motivator ends, will the activity continue?

Motivators of environmental stewardship are factors that prompt an individual to feel a responsibility to protect the environment (Deci and Ryan 1985). They are formed through the values and belief structures held by individuals and are based on factors such as the perceived responsibility, expected benefits, and knowledge of key issues and concepts held by the individual. Motivation by force, coercion, or anticipated financial benefit alone would not contribute to a true environmental stewardship ethic because it would not contain the attributes associated with stewardship that were discussed previously. However, behavior that was instigated by one of these motivators in conjunction with true environmental stewardship motivators still could be considered true stewardship behavior. Likewise, behavior initiated by a nonstewardship motivator could conceivably evolve into true stewardship behavior if the motivator was removed and the behavior continued.

Given the difficulty in interpreting behaviors based on their motivations, examples of activities that are voluntary (e.g., not mandated by law/regulation) and offer little tangible incentive (e.g., economic, social, etc.) may provide more salient measures of environmental stewardship for boaters. Several examples of this nature exist in the activities that are being promoted by the boating community.

Real World Examples

Reducing or stopping pollution

Reducing pollutants in waters is a highly visible effort of many boating organizations and government agencies. Generally, this revolves around stopping litter and debris from being discarded overboard, increasing the use of pumpout facilities for onboard toilets, and reducing the incidence of gasoline and petroleum spillages from boating activities.

One example of such an initiative is the Clean Marina program. This is a voluntary program that encourages coastal marina operators and recreational boaters to protect water quality by engaging in environmentally sound operating and maintenance procedures in marinas. Programs are customized by each state but all provide guidance to facilities on best management practices that must be followed to be designated as a "clean marina." Clean Marina programs are found in 20 jurisdictions nationwide (Figure 1).

According to the National Oceanic and Atmospheric Administration (see the National Oceanic and Atmospheric Administration's Web site regarding information on Clean Marinas, http://coastalmanagement.noaa.gov/marinas.html), there are several potential benefits for a facility participating in the Clean Marina program, including

- reduction of waste disposal costs;
- generation of new sources of revenue;

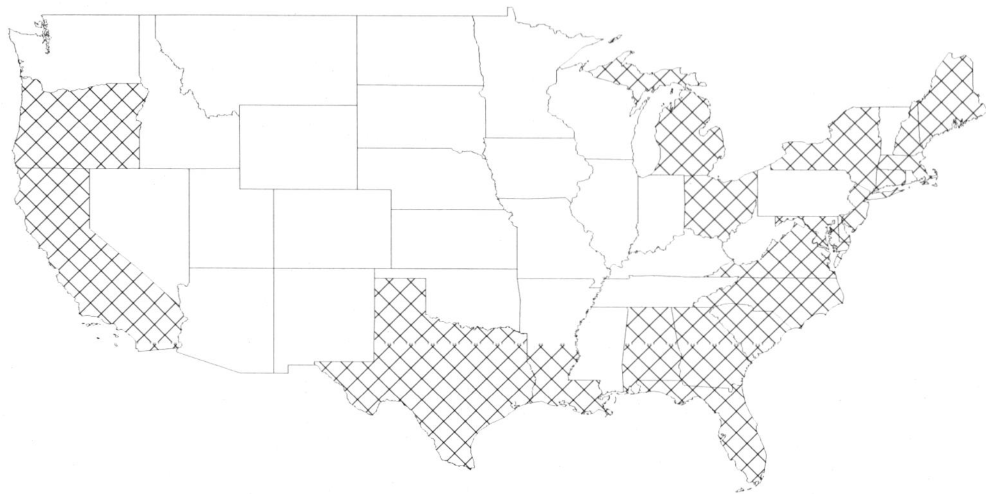

FIGURE 1. Distribution of Clean Marina programs in the United States.

- receiving free technical assistance;
- reducing legal liabilities;
- enjoying free publicity;
- attracting knowledgeable customers;
- improving water quality and habitat for living resources; and
- demonstrating that the marina is a good steward of the environment.

Participation in the program generally requires a financial investment by the facility operator and commonly results in higher fees for users of the facility. One test of whether the environmental benefits of a cleaner marina are supported by the users (boaters) as opposed to the service providers (marinas) is the reaction of boaters after the investments have been made. A study by the U.S. Environmental Protection Agency (USEPA; USEPA 1996) concluded that such investments in more environmentally-friendly marinas were supported by customers. Facilities in the USEPA study reported that common consumer response to their changes included a generally positive reaction of marina customers. Although some facilities reported an initial loss of a few customers as prices were increased, those lost customers were soon replaced by customers seeking the "new" environment. Further, testimonials from operators of facilities who had made the investment in Clean Marina technology and practices indicated that "marinas prospered with custom-

ers who remained and were happier with Clean Marina philosophy" and that in many cases, "….rates and occupancy are higher."

Reducing boaters' impacts on the biological community

Another potential measure of stewardship could be boaters' adoption of behaviors that prevent or mitigate any negative interactions that their activity may have on aquatic biological communities. This could include activities such as helping to prevent the spread of invasive species or reducing boaters' interactions with marine mammals. Often, these campaigns are localized, such as the education of boaters to reduce collisions with manatees in Florida. Other times, these efforts are broader in scope, including nationwide efforts by the federal intergovernmental Aquatic Nuisance Species (ANS) Task Force and others to reduce the rate of dispersal of invasive species such as zebra mussel. While the ultimate measure of success of these programs would be the achievement of their goal (e.g., no spread of invasive species by boaters), the measure of stewardship would be the degree to which acceptable behaviors were adopted. No evidence is available as to whether the actual intent (reducing dispersal rate of aquatic species by boaters) is being achieved by the ANS Task Force. However, the ANS Task Force lists 187 partners of their "Stop Aquatic Hitchhikers!"

campaign, with only 10 of those clearly being boater-oriented (seven organizations and three companies). This may indicate that current techniques to reach this audience are not working or the community is reluctant to join in the efforts as structured. It should be noted that while state and federal governments have expended considerable resources on campaigns to reduce boaters' impacts on biological communities, this classification of activity does not appear to be as prominently promoted by the large boating organizations as the other five classifications outlined earlier in this paper.

Supporting issues and policies that lead to enhancement of resources

Behaviors associated with aquatic stewardship may include "indirect" support of political organizations or political activism supporting environmental interests (Knuth and Siemer 2004). Such third party involvement by boaters in support of the environment is an important means for individual boaters and boating organizations to collectively express their views and further their positions in the political arena of a democratic society.

One of the preeminent programs supporting aquatic conservation and management in the United States during the past 55 years is the Federal Aid in Sport Fish Restoration (SFR) program (Rassam et al. 2000). Through SFR, funds generated by excise taxes on fishing equipment and fuels taxes generated through motorboat usage are reinvested into the natural resources and infrastructure supporting recreational fishing and boating activities. Since 1992, the SFR program has incorporated the Clean Vessel Act, which provides funding for pumpout facilities for boaters. In that time, grants have been awarded to install 2,200 pumpout stations and 1,400 dump stations, thereby reducing the incidence of sewage from boaters degrading water quality. Strong support by primary user groups (anglers and boaters) provided impetus for the original passage of this tax on their activities, and for the major amendments since then. This support continues to be vital to maintaining the effectiveness and integrity of this program.

User support of SFR is often interpreted as a sign of commitment to fisheries conservation (Fedler et al. 2001). The primary organization for maintaining political support for the program is the American League of Anglers and Boaters (ALAB). The ALAB coalition is composed of 32 individual organizations and is considered the watchdog organization for the program.

Membership in the ALAB coalition provides a relative indicator of the importance of the support that various industries place on this preeminent conservation program. Of the 32 members in ALAB, 18 of them hold boating as a primary focus (Table 2). Several of the other organizations also represent boating as a component of their mission. The fact that more than half of the

TABLE 2. Members of the American League of Anglers and Boaters (asterisk indicates organizations with a primary focus on boating).

American Fisheries Society
American Recreation Coalition
American Sportfishing Association
*American Watercraft Association
Aquatic Resources Educators Association
Atlantic States Marine Fisheries Commission
Bass Anglers Sportsman Society/ESPN
*Boat Owners Association of the U.S.
*Boating Trades Association of Texas
*Brunswick Corporation
*Coast Guard Auxiliary Association
Coastal Conservation Association
Congressional Sportsmen's Foundation
*Greater Coalition for Boating Safety
International Association of Fish and Wildlife
    Agencies
Izaak Walton League of America
*Marina Operators Association of America
*Marine Retailers Association of America
*National Association of State Boating Law
    Administrators
*National Boating Federation
*National Marine Manufacturers Association
National Recreation and Park Association
*National Safe Boating Council
*National Water Safety Congress
*Personal Watercraft Industry Association
Pure Fishing
Recreational Fishing Alliance
*Sail America
*States Organization for Boating Access
Trout Unlimited
*United States Power Squadrons
*U.S. Sailing Association

ALAB members are focused primarily on boating is a strong indicator that the boating community views this program as vitally important to their activity. Considering that the majority of boaters use their craft for fishing (Strategic Research Group 2003; Lydecker, personal communication), both the fisheries conservation provisions and the infrastructure development components are important to boaters. This significant presence in protecting what is believed to be a vital conservation program serves as an example of one measure of environmental stewardship among the boating community.

Direct support for cleaner aquatic environments

Although boater support of the SFR program is a demonstrable indicator of their willingness to pay for a cleaner environment, more direct measures of this trait are also available. This includes the boating community's direct financial support of private and/or nonprofit organizations whose mission is to enhance or protect aquatic resources. As an example, two of the most visible efforts of this nature which cover large geographic regions are the FishAmerica Foundation and the BoatU.S. Foundation for Boating Safety and Clean Water. FishAmerica was founded in 1983 by a subsidiary of the Brunswick Corporation, a prominent manufacturer of boats and equipment. Today, FishAmerica leverages the support of Brunswick and other boating equipment businesses, along with a broader section of the fishing and boating industries. Over the last 20 years, the FishAmerica Foundation has provided over $8 million for more than 750 grassroots fisheries conservation and research projects all across the United States and Canada and leveraged significantly more from partners on the ground.

Whereas FishAmerica is supported primarily by companies, the BoatU.S. Foundation for Boating Safety and Clean Water is supported by some of the more than 600,000 individual members of BoatU.S. The foundation is dedicated to promoting safe and environmentally-sensitive boating, and includes educational outreach as well as a Clean Water Grants program. This grant program was initiated in 1999 due to the de-

mand from individuals who wanted their organization to support projects which promote clean boating education.

A related measure of the boating community's stewardship ethic is the direct promotion of environmentally sensitive behavior. The Ethical Angler® Program, which is a joint education campaign between the National Oceanic and Atmospheric Administration, state natural resources agencies, and BoatU.S. is such an example. Although Ethical Angler® is designed to reach all types of anglers (mainly in marine environments) it focuses much of its message on boat-based fisheries through materials designed to educate anglers about equipment and practices that advance more environmentally friendly fishing and boating practices (Figure 2). BoatU.S., with more than 600,000 members, was a founder of this program and continues to actively promote it to members and nonmembers alike.

Ethical Angler®, the FishAmerica Foundation, and the BoatU.S. Foundation for Boating Safety and Clean Water are examples of programs that integrate boating and healthy aquatic resources. The boating community's continuing support of these and other similar initiatives could be utilized as one measure of aquatic stewardship from the boating perspective.

What are boaters willing to pay for clean water?

The previous examples provide indications that boaters may be willing to support political and nonprofit activities to improve the environment, but the question remains of how much more boaters are willing to invest into the environment. In a survey of Maryland registered boaters in 2000–2001, boaters were asked to rate their perception of water quality in the Chesapeake Bay as poor, fair, good, very good, or excellent. Subsequently, they were asked about their "willingness to pay for a one-step improvement in water quality" (Lipton 2004). Sixty-two percent of respondents indicated that they would be willing to pay extra for this improvement. The mean amount that they indicated they would be willing to pay annually was $54.68. Across all sailboats, in-water powerboats, and trailered power boats, the total that Maryland Chesapeake Bay boaters were will-

FIGURE 2. Materials provided through the Ethical Angler® Program promote behaviors consistent with environmental stewardship.

ing to pay amounted to $7.3 million per year to achieve higher water quality. In general, the poorer the water quality that boaters perceived currently, the more they were willing to pay to clean it up (Lipton 2004).

Does the End Justify the Means?

Whereas environmental stewardship behaviors among recreational boaters can be cataloged, the motivations behind them are uncertain. Hence, under the definition of stewardship requiring behaviors plus motivations, whether these observed activities constitute true stewardship is unknown. However, the applied practitioner of natural resources management must ask the following: does the motivator matter as long as the desired result is being obtained? Sometimes, the answer may be a definite *yes*, but often, the answer may be less clearly defined. Some natural resources managers will be very interested in the motivation, but to others, the "end may justify the means" regardless of motivation, particularly if the behavior is sustained for a substantial period of time.

For example, the motivation for achieving environmentally sound behavior may be viewed in a hierarchical manner as in Figure 3. Economic motivators, social pressures, and laws and regulations may be shared by the majority of boaters (some motivators being more common than others), but a motivator of "true environmental concern" may be a characteristic of a smaller number of boaters. If an action such as eliminating petroleum spills from recreational boats is desired, is it more effective for managers to work at the level where fewer boaters can be reached (the point of the pyramid) or at the broadest level (base of the pyramid)? Again, the answer will depend on the situation and may very well entail working at

Pure Environmental Concern

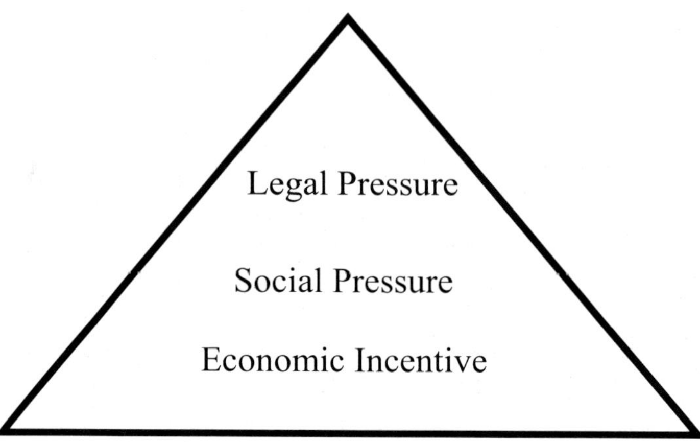

FIGURE 3. Hypothetical hierarchy of motivations for promoting environmental stewardship among boaters.

multiple levels of the pyramid. In making the decision of what level (or levels) of motivation to work, managers would need to consider a variety of factors, including

- resources available for the program (financial, personnel, etc.);
- duration of the effort necessary to achieve the desired behaviors;
- political will/public acceptance of both the desired behavior and the motivator; and
- alternative means to achieve the same result.

It is important to recognize the practical feasibility of achieving a desired behavior in the context of these factors. While zero emissions from boat motors is desirable, it is not technologically feasible. Therefore, reducing emissions by a certain degree may be the next best achievable result. A law may be the most effective means to achieve a behavior, but if the necessary enforcement costs cannot be sustained over time or political pressures will not allow the action, an alternative mechanism (or combination of mechanisms) would need to be implemented. A related consideration that natural resources practitioners should consider is the potential for barriers to motivation for environmental stewardship. The most simplistic example is to assume that all boaters are "intrinsic stewards of the resource." Despite this, barriers (or stronger motivators for other behaviors) may prevent boaters from practicing sound stewardship. Using the example of eliminating petroleum spills, if the natural tendency for boaters is to prevent such spillage, but all equipment to do so is beyond the economic means of the boater to obtain, then a lesser accomplishment (perhaps eliminating only a fraction of the spills) may be the best result that can be achieved until the economic barrier can be overcome.

In considering which motivators to utilize, managers may do well to spread their options across several levels of motivation. For example, if oil-spill prevention technology is available but expensive, a program may split limited financial resources between outfitting the ardent environmentally-conscious boater who is an opinion leader in the community with demonstration equipment as well as providing subsidies to those who may not be able to afford the equipment. In this way, a manager can approach the issue through peer pressure as well as economic incentives. To overcome barriers at various motivational levels, managers should be willing to reach out for professional expertise that they may not be accustomed to dealing with, such as consumer marketing and sales, small business financing, and others. Partnerships with other government agencies or with private sector entities in the boating field (e.g., manufacturers, associations, retailers, etc.) may be a way to accomplish this.

Summary

There is no single measure that alone can be used as an indicator of aquatic stewardship within the boating community. Based on review of the environmentally sound behaviors being promoted by boating organizations, there are a number of behaviors that overlap the traits associated with good stewardship. Specific to the boating community, these include

- trends in participation in programs such as "Clean Marina;"
- participation in debris clean-up programs, trends in pump-out usage, and trends in sales of clean technologies and chemicals;
- support of "environmentally friendly" governmental programs and legislation;
- degree of adoption of practices such as "stop aquatic hitchhikers" and other programs to lessen the boating impacts on the biological environment;
- support of nongovernmental organization environmental programs and so forth; and
- willingness to pay for environmental improvements.

It is clear that some behaviors associated with environmental stewardship are exhibited by the recreational boating community. These behaviors can be measured with some effort, but discerning the motivations is more difficult. The importance of these motivations is a matter that each practitioner of natural resources management must decide under each circumstance.

Acknowledgments

Several organizations and individuals assisted with the development of this paper. The Sport Fishing and Boating Partnership Council and the Recreational Boating and Fishing Foundation provided funding for the symposium and book publication. Barbara Knuth and William Siemer of the Cornell University Department of Natural Resources provided leadership in initiating and organizing the entire effort. The content of the paper was formed through discussions with, and the input of, Ryck Lydecker of BoatU.S. and Margaret Podlich of the BoatU.S. Foundation for Boating Safety and Clean Water.

References

Deci, E. L., and R. M. Ryan. 1985. Intrinsic motivation and self determination in human behavior. Plenum, New York.

USEPA (U.S. Environmental Protection Agency). 1996. Clean marinas clear value. U.S. Environmental Protection Agency, EPA report 841-R-96–003, Washington, D.C.

Fedler, A. J., W. F. Siemer, B. A. Knuth, and B. E. Matthews. 2001. Developing aquatic resource stewards. Taproot (Coalition for Education in the Outdoors) 12(4):9–15.

Geisler, C. C., O. B. Martinson, and E. A. Wilkening. 1977. Outdoor recreation and environmental concern: a restudy. Rural Sociology 42:241–249.

Knuth, B. A., and W. F. Siemer. 2004. Fostering aquatic stewardship: a key for fisheries sustainability. Pages 243–255 in E. E. Knudsen, D. D. MacDonald, and Y. K. Muirhead, editors. Sustainable management of North American fisheries. American Fisheries Society, Symposium 43, Bethesda, Maryland.

Lipton, D. 2004. The value of improved water quality to Chesapeake Bay boaters. Marine Resource Economics 19(2):265–270.

NMMA (National Marine Manufacturers Association). 2003. 2003 recreational boating abstract National Marine Manufacturers Association, Chicago.

Strategic Research Group. 2003. 2002 national recreational boating survey report. November 30, 2003. Prepared for the U.S. Coast Guard Office of Boating Safety, Washington, D.C.

Rassam, G. N., Loftus, A. J. and B. Tyler, editors. 2000. Celebrating 50 years of the Sport Fish Restoration Program. Fisheries (25) 7 (supplement).

American Fisheries Society Symposium 55:137–143, 2007

Measures of Aquatic Stewardship from a Fisheries Perspective

PHIL T. SENG[1]

D.J. Case & Associates
317 East Jefferson Boulevard, Mishawaka, Indiana 46545, USA

GWEN M. WHITE[2]

Indiana Department of Natural Resources
402 West Washington Street, Room W273, Indianapolis, Indiana 46204, USA

Abstract.—Fishing is an exciting, popular, family-oriented activity that can be ideal as an introduction to and long-term platform for achieving aquatic resources stewardship. Many agencies and stakeholder organizations have developed fishing programs for this purpose, and each year, millions of people participate in these programs across the country. This paper will identify best management practices for assessing and evaluating fishing programs for effectiveness in achieving that goal. It will address program goals, objectives, logic models and needs assessment, developing environmental sensitivity, and social context and support. Findings are based on extensive work conducted by educators and aquatic resources practitioners as part of the Recreational Boating and Fishing Foundation's Best Practices in Boating, Fishing, and Aquatic Resources Stewardship project.

Overview

For aquatics education professionals, few things match the emotional high of watching a wide-eyed, freckle-faced 6-year-old battle his first bluegill *Lepomis macrochirus*, particularly when it happens on your turf—at *your* big events. As mom and dad cheer encouragement and the ecstatic child strains to reel in what *must be* a whale, it is one of countless Kodak moments, ones which educators help create.

Across the nation, hundreds of thousands of families each year cast hook and bobber thanks to aquatic education programs hosted by fish and wildlife agencies, conservation organizations, communities, and related partners. Many of these programs—from fishing derbies to free youth fishing days—play a starring role in attempts to influence the awareness, knowledge, motivations, and lifelong activities of participants in areas of boating, fishing, and aquatic resources stewardship.

Fishing is unmatched in its potential to reach constituents. It is a popular, family-oriented activity—even for those who have never fished. Fishing is easy to do successfully and inexpensively at a beginner's level. It is largely free from hindering perceptions (ones that hunter education administrators routinely face) about being dangerous, complicated, or inhumane.

Fishing serves as the perfect portal to achieving multiple aquatic education goals. Educators want to affect awareness, knowledge, attitudes, skills, and levels of participation. You want people to fish and boat safely and often. You want to attract new anglers and retain others who will buy fishing licenses. Educators want constituents to think highly of agencies and organizations, supporting their budgets and aims.

Educators also want to foster aquatic resources stewardship, defined by the Recreational Boating and Fishing Foundation (RBFF) as "taking personal responsibility to sustain and enhance freshwater and marine resources, while accepting the obligation to the environment and future us-

---

[1] E-mail:phil@djcase.com
[2] E-mail: gwhite@dnr.in.gov

ers" (www.rbff.org) (see Table 1). But by and large, do fishing programs effectively promote these things? In particular, do they help create a stewardship ethic among participants?

According to a strong body of research, the answer is no. There is little direct evidence that the bulk of fishing programs improve aquatic stewardship (Fedler 2001).

"There's a difference between being effective versus just doing 'fun stuff,'" says Steve Huffaker, department director, Idaho Fish and Game Department. "A lot of stuff is fun for agencies to do and for people to participate in—but it might not be what is needed" (Recreational Boating and Fishing Foundation 2003).

As agencies and organizations tighten their budgetary belts, there is intense pressure to justify programs. This means especially that "soft" programs such as aquatic education come under hard scrutiny. Increasingly, staffs must prove the effectiveness of aquatic education programs, even efforts that have been around for years. For managers who never have been in the position of measuring whether programs are successful, it provides a challenging situation indeed.

The idea that a program might get a low grade presents a real fear factor to some program managers. But the truth is that internal and external stakeholders are more likely to take aquatic stewardship programs seriously—and provide funding and support—if they can see the promise in such programs and corrective actions to get them on the right course.

Educators often have felt at a loss to find research and tools to measure and engineer programs' effectiveness. Fedler (2001a:5) writes,

"Biologists can point to improved water quality, miles of streams or acres of lakes rehabilitated, increased fish populations, and the larger size of fish as measures of biological benefits." What proven measures do aquatic education professionals have? How can they build effective programs that show leaders, administrators, and constituents that efforts have a true impact on organizational missions and goals?

Best Practices Provide Solid Guidance

Guidance is available through a series of recommendations, research, data, and a suite of tools called "Best Practices for Boating, Fishing and Aquatic Stewardship," otherwise known as Best Practices. This chapter will identify Best Practices to assess and evaluate fishing programs. Unless referenced otherwise, the rest of this chapter is based upon research reported in the 2001 landmark work *Defining Best Practices in Boating, Fishing, and Stewardship Education* sponsored by the Recreational Boating and Fishing Foundation (RBFF; Fedler 2001b).

Best Practices are methods to derive specific outcomes that have been clearly defined, refined, and evaluated through repeated delivery; outcomes are supported by a substantial body of research (Seng and Rushton 2003). Best Practices are the latest and greatest knowledge available to develop aquatic education efforts. As educational efforts, research, and evaluation continue, Best Practices also will evolve to apply "tested, science-based practices to educational efforts, the same way biologists apply science to the management of fish, wildlife and

---

TABLE 1. Definitions of aquatic stewardship and ethics-based stewardship.

Aquatic stewardship is
- taking personal responsibility to sustain and enhance freshwater and marine resources, while accepting the obligation to the environment and future users (www.rbff.org).
- based upon the premise that use and enjoyment of the resource is a privilege not a right and that resource conservation and enhancement is achievable through thoughtful participation and ordinary use (www.rbff.org).

Ethics-based stewardship is a process of developing ethical competence and skills, including
- sensitivity to recognize a situation as posing one or more ethical considerations,
- knowledge of what responses are legal versus what responses might be ethical in that situation,
- willingness to act,
- judgment to weigh various considerations where there are no laws or moral guidelines, and
- humility to seek consultation and additional knowledge to guide one's action (Fedler 2001).

other natural resources" (Seng and Rushton 2003:1).

Best Practices guidelines are *not* a program unto themselves. Instead, Best Practices are tools to enhance the design, delivery, and implementation of your existing program's content. By using Best Practices as part of aquatic stewardship education programs, managers can

- plan, develop and implement aquatic education programs;
- conduct program evaluations at all levels of development and implementation;
- provide ongoing professional development for staff;
- identify and incorporate research to improve your educational efforts; and
- gain ongoing internal and external support and funding.

Best Practices are *process-based*, not content-based. Best Practices apply to *all* conservation education programs, even though they were developed for aquatic education. In addition, "Best Practices for Boating, Fishing and Aquatic Stewardship Education" pertains to all major aquatic education areas. Some educators focus exclusively on boating, fishing, or stewardship. Others emphasize fishing or boating but recognize the value of experiential fishing and boating to teach stewardship. Others offer programs that combine education in all three areas. Best Practices recommendations will benefit educators across the full spectrum of content types.

Background and Development

In 1998, the Department of Interior's Sport Fishing and Boating Partnership Council completed a strategic plan for their Outreach and Communication Program. The goal was to increase boating and fishing participation and aquatic resources stewardship to complement ongoing conservation efforts at agencies. RBFF was founded as a nonprofit organization that same year to fulfill that mission. It is largely funded through the Sport Fish Restoration Program as part of a multiyear national outreach and communication effort.

In 2000, national fisheries and aquatic education leaders came together as part of RBFF's Education Task Force, a working group charged to outline and solve problems affecting aquatic education. They formally recognized that aquatic resources education often misses the major components of evaluation and foundational research that should be an essential part of any program.

Starting that same year, RBFF's Education Task Force began developing Best Practices to help educators build, enhance, and evaluate programs based on proven research and techniques. RBFF commissioned 11 experts to develop summaries of existing research and recommendations. Experts came from diverse fields, including boating education, aquatic education, environmental education, marine education, youth development, stewardship and environmental ethics education, minority education, adventure recreation education, and outdoor education for people with disabilities. The summaries, compiled and edited by Fedler (2001b), distill practices to help managers set and reach goals for boating, fishing, and aquatic stewardship education programs. It is available at www.rbff.org.

In developing Best Practices, RBFF and RBFF's Education Task Force experts laid essential groundwork by overseeing development of (1) primary and secondary audiences for Best Practices efforts; (2) a database, inventory, and directory of existing educational programs, events, and curricula; (3) a Web site to maintain and update the database and research materials; and (4) an impressive suite of tools, including the centerpiece "Best Practices Workbook for Boating, Fishing, and Aquatic Stewardship Education" (Seng and Rushton 2003). Each of these Best Practices products and tools is outlined later in this chapter.

How to Make Aquatic Stewards

To understand why Best Practices are so essential, it is useful to reflect on why many aquatic education programs do not work. Why aren't the bulk of fishing or aquatic education programs improving aquatic stewardship among their participants? Best Practices tools address this topic in detail.

Program managers frequently misunderstand how to motivate change in people. They commonly assume that people will adopt a behavior simply after receiving information at a one-time event. However, knowledge and awareness are not enough to inspire long-lasting behavior changes.

Simply knowing that something is needed is *not* enough to inspire someone do it.

Promotional, marketing, or informational efforts are valued aspects of a campaign to create awareness—but media tactics cannot stand alone as a strategy to change behaviors. Information alone is not enough. Mass media tactics are important, but they are part of a much larger strategy.

So what does it take to make aquatic stewards? Researchers have identified a series of variables that contribute to environmentally responsible behaviors.

Entry level

The first step is to improve participants' environmental sensitivity and ecological knowledge. When a person lacks sensitivity and knowledge, programs must begin by providing basic information. For example, programs can raise awareness that, as a boater, you can spread aquatic plants, zebra mussels, and other nuisance species throughout lakes and waterways, and this can impact aquatic resources and recreation opportunities for yourself and other people. Without sensitivity and basic knowledge, a person is unlikely to progress to the next stage of ownership.

Ownership level

At this level, people internalize issues and problems. They create a personal connection with areas, an in-depth understanding of issues, and personal investment. (e.g., I love to go fishing and boating; *therefore*, I want to prevent the spread of aquatic nuisance species that could affect these activities).

Empowerment level

Empowerment gives people a sense they can make changes and help resolve important issues. For example, programs can empower people to prevent the spread of nonnative aquatic species by following key rules about dumping ballast water, cleaning plants and detritus from their boats, or participating in a volunteer program to help people check their boats and trailers at the local lake. People are empowered when they believe their personal actions can make a difference.

To be effective in each of these levels, pro-grams need to be socially relevant. If not grounded in the social context of the learner, stewardship education will remain abstract and ultimately irrelevant. Programs need to be specific to target audiences. Educators need a firm understanding of social, cultural, economic, and other sensitivities that guide how diverse groups approach issues, hold values, deal with problems, and have experiences. For example, fishing and aquatic stewardship programs for women (who may value cooperation) should be tailored differently than programs for men (who may prefer competition). The approaches used in working with largely Hispanic groups (with a maternalistic social center, generally) could be very different than approaches used with predominantly Caucasian groups (generally having a paternalistic structure).

Efforts also must be *repeated* to encourage long-term stewardship behaviors. Programs such as fishing derbies are short-term or one-time efforts. One-time efforts might create initial enthusiasm, but without the ability to sustain it long term, interest eventually withers.

Feedback, rewards, and penalties can produce short-term behavior change, but will not last without other efforts. Effective programs get learners to commit to target behaviors (e.g., prevent the spread of aquatic nuisance species) and select personal goals related to target behaviors (e.g., dump ballast water, check boat and trailers for aquatic nuisance species). Effective programs identify constraints to behaviors (e.g., unwillingness to take time, difficulty in identifying species, etc.) and work to eliminate constraints (e.g., teach boaters how to efficiently clean their equipment, provide opportunities for boaters to help other boaters, offer supplemental information).

How Best Practices Can Help

Best Practices offer the research and systematic methods to identify strengths and fill gaps in existing aquatic stewardship education efforts. This includes setting goals and objectives, applying precepts of a program logic model, evaluating activities and results, and making modifications as needed.

Goals and objectives

The top priority of applying Best Practices is to ensure a program has clear goals and objectives.

Your organization might have a mission statement such as "conserve aquatic resources and provide recreational opportunities." With such a broad statement, many programs are appropriate, but specific goals and objectives can help focus your efforts.

Goals should be broad, overarching statements that give a sense of purpose. A goal should answer the question, why are we doing this program (e.g., to increase license sales, to decrease the transport of aquatic nuisance species)?

Objectives must be specific and measurable; they usually are short-term. It is often helpful to think in terms of the statement, when a participant completes this program, he or she will know, feel or be able to ________." The blank is the objective (e.g., participants will know how to tie their own knots or clean a fish).

Program logic model

After setting goals and objectives, the next step is to develop a program logic model, which identifies how factors fit and relate. Figure 1 shows how it might look. A good way to use the model is to work backward—think about the outputs and outcomes based on goals and objectives, consider what methods or throughputs are appropriate to achieve them, and determine what resources or inputs are required to make them happen.

Managers should base their programs on a needs assessment or logic model that captures inputs, throughputs, outputs, and outcomes. Inputs are invested resources to implement a program (e.g., staff, money, equipment, facilities, administrative approvals, budget authority, agreements with co-operating agencies, volunteer support, in-kind services, donations, and environmental and community resources). Throughputs are mechanisms, including activities and participants (including staff) (e.g., a boating workshop, fishing derby or aquatic stewardship program). Outputs include concepts of how many participants attended, their evaluated level of satisfaction, and how many are exposed to key messages. Outcomes are results beyond outputs. Successful outcomes include increased environmental awareness, boating and fishing knowledge and skills, improved social support for boating and fishing, and changed attitudes about proper actions toward and care of the environment.

Measuring outcomes is a bigger challenge than the relatively simple task of measuring quantitative outputs. In order to measure outcomes, you need to build accurate and aggressive evaluation tactics.

Evaluation

Just as important as setting goals and objectives is evaluating whether they are achieved. Yet, evaluation typically is overlooked and neglected. According to the Best Practices Workbook, far too often programs are based, not on research evidence supporting their effectiveness or on an accepted education theory, but only on what another program or agency is doing. And most evaluation efforts rarely report more than simple program outputs such as the number of participants at an event, participant satisfaction, and cost of delivery. What do these simple outputs tell you about how well you are educating your audiences? If

Inputs	Throughputs		Outputs	Outcomes		
Resources	**Activities**	**Participation**	**Counts/Feedback**	**Short-term**	**Medium-term**	**Long-term**
				Learning	**Action**	**Conditions**
Staff	Curriculum	Participants	Number reached	Awareness	Practice	Social
Volunteers	design	Customers	Experiences	Motivations	Decisions	Economic
Curricula	Product dev.	Stakeholders	Satisfaction	Knowledge	Action	Political
Donors	Recruiting	Citizens	Surveys	Values	behavior	Civic
Time	Clinics	Volunteers	Other feedback	Attitudes	Stewardship	Environmental
Money	Workshops	Trainers	Service units	Opinions	Policies	Public relations
Materials	Meetings	Teachers	Cost per unit	Skills		
Equipment	Counseling	Youth	Service quality	Aspirations		
Technology	Facilitation	Families				
Partners	Assessments					
	Media work					
	Training					

INFLUENTIAL ENVIRONMENTAL FACTORS AND ASSUMPTIONS

FIGURE 1. Conceptual logic model for program development and evaluation.

you are asked what kind of impact your program is having on the knowledge, attitudes and behaviors of your audience, how will you answer? (Seng and Rushton 2003:4-1)

There are two primary types of evaluation. Formative evaluation is done when developing a program. It might include a needs assessment to identify performance measures before beginning the program. A program logic model is an excellent tool for formative evaluation because you must quantify all program delivery steps. Putting steps on paper can show where a program needs adjustment. Summative evaluation is what most people think of as traditional evaluation. After implementing a program, you check performance measures to see if the program achieved objectives. Then you adjust the program based on what you learned.

There are different ways to evaluate programs and efforts, but most effective evaluations are conducted during the program's planning stage, during implementation and upon completion. Table 2 highlights Best Practices rules for program evaluation.

It is commonly misunderstood that evaluation should happen every so often. Thus, a program might be implemented in multiyear segments with a one-time evaluation conducted between segments to make sure that things are on track. The reality is that programs, society, agencies, and activities are in continual flux. *Nothing* stays the same. That is what makes regular, on-going evaluation so important.

Best Practices suggest that continuous, integral evaluation is the only real measure of program effectiveness. It is the only way to be certain that a program is meeting agency goals and objectives, as well as needs of target audiences. Evaluation is the primary way to demonstrate a program's value to those to whom you are accountable.

There are many methods available for evaluation (see Table 3). Each type of evaluation has its strengths and weaknesses. Educators always should customize evaluation techniques to their specific program; they should use multiple and varied techniques where possible. This way, you can show evaluations from various angles based on actual performance.

Best Practices Tools

Best Practices described here are just a few within a suite of tools from RBFF. The tools can help you incorporate Best Practices into boating, fishing, and aquatic resources stewardship education programs.

Best Practices workbook

The primary tool is the *Best Practices Workbook for Boating, Fishing and Aquatic Resources Stewardship Education* (Seng and Rushton 2003). This comprehensive document shows how to plan, design, conduct, and evaluate programs according to Best Practices that researchers and other programs have proven effective. As you progress through the workbook, worksheets will help you to incorporate Best Practices at each stage of development.

Information sheets

Eleven information sheets give brief overviews of major segments within the Best Practices workbook.

TABLE 2. Best practices for effective program evaluation.

Effective program evaluation
- is based on program goals and objectives.
- explores and investigates the program's long-term benefits and impacts.
- is systematic and ongoing process that begins when a program is being planned and carries through implementation.
- encourages the use of multiple and varied assessment methods.
- is used as a learning tool to support program reflection, decision-making and improvement.
- uses national criteria to select, develop and/or revise curriculum materials.
- helps identify program outputs, such as number of participants and participant feedback.
- allows program staff to take advantage of professional development opportunities relating to evaluation.
- explores and investigates the program's short-term learning outcomes.

TABLE 3. Methods available for evaluation of aquatic stewardship education programs.

Method	Method synopsis
Experimental designs	Arguably the most effective tools for evaluating program outcomes, experimental evaluation includes manipulating an independent variable on a dependent or outcome variable while minimizing effects of other relevant factors.
Surveys	A series of questions asked of a sample group.
Testing	Commonly associated with school programs.
Focus groups	Small numbers of people assembled to discuss a topic.
Ethnographic methods	Researching a community (such as an ethnic or geographic community) by being part of the community to get the insider's view.
Longitudinal studies	Efforts to track a fixed number of individuals over time.
Portfolios or journals	Portfolios are collections of work that show how a student increases proficiency or understanding over time. Journals show students' thought processes regarding developing projects.
Projects	A display, Web site development, or group presentation with PowerPoint are examples. Projects encourage students to cooperate for a common goal, demonstrating the importance of achieving results.

You can review the fact sheets to decide which segments apply or use them to help convince others of the importance of using Best Practices.

PowerPoint presentation

The presentation, available online and on CD-ROM, has three different modules that you can customize to a target audience to communicate the importance of Best Practices.

Trainer's guide

The best way to get partners to incorporate Best Practices is to show them how to do it. The trainer's guide helps do just that. It uses a "cookbook" approach to identify key points and appropriate tools to communicate with various target audiences. The guide also contains outlines and instructions for 1-d and 2-d workshops. In addition, RBFF also offers "train-the-trainer" workshops to show facilitators how to present and use Best Practices materials.

Best Practices tools are part of a proven recipe for success in boating, fishing, and aquatic resources stewardship education programs. It's just ready and waiting for you to start cooking! The best way to obtain these materials is to visit the resources section of the RBFF Web site at www.rbff.org. You can order or download materials. Single review copies are available free, and bulk orders are available at cost.

References

Fedler, A. J. 2001a. Fishing, boating, and aquatic stewardship education: framework and best practices recommendations. Pages 4–17 *in* A. J. Fedler, editor. Defining best practices in boating, fishing, and stewardship education. Recreational Boating and Fishing Foundation, Alexandria, Virginia.

Fedler, A. J., editor. 2001b. Defining best practices in boating, fishing, and stewardship education. Recreational Boating and Fishing Foundation, Alexandria, Virginia.

Recreational Boating and Fishing Foundation. 2003. Reel Tips Newsletter. August. Recreational Boating and Fishing Foundation. Alexandria, Virginia.

Seng, P. T. and S. Rushton, editors. 2003. Best practices workbook for boating, fishing, and aquatic resources stewardship education. Recreational Boating and Fishing Foundation, Alexandria, Virginia.

American Fisheries Society Symposium 55:145–155, 2007

Does Angling or Boating Improve the Stewardship Ethic of Participants?

STEVE L. MCMULLIN[1]
*Department of Fisheries and Wildlife Sciences, Virginia Tech
Blacksburg, Virginia 24061, USA*

KAREN S. HOCKETT[2] AND JULIE A. MCCLAFFERTY[3]
*Conservation Management Institute, Virginia Tech
Blacksburg, Virginia 24061, USA*

Abstract.—We conducted a mail survey of U.S. citizens to test numerous indicators of natural resource stewardship and the frequently stated hypothesis that participation in angling or boating increases stewardship behavior. Due to the large sample size of our survey, nearly all indicators of stewardship yielded significant relationships with measures of stewardship behaviors. However, five indicators stood out from the rest: ownership, sense of personal responsibility/locus of control, verbal commitment to the environment, awareness of the consequences of human actions for the environment, and environmental concern (as measured with a variation of the New Environmental Paradigm). Among the five indicators that appeared to be most significantly related to activism behaviors, active (fished or boated within the last 5 years) and lapsed (fished or boated at some point during their lives but not in the last 5 years) participants were more likely than nonparticipants (never fished or boated) to rate highly in three: sense of ownership, sense of personal responsibility/locus of control, and awareness of consequences of human actions. Survey findings suggest that the relationship between participation in angling or boating and stewardship behavior is complex and that simply recruiting new participants does not guarantee overall improvement in stewardship behavior. We suggest that recruitment and education efforts should strive to enhance the sense of personal ownership among all citizens that currently is more prevalent among anglers and boaters. We also suggest that educators and managers exercise caution in touting the link between stewardship and participation in boating and/or angling.

Introduction

Declining participation rates throughout the United States in recreational fishing in the late 20th and early 21st centuries (U.S. Fish and Wildlife Service 2001) have concerned fisheries managers for at least two reasons. Their first concern focuses on the implications of declining participation for agency funding as fewer anglers purchase fishing licenses. Their second concern focuses on an expected decrease in environmental stewardship as fewer people participate in recreation tied to a clean environment. The latter concern derives from the commonly held assumption that participation in outdoor recreation increases attitudes and behaviors associated with stewardship and environmental concern (Dunlap and Heffernan 1975; Tanner 1980).

Dunlap and Heffernan (1975) proposed and tested three hypotheses regarding the relationship between participation in outdoor recreation and environmental concern:

1. There is a positive association between involvement in outdoor recreation and environmental concern.

[1] E-mail: smcmulli@vt.edu

[2] E-mail: khockett@vt.edu

[3] E-mail: jmcclaff@vt.edu

2. The association is stronger between appreciative activities (e.g., wildlife watching) and environmental concern than between consumptive activities (e.g., hunting) and environmental concerns.

3. There is a stronger association between outdoor recreation and concern with protecting aspects of the environment necessary for pursuing such activities than between outdoor recreation and other environmental issues such as air and water pollution.

Dunlap and Heffernan's research and other empirical studies conducted since 1975 have found little support for the first hypothesis (Dunlap and Heffernan 1975; Geisler et al. 1977; Pinhey and Grimes 1979; Van Liere and Noe 1981). More recent studies that focused on the relationship between participation in outdoor recreation and pro-environmental behavior, rather than environmental concern, had more positive findings. For example, Nord et al. (1998) found that Pennsylvania landowners who participated in forest-related outdoor recreation were more likely to purchase "green" products, watch nature programming on television, and belong to environmental organizations. Theodori et al. (1998) obtained similar results and found that Pennsylvania residents who engaged in outdoor recreation also were more likely to contribute to environmental organizations, read conservation-related magazines, attend public meetings, and vote for candidates for environmental reasons.

In this paper, we report on aspects of a survey of U.S. citizens designed to test Dunlap and Heffernan's (1975) first hypothesis. Although our research addressed all three of the hypotheses (as well as other factors), we limit our discussion here to indicators of environmental stewardship and the effects of participation in angling and boating on stewardship. The Recreational Boating and Fishing Foundation (which funded this research) defined aquatic stewardship as "taking personal responsibility to sustain, and enhance freshwater and marine resources, while accepting an obligation to the environment." Despite the presumed relationship between participation in angling or boating and stewardship, these recreational activities have received little attention from researchers (Fedler 2001). We tested effects of participation in angling and boating on both environmental concern and pro-environmental behavior. Information presented here is taken from a much larger study (Hockett et al. 2005). Upon completion of the project, all reports and survey data will be available through the Recreational Boating and Fishing Foundation at www.rbff.org.

Methods

We sent a self-administered mail survey to 5,500 randomly selected households in each of four regions in the United States during Fall 2004. Survey administration followed Dillman's (2000) Tailored Design Method. We conducted telephone interviews with approximately 25 nonrespondents per region to assess nonresponse bias. In addition, we compared demographic data for respondents to U.S. Census data to determine how well respondent characteristics compared to those of U.S. citizens.

The questionnaire included items designed to assess the efficacy of numerous indicators of environmental stewardship, including demographic characteristics, commitment, ownership, locus of control, sense of personal responsibility, religion/spirituality, affect/emotion, the role of government in environmental protection, threat perception, awareness of the consequences of human actions, environmental concern (New Environmental Paradigm), perceived seriousness of depreciative actions, constraints to pro-environmental behavior, and participation in recreational boating and fishing. In this paper, we discuss findings related to ownership, commitment, sense of personal responsibility/locus of control, awareness of consequences, and environmental concern.

We assessed ownership (personal investment in and identification with environmental issues) with a single item that asked respondents to self-assess to what degree they considered themselves to be natural resource stewards. The response scale was anchored at each end by "No, not at all" (1), and "Yes, very much" (7).

Cottrell and Graefe (1997) found verbal commitment to acting pro-environmentally to be a relatively strong predictor of environmental concern and behavior. We assessed verbal commitment to environmental stewardship with two items: willingness to volunteer time to help the environment, and willingness to pay more for products if that would improve the environment (Cronbach's alpha = 0.54). We used a 5-point agreement–disagreement scale, with strongly agree coded as 5, neutral coded as 3, and strongly disagree coded as 1. We then summed responses to the two items to form a commitment score.

Personal responsibility is a concept that describes a person's feelings of duty or obligation to engage in helping behavior. People who internalize responsibility for their actions are more likely to engage in helping behavior, either toward others or to the environment (Granzin and Olsen 1991). Locus of control has been defined as an individual's perception of whether or not he or she has the ability to bring about change through his or her behavior (Hines et al. 1987). Individuals with greater internal locus of control are expected to be more likely to act on their attitudes and beliefs than those with an external locus of control. Those who believe they are capable of acting (i.e., know how to act and can physically perform the behavior) in pro-environmental ways are more likely to attempt to act on any pro-environmental beliefs that they have. Four items assessed personal responsibility/locus of control: feeling of personal control over whether or not daily activities of the individual harm the environment; importance of reducing one's personal impact on the environment; perception that because one person's contribution to environmental problems is small, the individual has little responsibility for causing environmental problems; and perception that the conservation efforts of one person are insignificant as long as others refuse to conserve resources (Cronbach's alpha = 0.64). These items also used a 5-point agreement–disagreement scale. We summed the four items (with one item reverse-coded) to form a personal responsibility/locus of control score.

Eight items assessed awareness of the consequences of human actions on the environment. They included effects of human actions on water quantity, water quality, air quality, biodiversity, and human health. For these items, we used a 4-point agreement-disagreement scale with an additional "not sure" response option. Although no definitive right or wrong answers existed for some of the items, responses nevertheless indicated the level of environmental concern. We coded responses indicating pro-environmental concern (e.g., answering strongly agree or agree to "Driving a car contributes to global warming") as 1 and all other responses as 0. We then generated an awareness score by summing coded responses to all eight questions.

The New Environmental Paradigm (NEP) scale, originally developed by Dunlap and Van Liere (1978), has been used frequently to assess overall environmental concern. We used 10 items from the 15-item revised New Environmental Paradigm scale (Dunlap et al. 2000) to assess environmental concern. The 10 items included items from all five subscales of the revised NEP. However, due to high internal reliability (Cronbach's alpha = 0.80) and factor analysis that showed all 10 items loading on the first factor, we combined all 10 items into a single NEP score.

We also assessed pro-environmental behavior of respondents in two categories that we labeled "lifestyle" and "activism." The lifestyle category included seven questions assessing the frequency (always, sometimes, never) with which respondents engaged in conservation-related behaviors. Behaviors included recycling, encouraging others to recycle, conserving water and electricity in the home, picking up others' litter, purchasing recycled products, and trying to purchase and use products that are less harmful to the environment. We developed a lifestyle behaviors score for each individual by calculating the mean of all lifestyle behavior items answered (range of possible scores = 0 [never] to 2 [always]). In addition, we calculated lifestyle subscale scores for consumer decisions (e.g., buying recycled products, buying products that are perceived as less harmful to the environment, using energy efficient light bulbs), recycling (including encouraging others to recycle), and personal actions (picking up others' litter, conserving water in the home). Activism behaviors included seven yes/no items related to political and environmental activism. The activities included ceasing to buy products that cause environmental problems, contributing money or one's time to environmental organizations or projects, assisting in stream or beach clean-up projects, contacting a government official in support of an environmental issue, actively opposing an environmentally damaging project, and voting for a candidate largely because of his/her pro-environmental views. We generated an activism score by summing the number of "yes" responses for each individual (range of possible scores = 0–7).

We tested the relationship between each indicator and stewardship behavior by categorizing respondents as high (as close to the upper 25% of responses as possible), medium (middle 50% of responses) or low (bottom 25% of responses) on each indicator and performing a one-way analysis of variance (ANOVA) with either lifestyle behavior or activism behavior as the dependent variable. We then tested the relationship between participation in fishing and/or boating and the indicators using Chi-square contingency table analyses on cross-tabulations of participation and percent of respondents in the low, medium, and high categories of each indicator. We defined participation as active if the respondent had engaged in fishing or boating in the last 5 years and lapsed if the respondent had engaged in one or both activities at some point in his/her life but not in the last 5 years. Nonparticipants had never fished or boated.

Results

Response rates and nonresponse bias

After adjustment for undeliverable questionnaires, 17.2% of the survey subjects responded. The low response rate could have been problematic if our goal was to make inferences regarding the U.S. population as a whole. However, our primary objective was to compare active participants in angling and boating to lapsed participants and nonparticipants. Analysis of demographic data showed that respondents were older, less likely to be minorities, more likely to be male, and more likely to be anglers than the U.S. population as a whole. The demographic profile of respondents approximated that of anglers except that respondents tended to be older than the U.S. angling population. We were unable to find reliable statistics on demographics of the U.S. boating population. We weighted the sample to adjust for the older age distribution because age was the only demographic variable that showed atypical patterns among participant levels, and age was shown to affect stewardship behaviors in a com-

plex, nonlinear fashion. The weighted sample closely resembled the U.S. Census data for age. Sample sizes of the three groups of interest were large enough to allow for valid comparisons among the groups (444 nonparticipants, 691 lapsed participants, 2,112 active participants).

Indicators of stewardship and their relationships to behavior

Although most indicators tested against the lifestyle and activism behaviors yielded significant results (likely due to the large sample size), five indicators stood out for their relationships to behavior in our preliminary analysis: ownership, sense of personal responsibility/locus of control, verbal commitment to the environment, awareness of the consequences of human actions for the environment, and environmental concern (NEP). In the following sections, we discuss these five indicators in more detail.

Ownership.—Fifty-two percent of respondents placed themselves above the midpoint of the ownership scale, compared to only 21% who placed themselves below the midpoint of the scale. ANOVA of self-assessed ownership (broken into four categories) versus stewardship behaviors yielded significant results for nearly all comparisons (Table 1). Respondents who strongly identified with natural resource stewardship engaged in nearly 2.5 times more activism behaviors, on average, than respondents who had little or no identification with the term. Although the relationship between ownership and lifestyle behaviors was less dramatic, respondents who strongly identified with natural resource stewardship engaged in lifestyle behaviors 30% more frequently than those who weakly identified with the term. Active participants were much more likely than nonparticipants to place themselves above the midpoint of the ownership scale (60% versus 42%; Table 2). Conversely, nonparticipants were much more likely than active participants to place themselves below the midpoint of the ownership scale (28% versus 17%).

Personal responsibility/locus of control.—Respondents who scored low, medium, or high for sense of personal responsibility/locus of control differed significantly in all behavior categories (Table 3). Although all comparisons were statistically significant, the differences were most

TABLE 1. Mean overall lifestyle behavior scores, lifestyle subscale behavior scores and activism behavior scores for respondents in four categories of self-assessed ownership. Respondents in the low category chose 1, 2, or 3 in responding to the question, "Do you consider yourself to be a natural resource steward?" Respondents in the moderate category chose 4. Respondents in the moderately high category chose 5, and respondents in the high category chose 6 or 7. Superscripts indicate significant differences in paired comparisons (Tukey's).

| | Response to ownership item | | | | Analysis of variance | |
Behavior scale	Low ($n = 678$)	Moderate ($n = 845$)	Moderately high ($n = 1,010$)	High ($n = 656$)	F	p-value
Lifestyle[a]	1.13[1]	1.26[2]	1.32[3]	1.47[4]	121.38	<0.0005
Consumer decisions	1.04[1]	1.13[2]	1.19[3]	1.36[4]	82.54	<0.0005
Recycling	1.12[1]	1.36[2]	1.44[3]	1.58[4]	81.56	<0.0005
Personal actions	1.27[1]	1.33[1]	1.40[2]	1.50[3]	33.04	<0.0005
Activism[b]	1.51[1]	2.16[2]	2.89[3]	3.74[4]	209.54	<0.0005

[a] Score = mean responses on scale of 0 = never, 1 = sometimes, and 2 = always.

[b] Score = mean sum of yes responses.

TABLE 2. Percent of nonparticipants, lapsed participants, and active participants (participant levels), as well as active anglers, active boaters, and active anglers and boaters (participant types) in the low, medium, medium high, and high categories of self-assessed ownership. Chi-square = 64.73, $p < 0.0001$ for participant levels. Chi-square = 21.76, $p = 0.001$ for participant types.

| | Response to ownership item | | | |
Participation level/type	Low	Moderate	Moderately high	High
Participation level				
Nonparticipant ($n = 434$)	30.0	32.5	22.1	15.4
Lapsed participant ($n = 679$)	23.9	29.0	28.6	18.6
Active participant ($n = 2,067$)	18.6	24.5	34.6	22.2
Participation type				
Angler only ($n = 233$)	24.9	31.3	25.3	18.5
Boater only ($n = 439$)	18.5	23.9	37.8	19.8
Angler and boater ($n = 1,396$)	17.7	23.5	35.2	23.6

TABLE 3. Mean overall lifestyle behavior scores, lifestyle subscale behavior scores and activism behavior scores for respondents who had low, medium, and high personal responsibility/locus of control scores. Superscripts indicate significant differences in paired comparisons (Tukey's).

| | Personal responsibility/locus of control score | | | Analysis of variance | |
Behavior scale	Low ($n = 708$)	Medium ($n = 1,566$)	High ($n = 921$)	F	p-value
Lifestyle[a]	1.19[1]	1.29[2]	1.41[3]	85.47	<0.0005
Consumer decisions	1.10[1]	1.17[2]	1.25[3]	34.36	<0.0005
Recycling	1.21[1]	1.37[2]	1.55[3]	74.58	<0.0005
Personal actions	1.30[1]	1.35[2]	1.48[3]	37.39	<0.0005
Activism[b]	1.79[1]	2.24[2]	3.41[3]	168.65	<0.0005

[a] Score = mean responses on scale of 0 = never, 1 = sometimes, and 2 = always.

[b] Score = mean sum of yes responses.

notable for activism behaviors (high respondents engaged in these behaviors nearly twice as often as low respondents). Respondents with a high sense of personal responsibility/locus of control engaged in the lifestyle behaviors nearly 20% more often than those with a low sense of personal responsibility/locus of control. Active participants were less likely than lapsed participants and nonparticipants to have low scores for personal responsibility/locus of control and nonparticipants were less likely to have high scores (Table 4). Active participants who engaged only in boating were more likely to have high scores and less likely to have low scores than people who engaged only in fishing or in both activities.

Verbal commitment to the environment.—Respondents who scored low, medium, or high for verbal commitment to the environment (stated willingness to donate time or money to environmental causes or organizations) differed significantly in all behavior categories (Table 5). Respondents with high commitment scores engaged in activism behaviors nearly 2.5 times more often than those with low commitment scores and they engaged in lifestyle behaviors 20% more frequently. Only minor differences existed among active participants, lapsed participants and nonparticipants with respect to verbal commitment (Table 6).

Awareness of the consequences of human actions on the environment.—Respondents who scored low, medium or high for awareness of the

TABLE 4. Percent of nonparticipants, lapsed participants, and active participants (participant levels), as well as active anglers, active boaters, and active anglers and boaters (participant types) in the low, medium, and high categories of personal responsibility/locus of control. Chi-square = 12.52, $p = 0.014$ for participant levels. Chi-square = 7.21, $p = 0.125$ for participant types.

	Personal responsibility/locus of control score		
Participation level/type	Low ($n = 708$)	Medium ($n = 1,566$)	High ($n = 921$)
Participation level			
Nonparticipant	27.6	47.0	25.5
Lapsed participant	23.9	47.1	29.0
Active participant	20.5	50.1	29.4
Participation type			
Angler only	22.8	50.9	26.3
Boater only	16.6	50.6	32.9
Angler and boater	21.3	49.8	28.8

TABLE 5. Mean overall lifestyle behavior scores, lifestyle subscale behavior scores, and activism behavior scores for respondents who had low, medium, and high verbal commitment scores. Superscripts indicate significant differences in paired comparisons (Tukey's).

	Verbal commitment score			analysis of variance	
Behavior scale	Low ($n = 442$)	Medium ($n = 962$)	High ($n = 1,830$)	F	p-value
Lifestyle[a]	1.17[1]	1.28[2]	1.41[3]	145.59	<0.0005
Consumer decisions	1.06[1]	1.15[2]	1.29[3]	101.44	<0.0005
Recycling	1.21[1]	1.37[2]	1.53[3]	94.05	<0.0005
Personal actions	1.28[1]	1.36[2]	1.46[3]	48.67	<0.0005
Activism[b]	1.43[1]	2.47[2]	3.56[3]	461.59	<0.0005

[a] Score = mean responses on scale of 0 = never, 1 = sometimes, and 2 = always.
[b] Score = mean sum of yes responses.

TABLE 6. Percent of nonparticipants, lapsed participants, and active participants (participant levels), as well as active anglers, active boaters, and active anglers and boaters (participant types) in the low, medium, and high categories of verbal commitment. Chi-square = 9.25, p=.055 for participant levels. Chi-square = 18.63, p=.001 for participant types.

	Verbal commitment score		
Participation level/type	Low ($n = 442$)	Medium ($n = 962$)	High ($n = 1,830$)
Participation level			
Nonparticipant	35.2	27.1	37.7
Lapsed participant	34.4	29.1	36.5
Active participant	30.4	27.7	41.9
Participation type			
Angler only	40.7	28.1	31.2
Boater only	26.5	30.6	42.9
Angler and boater	29.9	26.8	43.3

consequences of human actions on the environment differed significantly in all behavior categories (Table 7). Respondents with high awareness scores engaged in more than twice as many activism behaviors, on average, as respondents with low awareness scores. Nonparticipants were more likely than active participants or lapsed participants to have low awareness scores and less likely to have high awareness scores (Table 8).

Environmental concern.—Respondents who scored low, medium or high on the NEP scale differed significantly in all behavior categories (Table 9). Respondents with high NEP scores engaged in nearly twice as many activism behaviors, on average, as respondents with low NEP scores. However, NEP scores of active participants, lapsed participants, and nonparticipants were nearly identical (Table 10).

Participation and behavior.—Active participants engaged in 2.77 activism behaviors, on average, compared to 2.29 for lapsed participants and 2.06 for nonparticipants (Table 11). The three groups did not differ in the frequency in which they engaged in lifestyle behaviors overall, but nonparticipants tended to engage in recycling behavior more frequently than active participants. Active participants who engaged only in fishing had lower lifestyle behavior scores than boaters or active participants who both fished and boated (Table 12).

Discussion

Our findings suggest that the link between participation in angling or boating and natural resource stewardship is complex and that conservation educators and natural resource manag-

TABLE 7. Mean overall lifestyle behavior scores, lifestyle subscale behavior scores, and activism behavior scores for respondents who had low, medium, and high awareness of consequences scores. Superscripts indicate significant differences in paired comparisons (Tukey's).

	Awareness of consequences			Analysis of variance	
Behavior scale	Low ($n = 929$)	Medium ($n = 1,184$)	High ($n = 1,131$)	F	p-value
Lifestyle[a]	1.19[1]	1.30[2]	1.39[3]	84.74	<0.0005
Consumer decisions	1.08[1]	1.18[2]	1.26[3]	58.86	<0.0005
Recycling	1.23[1]	1.39[2]	1.50[3]	55.61	<0.0005
Personal actions	1.30[1]	1.37[2]	1.45[3]	30.88	<0.0005
Activism[b]	1.63[1]	2.47[2]	3.44[3]	272.23	<0.0005

[a] Score = mean responses on scale of 0 = never, 1 = sometimes, 2 = always

[b] Score = mean sum of yes responses

TABLE 8. Percent of nonparticipants, lapsed participants, and active participants (participant levels), as well as active anglers, active boaters, and active anglers and boaters (participant types) in the low, medium, and high categories of awareness of consequences. Chi-square = 11.70, p = 0.021 for participant levels. Chi-square = 14.44, p = 0.0006 for participant types.

	Awareness of consequences score		
Participation level/type	Low (n = 929)	Medium (n = 1,184)	High (n = 1,131)
Participation level			
Nonparticipant	33.9	37.0	29.1
Lapsed participant	26.5	35.6	37.9
Active participant	28.3	36.6	35.1
Participation type			
Angler only	33.9	27.0	39.1
Boater only	26.3	35.3	38.4
Angler and boater	28.1	38.6	33.4

TABLE 9. Mean overall lifestyle behavior scores, lifestyle subscale behavior scores, and activism behavior scores for respondents who had low, medium, and high environmental concern (NEP) scores. Superscripts indicate significant differences in paired comparisons (Tukey's).

	Environmental concern (NEP) score			Analysis of variance	
Behavior scale	Low (n = 797)	Medium (n = 1,537)	High (n = 771)	F	p-value
Lifestyle[a]	1.20[1]	1.30[2]	1.41[3]	72.90	<0.0005
Consumer decisions	1.06[1]	1.18[2]	1.29[3]	67.02	<0.0005
Recycling	1.27[1]	1.38[2]	1.52[3]	36.21	<0.0005
Personal actions	1.32[1]	1.37[2]	1.46[3]	21.84	<0.0005
Activism[b]	1.83[1]	2.47[2]	3.58[3]	192.63	<0.0005

[a] Score = mean responses on scale of 0 = never, 1 = sometimes, and 2 = always.
[b] Score = mean sum of yes responses.

TABLE 10. Percent of nonparticipants, lapsed participants, and active participants (participant levels), as well as active anglers, active boaters, and active anglers and boaters (participant types) in the low, medium, and high categories of environmental concern (NEP score). Chi-square = 7.43, p = 0.115 for participant levels. Chi-square = 24.05, p < 0.0005 for participant types.

	Environmental concern (NEP) score		
Participation level/type	Low (n = 797)	Medium (n = 1,537)	High (n = 771)
Participation level			
Nonparticipant	24.6	53.0	22.4
Lapsed participant	23.2	52.5	24.3
Active participant	26.7	47.8	25.5
Participation type			
Angler only	26.9	45.2	27.9
Boater only	23.9	42.0	34.1
Angler and boater	27.6	49.9	22.5

TABLE 11. Mean overall lifestyle behavior scores, lifestyle subscale behavior scores and activism behavior scores for active participants, lapsed participants and nonparticipants. Superscripts indicate significant differences in paired comparisons (Tukey's).

| Behavior scale | Participation level | | | Analysis of variance | |
	Nonparticipant (n = 444)	Lapsed participant (n = 691)	Active participant (n = 2,112)	F	p-value
Lifestyle[a]	1.34	1.29	1.30	2.81	0.060
Consumer decisions	1.22	1.17	1.18	2.36	0.094
Recycling	1.46[1]	1.43[1]	1.36[2]	7.64	<0.0005
Personal actions	1.37[1, 2]	1.33[1]	1.39[2]	4.50	0.011
Activism[b]	2.06[1]	2.29[1]	2.77[2]	36.62	<0.0005

[a] Score = mean responses on scale of 0 = never, 1 = sometimes, and 2 = always

[b] Score = mean sum of yes responses

TABLE 12. Mean overall lifestyle behavior scores, lifestyle subscale behavior scores, and activism behavior scores for active participants who participated only in angling, only in boating, or both angling and boating. Superscripts indicate significant differences in paired comparisons (Tukey's).

| Behavior scale | Participation type | | | Analysis of variance | |
	Angler only (n = 444)	Boater only (n = 691)	Angler and boater (n = 2,112)	F	p-value
Lifestyle[a]	1.25[1]	1.35[2]	1.29[2]	6.81	0.001
Consumer decisions	1.14	1.19	1.18	1.51	0.221
Recycling	1.28[1]	1.48[2]	1.33[1]	12.62	<0.0005
Personal actions	1.35	1.41	1.39	1.53	0.216
Activism[b]	2.14[1]	2.87[2]	2.85[2]	14.39	<0.0005

[a] Score = mean responses on scale of 0 = never, 1 = sometimes, and 2 = always.

[b] Score = mean sum of yes responses.

ers should exercise caution in touting that link. Although we found some evidence to support Tanner's (1980) and Dunlap and Heffernan's (1975) hypotheses that significant life experiences in the outdoors shape individuals' natural resource stewardship ethic, the evidence was mixed and not compelling. Although a statistically significant relationship between participation in angling or boating and activism behavior existed, the effect was far less significant for participation than it was for many other indicators. Participation level had no significant effect on lifestyle behaviors.

Among the five indicators that appeared to be most significantly related to activism behaviors, active and lapsed participants were more likely than nonparticipants to rate highly in three: sense of ownership, sense of personal responsi-bility/locus of control, and awareness of consequences of human actions. It should be comforting to natural resource managers that active participants are far more likely than nonpartici-pants (57% versus 38%) to assume high or moderately high levels of personal ownership and that people who assume higher levels of ownership are much more likely to engage in both lifestyle and activism stewardship behaviors. This finding helps to justify efforts to increase future recruitment of anglers and boaters. However, for many other indicators, active participants did not differ greatly from nonparticipants in stewardship behavior. Although differences in proportions of active participants and nonparticipants rating high or low in personal responsibility/locus of control and awareness of consequences of human actions were significant, they were much less dramatic than the difference in personal ownership. Furthermore, the percentage of active participants rating high in verbal commitment and environmental concern (NEP) did not differ from the percentage of nonparticipants rating high for those indicators.

Differences between active participants and nonparticipants consistently were more dramatic for activism behaviors than they were for lifestyle behaviors. Compared to nonparticipants, active participants more frequently wrote letters to government officials in support of an environmental issue, contributed money to an environmental or conservation organization, volunteered their time to environmental groups, actively opposed environmentally damaging projects and helped to clean up local beaches or streams. However, active participants did not differ significantly in the frequency with which they (1) voted for candidates largely because of their pro-environmental views, or (2) ceased to buy products because they caused environmental problems. Although these findings demonstrate an association between active participation and stewardship behavior, particularly in some aspects of the political arena and in personal time or money devoted to specific resources of concern to participants, they do not establish a causal relationship. No clear relationship between participation in fishing or boating and a broader environmental ethic (as indicated by behaviors such as recycling and consumer decisions) was evident. This is consistent with Dunlap and Heffernan's (1975) third hypothesis that participants are more willing to engage in stewardship that protects resources that support their recreation than they are to protect the environment in general.

Differences between active participants who engaged only in boating or only in angling likely were due to demographic differences between the two groups. Respondents who only boated were significantly more likely to be female, younger, and better educated and to live in an urban environment than respondents who only fished. Each of these demographic differences contributed to boaters having higher scores for the personal responsibility/locus of control indicator and for the lifestyle behaviors score.

Our findings suggest many implications for natural resource managers and educators. We present three implications here. First, our findings suggest that efforts to increase recruitment of future anglers and boaters (if they are successful) should increase the sense of personal ownership of natural resources. The impact should be felt most in terms of personal and political involvement in conservation causes. Second, although conservation educators and resource managers appear to be safe in contending that participation in boating and fishing is associated with some stewardship activities, they should not portray participation as a major determining factor of stewardship behaviors. Finally, the relatively strong relationship between personal ownership and stewardship behavior suggests that an educational strategy designed to expand the sense of ownership to more people (not just active participants) could yield significant benefits.

As is usually the case, our research raised questions as well as provided answers. The question of whether participation in angling or boating improves the stewardship ethic of participants is complicated. Some of the indicators and behaviors we tested suggested that a positive relationship existed whereas other indicators did not. However, respondents who said that fishing and boating experiences were very important in shaping their environmental views were more likely to engage in both lifestyle and activism behaviors. Further analysis of our findings and future research should attempt to clarify the complicated relationship between stewardship and participation in fishing and/or boating. Much work remains to be done by researchers and conservation educators.

Acknowledgments

We thank the Recreational Boating and Fishing Foundation for funding this research. Special thanks to Marla Hetzel, Kristen Chambers, Jen Levin, and the many members of the foundation's stewardship advisory team, all of whom contributed substantially to the project.

References

Cottrell, S. P., and A. R. Graefe. 1997. Testing a conceptual framework of responsible environmental behavior. The Journal of Environmental Education 29:17–27.

Dillman, D. A. 2000. Mail and internet surveys: the tailored design method. Wiley, New York.

Dunlap, R. E., and R. B. Heffernan. 1975. Outdoor recreation and environmental concern: an empirical examination. Rural Sociology 40:18–30.

Dunlap, R. E., and Van Liere, K. D. 1978. The "New Environmental Paradigm." The Journal of Environmental Education 9:10–19.

Dunlap, R. E. , K. D. Van Liere, A. G. Mertig, and R. E. Jones. 2000. Measuring endorsement of the New Ecological Paradigm: a revised NEP scale. Journal of Social Issues 56:425–442.

Fedler, A. J. 2001. An examination of the relationship between recreational boating and fishing participation and aquatic resource stewardship. Recreational Boating and Fishing Foundation, Alexandria, Virginia.

Geisler, C. C., O. B. Martinson, and E. A. Wilkening. 1977. Outdoor recreation and environmental concern: a restudy. Rural Sociology 42:241–249.

Granzin, K. L., and J. E. Olsen. 1991. Characterizing participants in activities protecting the environment: a focus on donating, recycling, and conservation behaviors. Journal of Public Policy & Marketing 10:1–27.

Hines, J. M., H. R. Hungerford, and A. N. Tomera. 1987. Analysis and synthesis of research on responsible environmental behavior: a meta-analysis. The Journal of Environmental Education 18:1–8.

Hockett, K. S., J. A. McClafferty, and S. L. McMullin. 2005. The making of a resource steward: defining the relationship between aquatic recreation and aquatic stewardship. Virginia Tech, Conservation Management Institute and Department of Fisheries and Wildlife Sciences, Blacksburg, Virginia.

Nord, M., A. E. Luloff, and J. C. Bridger. 1998. The association of forest recreation with environmentalism. Environment and Behavior 30:235–246.

Pinhey, T. K. and M. D. Grimes. 1979. Outdoor recreation and environmental concern: a reexamination of the Dunlap-Heffernan thesis. Leisure Sciences 2:1–11.

Tanner, T. 1980. Significant life experiences: a new research area in environmental education. Journal of Environmental Education 11(4):20–24.

Theodori, G. L., A. E. Luloff, and F. K. Willits. 1998. The association of outdoor recreation and environmental concern: re-examining the Dunlap-Heffernan thesis. Rural Sociology 63. 94–108.

U.S. Fish and Wildlife Service. 2002. 2001 national survey of fishing, hunting and wildlife-associated recreation. Government Printing Office, Washington D.C.

Van Liere, K. D., and F. P. Noe. 1981. Outdoor recreation and environmental attitudes: further examination of the Dunlap-Heffernan thesis. Rural Sociology 46:505–513.

American Fisheries Society Symposium 55:157–167, 2007

The Influence of Angler Value Orientations on Fisheries Stewardship Norms

JEREMY T. BRUSKOTTER[1]

*Minnesota Cooperative Fish & Wildlife Research Unit, University of Minnesota
1980 Folwell Avenue, St. Paul, Minnesota 55108, USA*

DAVID C. FULTON[2]

*U.S. Geological Survey, Minnesota Cooperative Fish & Wildlife Research Unit
University of Minnesota, 1980 Folwell Avenue, St. Paul, Minnesota 55108, USA*

Abstract.—In this paper, we describe a fishing ethic, conceptualized as Minnesota anglers' normative beliefs regarding various stewardship behaviors. We use structural equation modeling to determine the extent to which angler's value orientations, measured along an anthropocentric–biocentric continuum, can be used to predict social norms regarding angling and endorsement or opposition to the use of technological angling aids. Data were obtained from a statewide mail survey of Minnesota anglers conducted in the spring of 2003 ($n = 457$). Results show a modest, positive relationship between biocentric value orientations and stewardship norms and a modest, negative relationship between biocentric value orientations and support for the use of technological angling aids. Consistent with previous research, our results indicated that norms regarding angling may be positioned along a bio-anthropocentric continuum and support the use of the cognitive hierarchy as a framework for understanding and predicting anglers' normative beliefs. Results further suggest fisheries managers interested in promoting stewardship could benefit from recognizing the underlying values that help guide our behavior regarding natural resources.

Introduction

As the next generation of anglers prepares to enter the waters they will have access to an increasingly sophisticated set of tools (i.e., equipment for pursuing, finding, and catching fish), including sonar, global position devices (GPS), digital compasses, and underwater cameras. The use of such devices may not only change how people fish, but how they interact with other anglers while fishing. For instance, rather than simply returning to their favorite "fishing holes," anglers equipped with these devices may travel around lakes in search of a hot spot and conceivably congregate in high densities as they follow fish, thus increasing the likelihood of conflicts.

In contrast to past innovations, this most recent series of devices represents a significant leap in terms of their sophistication and capacity to aid anglers in finding and ultimately landing fish. Yet, to some extent, fish-finders and underwater cameras may be seen as providing those who use them with an unfair advantage, threatening the ideal of fair chase.

Nearly a half century ago, Aldo Leopold lamented the use of such technological aids among outdoorsmen. Leopold worried that these technologies or "gadgets" could threaten the purity of the outdoor experience:

> Then came the gadgeteer, otherwise known as the sporting-goods dealer. He has draped the American outdoors man with an infinity of contraptions, all offered as aids to self-reliance, hardihood, woodcraft, or marksmanship, but too often functioning as substitutes for them. [Leopold 1949]

[1] E-mail: brus0105@umn.edu
[2] E-mail: dcfulton@umn.edu

Leopold (1949:178) argued that the "voluntary adherence to an ethical code elevates the self-respect of the sportsman." Though an ethic denotes personal, prescriptive judgments as to rightness or wrongness (Runes 1983; cited in Manning et al. 1999) these judgments are only enforceable to the extent that they are shared among members of a group. Formal and informal sanctions of behaviors that anglers judge to be wrong provide a mechanism for the establishment and maintenance of behavioral norms regarding the use of technologies (Heywood 2002).

What would Leopold make of the technologies available to anglers today? More importantly, how do current anglers feel about these advances? The latter question may be determined, in part, by examining how current anglers spend their money. In 2001, anglers spent approximately $35 billion on trips, equipment, licenses, or other items related to fishing (USFWS 2001). According to the U.S. Fish and Wildlife Service, nearly half (48%) was spent on various kinds of angling-related equipment (USFWS 2001). Considering the high costs of the latest technologies, this number seems likely to rise.

However, attitudes and social norms regarding the use of such devices are too complex to be fully understood by simply looking at angler's expenditures. The cognitive hierarchy provides a conceptual framework for understanding the formation of norms regarding angling, positing that values and basic beliefs provide a foundation upon which group norms and attitudes are formed and changed (Fulton et al. 1996). In short, this framework suggests that in the absence of established attitudes and norms regarding the acceptability of technological aids people may turn inward, accessing deeply held values regarding the environment to help them sort out what types of behaviors are acceptable.

In this chapter, we use structural equation modeling (SE) to determine the extent to which angler's value orientations, measured along an anthropocentric–biocentric continuum, can be used to predict behavioral norms regarding angling and endorsement or opposition to technological aids. Data were taken from a statewide mail survey of Minnesota anglers conducted in the spring of 2003.

Theoretical Framework

Similar to other cognitive consistency theories, the cognitive hierarchy posits that, in general, an individual's thoughts (i.e., their values, beliefs, attitudes, norms, and behavioral intentions) regarding a given topic will tend to be evaluatively consistent with one another (Rokeach 1973; Homer and Kahle 1988; Fulton et al. 1996). Fulton et al. (1996) used an inverted pyramid (Figure 1) to represent the cognitive hierarchy, which consists of values (at the bottom) followed by basic beliefs (i.e., value orientations), attitudes and norms, behavioral intentions, and behaviors. Lower order components (i.e., values and basic beliefs) are limited in number, centrally held, and slow to change, whereas higher order components (i.e., behavioral intentions and behaviors) are much more numerous, peripheral, and flexible (Fulton et al. 1996).

Rokeach (1973:5) defined a value as an "enduring belief that a specific mode of conduct or end-state of existence is personally or socially preferable to an opposite or converse mode of conduct or end state of existence." Values differ from attitudes in that they are more centrally held and thus more stable within individuals (Rokeach 1969, 1973; Fulton et al. 1996). Rokeach (1969) argued that while attitudes focus our attention on specific objects or situations, values transcend these fine distinctions, acting as guides for attitudes and evaluations as well as behaviors.

Values are seen as providing a foundation for a person's basic beliefs, which, in turn, guide the formation of attitudes, norms, and ultimately, behaviors (Rokeach 1973; Homer and Kahle 1988; Fulton et al. 1996). However, as values tend to be widely shared within societies, they are unlikely to account for much of the variability in higher order cognitions. Instead, values impact our attitudes and behavior indirectly by their influence on our basic beliefs (Vaske and Donnelly 1999). Patterns of related beliefs can be aggregated to create value orientations.

Value orientations

Shindler et al. (1993) proposed that people's value orientations regarding the environment could be represented as points on a continuum ranging from

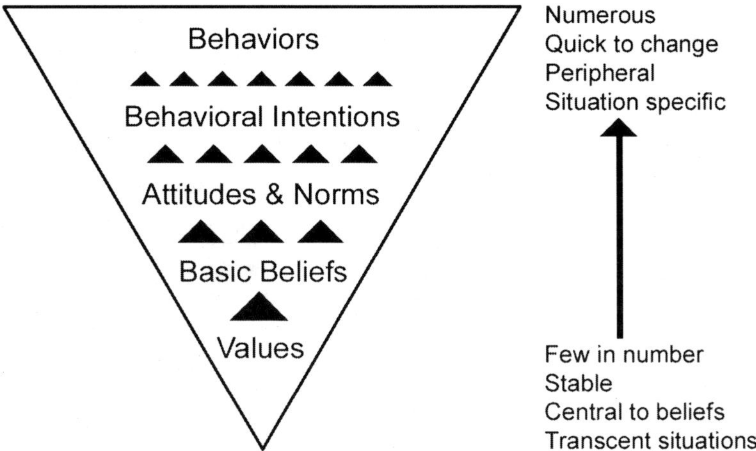

FIGURE 1. The cognitive hierarchy model (adapted from Fulton et al. 1996 and Vaske and Donnelly 1999).

biocentric to anthropocentric (see also Steel et al. 1994; Vaske and Donnelly 1999; Vaske et al. 2001). People who see natural resources as having inherent value beyond any economic or human benefit are said to have more of a biocentric value orientation, while those who view natural resources as valuable only to the extent that they provide some material benefit to human beings are said to have more of an anthropocentric value orientation (Vaske and Donnelly 1999). An anthropocentric orientation toward nature presumes that while people have ethical obligations to each other, they have no such obligations regarding the nonhuman parts of the environment (Steel et al. 1994). In contrast, a biocentric orientation "elevates the requirements and values of all natural organisms, species, and ecosystems to center stage, and, in some versions, makes the earth or nature as a whole the focus of moral considerability" (Steel et al. 1994:139).

Previous research has shown people's value orientation toward wildlands can be positioned along this anthropocentric–biocentric continuum (Vaske and Donnelly 1999), and these value orientations can be used to explain people's normative beliefs regarding national forest management (Vaske et al. 2001).

In addition, Vaske and Donnelly (1999) noted the conceptual similarity between the anthropocentric–biocentric value orientation and the protection-use value orientation proposed by Fulton et al. (1996) to describe people's values regarding wildlife. The protection-use value orientation was used to explain voting behavior regarding a wildlife trapping initiative in Colorado (see Manfredo et al. 1997). However, it is important to note that values are not seen as directly impacting behaviors; rather, they are viewed as indirectly influencing behavior by affecting normative beliefs and attitudes that are viewed as directly influencing behavioral intentions, which in turn predict behaviors (Fulton et al. 1996; Vaske and Donnelly 1999).

Normative beliefs

Normative beliefs, or social norms, are evaluative standards for how one ought to behave in a given situation (Donnelly et al. 2000; Heywood 2002). Through social involvement with various groups, people learn they are obligated to behave in a certain manner, and a norm is established for a particular situation. This behavior is then reinforced by peers or significant others who sanction violators of the norm and reward those who abide by it, thus perpetuating the norm (Heywood 2002). Norms are internalized through socialization and repeated sanctioning and may eventually develop the power to influence behavior even when no one else is present (Grasmick and Bursik 1990).

When in novel or ambiguous situations in which there is no established norm to guide behavior, individuals have no objective, external reality for determining "right" and "wrong." In such situations people can be especially influenced by group members (Khoury 1985). Through interactions with group members individuals become aware of each other's judgments and a norm is established. Yet, in the absence of established norms, people must use some criteria for determining appropriate behavior. In such situations, the cognitive hierarchy suggests that individuals' basic beliefs, or value orientations, may help guide their judgments concerning the appropriateness of behaviors.

We reasoned that, to the extent that value orientations guide the development of social norms regarding angling, understanding individuals' value orientations could help predict their ratings of the acceptability of various technological aids, as well as their normative beliefs regarding angling practices. First, we describe angler's normative judgments regarding angling behaviors and the acceptability of technological aids. We then use Confirmatory Factor Analysis to validate the bio-anthropocentric scale, and SE to determine the extent to which angler's value orientations can be used to predict endorsement or opposition to these norms. Based on theory and prior research, we identified and tested the following hypotheses:

H1.—Basic beliefs concerning angling can be represented by two dimensions, anthropocentric and biocentric, which when combined constitute a single, continuous bio-anthropocentric value orientation.

H2.—Biocentric value orientation will be negatively related with the acceptability of technological aids for angling.

H3: Biocentric value orientation will be positively related with acceptability of technological aids for angling.

One approach to promoting good stewardship of aquatic resources is to focus efforts on changing anglers' attitudes and norms regarding various angling practices. However, to the extent that norms and attitudes regarding stewardship behaviors are guided by more fundamental values, they may prove resistant to change, ultimately frustrating the efforts of stewardship educators. This research attempts to empirically assess the extent to which angler value orientations guide more peripheral norms regarding stewardship behaviors.

Methods

Researchers from the Minnesota Cooperative Fish and Wildlife Management Unit collected data for this study. We obtained a random sample of 900 anglers from the Minnesota Department of Natural Resources, drawn from the Minnesota's Electronic Licensing System licensee database. The licensee database consisted of individuals over the age of 16 who purchased a resident fishing license in Minnesota during the 2002–2003 fishing season. We used probabilistic sampling techniques to ensure an unbiased sample, and we used Dillman's (2000) Tailored Design Method in the mail survey. The first mailings occurred in early April 2003. We initially sent anglers a questionnaire, cover letter, and postage-paid return envelope. Two weeks after the first mailing, we sent a reminder postcard to anglers who had not yet returned the completed questionnaire. Six weeks after the initial mailing, we mailed another questionnaire and cover letter to nonrespondents. Finally, we sent a third replacement questionnaire to those who had not responded 13 weeks after the first mailing.

A total of 839 anglers were contacted by mail. We dropped 17 anglers from the sample because they were physically unable to fish, did not fish, were deceased, were under the age of 16, or indicated that they were would not participate in the survey. Of the 822 remaining mailback questionnaires, 27 were returned as undeliverable. In total, 457 completed surveys were returned resulting in a response rate of 57.5%.

Operationalization of variables. Anglers' value orientations were assessed based on their responses to 14 items, largely adapted from Vaske and Donnelly (1999) and Steel et al. (1994). They included items such as "fish are valuable in their own right, regardless of people," and were measured on seven point scales ranging from strongly disagree (1) to strongly agree (7). These items included six statements designed to measure biocentric beliefs and eight statements designed to measure anthropocentric beliefs.

Two dependent variables were also assessed in this study: (1) angler's normative judgments regarding the use of technological aids while fishing, and (2) angler's behavioral norms regarding fisheries stewardship. We assessed anglers' judgments about the appropriateness of 16 technological aids by asking respondents how acceptable it was for anglers to use each of the technologies while fishing. Responses were measured on five point scales that ranged from (1) always unacceptable to (5) always acceptable. Similarly, stewardship norms were assessed based on responses to 14 items that asked anglers how often they should engage in various behaviors while fishing. These 14 items were selected from a list of 47 original items as they were believed to represent a range of behaviors related to fisheries stewardship. We adopted Heywood's (2002) method of measuring behavioral norms. Briefly, respondents were asked how often angler's felt obligated to engage in various behaviors while fishing; scales ranged from (1) "should never" to (5) "should always."

Data analysis

Using the Statistical Program for the Social Sciences (SPSS/PC v12) we computed descriptive statistics for each of the items, as well as Cronbach's alpha reliability coefficient, a measure of internal consistency of the scale items, for each of the scales. We conducted a confirmatory factor analysis to test whether the bio/anthropocentric value orientation provided a reasonable fit to the data. Structural equation path analyses were then used to regress each of the latent norm constructs on value orientation, providing a measure of the relationship between these constructs. For factor and structural equation analyses a covariance matrix was computed using Lisrel v. 8.72, and data were analyzed using Maximum Likelihood estimation.

Results

Angler norms

Results indicate that Minnesota anglers hold similar views regarding which behaviors constitute appropriate fisheries stewardship (Table 1). The behaviors most supported were (1) treating private property and other anglers with respect, (2) helping to maintain a clean environment, (3) following fishing rules and regulations, and (4) teaching youth and other family members about appropriate fishing behavior. More than 85% of respondents felt that anglers should always engage in these behaviors. Respondents indicated strong opposition to (1) releasing fish in different waters than they were caught, (2) boating through spawning areas, or (3) boating through bulrush and other plants. At least 40% of respondents felt that anglers should never engage in these activities.

Anglers were also relatively consistent in which technological aids or equipment they deemed acceptable for use while fishing. Mean scores ranged from 4.6 to 2.4 (out of 5), indicating that technological aids ranged from always acceptable to usually unacceptable (Table 2). No items had a mean score that indicated the technology was always unacceptable. Artificial lures/flies, live baits, fish locators/finders, four-stroke outboard motors, GPS units, and both barbed and barbless hooks were all considered acceptable by at least 65% of respondents. More than 50% of respondents opposed the use of more than one line, electronic noise attractors, chumming, and floodlights at night.

Table 3 displays the standardized factor loadings, standard errors, and t values for both normative scales. Factor loadings for items in the *acceptability of technologies* scale ranged from 0.22 to 0.78, and all factors were significant ($p < 0.001$). The reliability coefficient for the acceptability of technologies scale was 0.80. Factor loadings for items in the *fisheries stewardship* scale ranged from 0.44 to 0.88, and all factors were again significant ($p < 0.001$). The reliability coefficient for the fisheries stewardship scale was 0.76.

Angler value orientations

On the whole, respondents tended to agree more with biocentric value statements as opposed to anthropocentric statements. Mean values for biocentric statements ranged from 3.7 to 6.4, whereas mean values for anthropocentric items ranged from 2.6 to 4.9 (Table 4), supporting the notion that anglers believe fishing resources have intrinsic value, that is, value beyond their utility to human beings.

Initial analysis of the biocentric value orientations and anthropocentric scales demonstrated that both scales were internally consistent;

TABLE 1. Respondents' norms regarding fisheries stewardship.

Response item[a]	N	Mean	Percent of respondents by category[b]				
			1	2	3	4	5
Treat private property with respect	402	4.9	0.0	0.0	0.2	6.0	93.8
Help maintain a clean environment	408	4.9	0.0	0.0	0.5	5.9	93.6
Follow fishing rules and regulations	407	4.9	0.0	0.0	1.2	6.9	91.9
Teach family members about appropriate fishing behavior	403	4.9	0.0	0.0	1.2	8.9	89.8
Treat other anglers with respect	408	4.9	0.0	0.2	0.7	11.3	87.7
Teach youth about appropriate fishing behavior	402	4.8	0.0	0.0	1.7	12.7	85.6
Turn in poachers	408	4.7	0.2	0.2	6.1	18.6	74.8
Clean up litter left by others	407	4.4	0.2	1.0	12.0	32.4	54.3
Teach other anglers about appropriate fishing behavior	401	4.4	0.0	0.5	19.0	24.2	56.4
Play and land fish as quickly as possible	406	4.3	1.0	1.7	16.0	30.3	51.0
Volunteer time to clean up and improve fish habitat	407	3.6	0.5	2.9	48.2	30.2	18.2
Boat through bulrush and other plants	400	1.9	41.5	32.3	24.0	1.5	0.8
Boat through spawning areas	400	1.7	51.8	30.0	15.5	1.8	1.0
Release fish in different waters than they were caught	402	1.4	71.1	18.4	9.0	0.7	0.7

[a] Order of actions based on mean.
[b] Categories: 1 = should never, 2 = maybe never, 3 = no obligation either way, 4 = maybe always, and 5 = should always.

TABLE 2. Respondents' norms regarding the use of various technologies while angling.

Fishing technology and equipment[a]	N	Mean	Percent of respondents by category[b]				
			1	2	3	4	5
Artificial lures/flies	387	4.6	0.5	0.5	3.1	28.4	67.4
Live bait	390	4.5	0.5	1.3	3.1	39.2	55.9
Fish locators/finders	390	4.3	2.8	1.8	6.4	35.6	53.3
Four-stroke outboard motors	378	4.2	2.1	1.9	22.0	26.5	47.6
GPS units	377	4.1	2.9	4.0	17.2	27.9	48.0
Barbless hooks	384	4.0	2.3	2.6	27.9	22.9	44.3
Barbed hooks	387	3.9	1.3	5.4	16.0	53.2	24.0
two-stroke outboard motors	377	3.8	2.4	6.9	25.2	39.3	26.3
Treble hooks	386	3.8	1.3	7.3	24.9	47.2	19.4
Lighted lures	387	3.2	8.8	11.6	36.4	33.9	9.3
Lead sinkers and lures	388	3.2	12.9	12.1	30.2	28.9	16.0
Underwater cameras	382	3.1	12.8	15.2	33.2	22.8	16.0
Using more than 1 line	386	2.5	28.2	23.6	23.1	16.6	8.5
Electronic noise attractors	387	2.5	23.8	14.7	50.4	8.5	2.6
Chumming	373	2.5	26.3	15.8	46.9	7.2	3.8
Floodlights at night	384	2.4	28.4	26.3	31.3	7.3	6.8

[a] Order of actions based on mean.
[b] Categories: 1 = never acceptable, 2 = usually unacceptable, 3 = uncertain, 4 = usually acceptable, and 5 = always acceptable.

TABLE 3. Factor analysis and reliability of fisheries stewardship and technology norms.

Response item	Standardized factor loading	SE	t value	Cronbach's alpha
Acceptability of technologies				0.80
Artificial lures/flies	0.60	0.06	10.84	
Live bait	0.56	0.06	9.53	
Fish locators/ finders	0.78	0.03	23.20	
Four-stroke outboard motors	0.62	0.05	12.66	
GPS units	0.75	0.04	18.94	
Barbless hooks	0.41	0.07	6.08	
Barbed hooks	0.57	0.06	10.26	
Two-stroke outboard motors	0.62	0.05	12.50	
Treble hooks	0.58	0.05	10.65	
Lighted lures	0.52	0.05	10.46	
Lead sinkers and lures	0.45	0.05	8.54	
Underwater cameras	0.57	0.04	13.24	
Electronic noise attractors	0.35	0.06	5.62	
Chumming	0.28	0.06	4.53	
Using more than one line	0.25	0.06	4.00	
Floodlights at night	0.22	0.06	3.41	
Stewardship norms				0.76
Follow fishing rules and regulations	0.55	0.09	6.27	
Help maintain a clean environment	0.69	0.08	8.69	
Treat other anglers with respect	0.67	0.07	9.03	
Treat private property with respect	0.70	0.08	8.91	
Teach family members about appropriate fishing behavior	0.88	0.04	22.49	
Teach youth about appropriate fishing behavior	0.80	0.05	16.74	
Turn in poachers	0.60	0.07	9.12	
Release fish in different waters than they were caught[a]	0.44	0.07	6.74	
Clean up litter left by others	0.57	0.06	9.02	
Teach other anglers about appropriate fishing behavior	0.76	0.04	19.05	
Play and land fish as quickly as possible	0.46	0.07	7.11	
Boat through spawning areas[a]	0.51	0.06	8.33	
Boat through bulrush and other plants[a]	0.51	0.06	8.67	
Volunteer time to clean up and improve fish habitat	0.45	0.06	7.84	

[a] Items were reverse-coded for analysis.

Cronbach's alpha was 0.73 and 0.72 for these scales, respectively. Consistent with theory and supporting hypothesis one, a subsequent confirmatory factor analysis revealed a strong negative relationship between the two factors ($\beta = -0.56$). However, the analysis also indicated a relatively poor fit to the data ($\chi^2 = 657.07$, df = 76, $p < 0.001$; root mean square error of approximation [RMSEA] = 0.133; goodness of fit index [GFI] = 0.75; adjusted goodness of fit index [AGFI] = 0.65).

In an effort to specify a model that offered a reasonable fit to the data, while remaining consistent with our initial conceptualization, we ran a series of analyses whereby we removed a low loading item in each analysis and continued removing items until the model offered a reasonable fit.

TABLE 4. Factor analysis and reliability of initial angler value orientation scales.

Response item	Item mean	Standardized factor loading	SE	t value	Cronbach's alpha
Anthropocentric value orientation					0.73
The primary value of fisheries is to provide recreation for people	4.9	0.35	0.06	5.56	
Fish are primarily valuable as food for people	4.6	0.43	0.06	7.45	
Humans were meant to rule over the rest of nature	4.0	0.55	0.05	10.65	
Fish should primarily be managed for human benefit	3.5	0.81	0.03	23.12	
Nature's primary value is to provide things that are useful to people	3.5	0.53	0.06	9.61	
Fish are valuable only if people get to use them in some way	2.8	0.58	0.06	10.20	
Humans have a right to change the natural world to suit their needs	2.7	0.63	0.05	12.78	
Fisheries are valuable only if they produce jobs and income for people	2.6	0.32	0.06	4.99	
Biocentric value orientation					0.72
People have a duty to protect fish and other parts of nature	6.4	0.59	0.05	11.15	
Fish are valuable in their own right, regardless of people	5.4	0.69	0.05	14.96	
Protecting the environment is more important than providing fishing opportunities	5.1	0.68	0.04	16.09	
Management should focus on doing what is best for nature instead of what is best for people	4.8	0.64	0.05	13.72	
Fish have as much right to exist as people	4.7	0.59	0.05	12.01	
Humans are no more important than other parts of nature	3.7	0.54	0.06	9.12	

The final scales included four biocentric items (alpha = 0.67) and three anthropocentic items (alpha = 0.71; Table 5). Factor loading for the final scales ranged from 0.45 to 0.76, and all factors were again significant ($p < 0.001$). In contrast to the initial model, this model provided a close fit to the data ($\chi^2 = 37.45$, df = 13, $p < 0.001$; RMSEA = 0.047; GFI = 0.97; AGFI = 0.93). Similar to the initial model, and consistent with theory, the two factors again showed a strong negative relationship ($\beta = -0.57$; Figure 2).

Following the methods of Vaske and Donnelly (1999), these items were used to construct a singe scale by reverse coding anthropocentric items, which provided an index of biocentricity. Cronbach's alpha for the items in the combined index was 0.74.

Predicting angler norms

The cognitive hierarchy posits that patterns of basic beliefs, or value orientations, provide a foundation for individuals' normative judgments. Consistent with this theory, we proposed that anglers' ecological value orientations would be a significant predictor of normative judgments regarding fishing. Specifically, we hypothesized that biocentricity would be negatively related with

TABLE 5. Factor analysis and reliability of revised angler value orientation scales.

Response item	Item mean	Standardized factor loading	SE	t value	Cronbach's alpha[a]
Biocentric value orientation					0.67
Fish have as much right to exist as people	2.8	0.75	0.05	15.54	
Fish are valuable in their own right, regardless of people	4.7	0.68	0.05	13.61	
Humans are no more important than other parts of nature	3.7	0.71	0.06	12.39	
Protecting the environment is more important than providing fishing opportunities	5.1	0.45	0.05	8.28	
Anthropocentric value orientation					0.71
Humans were meant to rule over the rest of nature	4.0	0.68	0.05	13.61	
Humans have a right to change the natural world to suit their needs	2.7	0.76	0.04	17.31	
Fish should primarily be managed for human benefit	3.5	0.75	0.05	14.53	

[a] Combined alpha for biocentric and anthropocentric scales = 0.74.

norms concerning the acceptability of technological aids and positively related with stewardship norms.

Figure 3 diagrams the relationship between the value orientation and norm constructs. Consistent with hypothesis two, angler norms regarding technological aids were modestly, but significantly related with value orientations (β = –0.24, t = 2.93, p < 0.01). The negative coefficient suggests that anglers with biocentric value orientations are less supportive of using technological aids while angling. However, value orientation accounted for only approximately 6% of the variance in normative judgment.

Similarly, stewardship norms were also significantly related with value orientations (β = 0.20, t = 2.56, p < 0.05). Consistent with hypothesis three, the positive coefficient suggests that anglers with biocentric value orientations were more likely to support fisheries stewardship practices. However, value orientation accounted for only 4% of the variance in stewardship norms, suggesting that other factors may be more important in determining anglers' judgments concerning appropriate fisheries stewardship.

Discussion

Previous empirical research has demonstrated that people's value orientations regarding natural resources can influence their attitudes, norms, and behavioral intentions (Fulton et al. 1996; Manfredo et al. 1997; Vaske and Donnelly 1999). Consistent with these models, our findings support the conceptual relationship between basic beliefs and normative judgments.

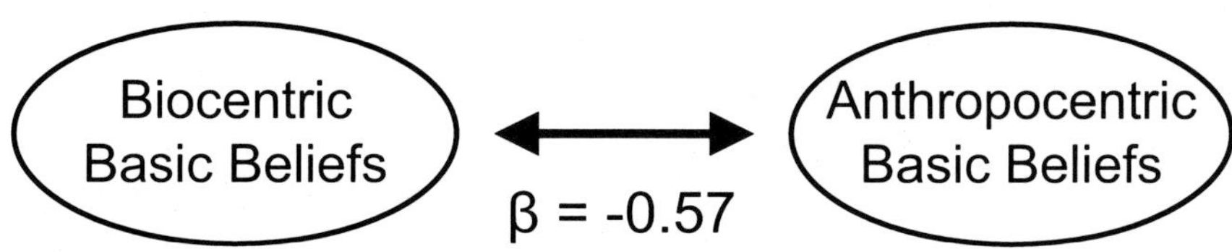

FIGURE 2. Relationship between biocentric and anthropocentric constructs.

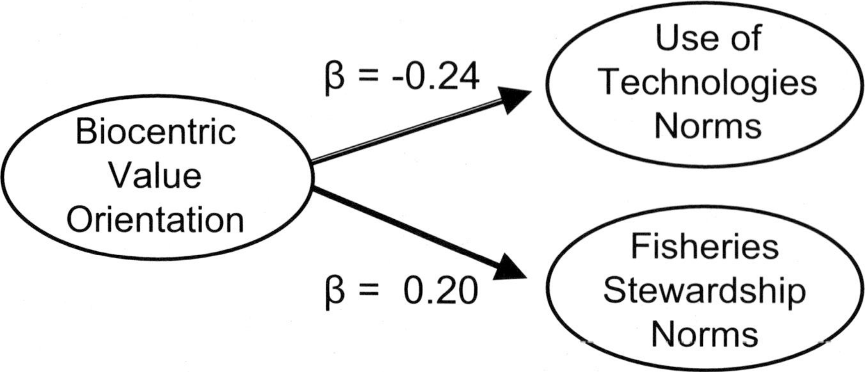

FIGURE 3. The relationship between value orientation and norms.

In addition, research has shown that value orientations regarding natural resources can be arrayed along a continuum from biocentric to anthropocentric (Vaske and Donnelly 1999; Vaske et al. 2001). Consistent with this line of research, our results indicate that anglers' ecological value orientations can also be arrayed along this continuum.

From the standpoint of fisheries managers, our findings suggest that the cognitive hierarchy may be useful in helping predict support or opposition to the use of new angling-related technologies as well as various policies related to angling practices. For instance, researchers have shown the biocentric value orientation is negatively related to length of residence (Vaske et al. 2001), age (Steel et al. 1994), and conservative political ideology and positively related with urban residency (Steel et al. 1994), education (Vaske et al. 2001), and gender (i.e., being male: Steel et al. 1994; Vaske et al. 2001). Thus, increasing urbanism and education levels, for example, might signal increasing opposition to new technologies and support for policies that promote angler stewardship.

Although this study helps to elucidate the relationship between value orientation and fishing-related norms, it was not our intent to provide a full, predictive model of stewardship norms. Past research suggests incorporating demographic and sociopolitical variables, as well as other components of the cognitive hierarchy (i.e., attitudes, behavioral intentions) in such a model. Rather, this study supports the empirical link between basic beliefs and norms found in previous studies. Furthermore, by using similar items to those employed by Vaske and Donnelly (1999) and Steel et al. (1994), our research demonstrates that the bio-anthropocentric value orientation may be useful for predicting attitudes and norms across a host of different natural resource-related contexts.

A caveat regarding our findings concerns the items used to measure respondents' value orientations. As our work built on existing empirical research regarding bio-anthropocentric beliefs, we attempted to modify previously used items to fit the angling context. Because these scales had been validated by prior research, we concluded that a confirmatory rather than exploratory factor analysis would be most appropriate. The fact that the initial, two-factor conceptualization did not provide an adequate fit to the data suggests that an alternative conceptualization may be more appropriate. Future researchers may wish to more fully explore the relationships among these basic beliefs.

When compared to previous research, our models show relatively modest relationships between the bio-anthropocentric value orientation and behavioral norms regarding fishing. In part, this may be due to low variability in the dependent variables; that is, because endorsement of stewardship behavioral norms was very high among anglers the resulting reduction in variability leaves less variance to be explained by the independent variables in the model.

Although high endorsement of stewardship behaviors is a statistical nuisance, it may prove good news for those wishing to promote stewardship of aquatic resources. High endorsement of these behaviors suggests that anglers already perceive a strong obligation to care for aquatic resources. Consequently, maximizing the benefits of stewardship education programs could require educators to look beyond anglers to other groups of aquatic recreation enthusiasts.

In addition, the relatively modest relationships between values and norms might also indicate basic beliefs play a less important role in shaping higher order cognitions in this specific context. This finding may also be of interest to stewardship educators, as it indicates that stewardship norms may be susceptible to educational interventions designed to promote good stewardship of aquatic resources.

References

Dillman, D. A. 2000. Mail and internet surveys: the tailored design method. Wiley, New York.

Donnelly, M. P., J. J. Vaske, D. Whittaker, and B. Shelby. 2000. Toward an understanding of norm prevalence: a comparative analysis of 20 years of research. Environmental Management 25:403–414.

Fulton, D. C., M. J. Manfredo, and J. Lipscomb. 1996. Wildlife value orientations: a conceptual and measurement approach. Human Dimensions of Wildlife 1(2):24–47.

Grasmick, H. G., and R. J. Bursik. 1990. Shame and embarrassment as deterrents to noncompliance with the law: the case of an antilittering campaign. Environment and Behavior 23:233–251.

Heywood, J. L. 2002. The cognitive and emotional components of behavior norms in outdoor recreation. Leisure Sciences 24:271–281.

Homer, P. M., and L. R. Kahle. 1988. A structural equation test of the value-attitude-behavior hierarchy. Journal of Personality & Social Psychology 54(4):638–646.

Khoury, R. M. 1985. Norm formation, social conformity and the confedarating function of humor. Social Behavior and Personality 13(2):159–165.

Leopold, A. 1949. A sand county almanac, and sketches here and there. Oxford University Press, New York.

Manfredo, M. J., D. C. Fulton, and C. L. Pierce. 1997. Understanding voter behavior of wildlife ballot initiatives: Colorado's trapping amendment. Human Dimensions of Wildlife 2:22–39.

Manning, R., W. Valliere, and B. Minteer. 1999. Values, ethics, and attitudes toward National Forest management: an empirical study. Society and National Resources 12:421–436.

Rokeach, M. 1969. The role of values in public opinion research. The Public Opinion Quarterly 32(4):547–559.

Rokeach, M. 1973. The nature of human values. Free Press, New York.

Runes, D. 1983. Dictionary of philosophy. Philosophical Library, New York.

Shindler, B., P. List, and B. S. Steel. 1993. Managing federal forests: public attitudes in Oregon and nationwide. Journal of Forestry 91:36–42.

Steel, B. S., P. List, and B. Shindler. 1994. Conflicting values about federal forests: a comparison of national and Oregon publics. Society & Natural Resources 7:137–153.

USFWS (U.S. Fish and Wildlife Service). 2001. National survey of fishing, hunting, and wildlife-associated recreation. U.S. Department of the Interior, Fish and Wildlife Service and U.S. Department of Commerce, U.S. Census Bureau, Washington D.C.

Vaske, J. J., and M. P. Donnelly. 1999. A value-attitude-behavior model predicting wildland preservation voting intentions. Society & Natural Resources 12:523–537.

Vaske, J. J., M. P. Donnelly, D. R. Williams, and S. Jonker. 2001. Demographic influences on environmental value orientations and normative beliefs about national forest management. Society & Natural Resources 14:761–776.

American Fisheries Society Symposium 55:169–175, 2007

A Test of Aquatic Education and Stewardship Relationships among Youth

ANTHONY J. FEDLER

Human Dimensions Consulting
9707 SW 55th Road, Gainesville, Florida 32608, USA

Abstract.—The common notion that aquatic education programs, typically consisting of fishing skill development and aquatic ecology units, change student desire to care for and protect aquatic resources (i.e., stewardship responsibility) has been generally accepted for many years. However, in recent years, the value of aquatic education programs has increasingly been questioned primarily because there have been few attempts to test the hypothesized relationships. The objectives of this study were to determine if comprehensive fishing curricula could change student perceptions of skill competency, interest in fishing, and attitudes toward aquatic stewardship. Specifically, the relationship among change in skills and interest in fishing, and aquatic stewardship attitudes was examined. Students in fourth to twelfth grade school physical education programs with fishing units, and Hooked on Fishing – Not on Drugs programs, were the subjects of this research. Results of the study showed that as student skill level increased from "weak" to "very strong," interest in fishing also increased. Likewise, as skill changed from "worse" to "much better," interest in fishing increased. The relationship of skills and interest with stewardship attitudes followed this same pattern. Skill level, skill change, and interest were all positively related to stewardship attitudes. These results show clear support for the common notion that teaching fishing skills and aquatic ecology does strengthen student attitudes for protecting aquatic resources.

Introduction

The goal of many state aquatic resource education programs is to foster a stewardship ethic among citizens. The implicit assumption is that participation in these programs will increase awareness of and build positive attitudes toward aquatic resources and that, ultimately, it will lead to individuals taking actions to protect and enhance fisheries and their habitats. This assumption has gone largely untested.

The assumption emanates from the popular writings of Aldo Leopold (1949), Rachel Carson (1962), and others that suggest that developing a relationship with nature builds a sense of responsibility and caring for the environment. Scientific support comes in the work by Tanner (1980) and others on early life experiences. These experiences place the participant in direct contact with nature and, according to Geisler et al. (1977), heighten environmental awareness and concern. Creating a sense of place over time, through building personal histories that link people and places, and the experiences that occur within the setting, helps children come to recognize and ultimately value their environment (Nabhan and Trimble 1994). Further, research by Palmberg and Kuru (2000) has shown that teaching outdoor skills and incorporating discussions of relevant environmental issues with students resulted in a strong and clearly definable empathetic relationship with nature. Further, students involved in the environmental education program also exhibited better social behavior and higher moral judgments.

Knuth and Siemer (2004) built upon the

____

[1] E-mail: tfedler@gru.net

pioneering work of Hungerford and Volk (1990), Hines et al. (1987), and Knapp et al. (1997) to develop a stewardship education model consisting of entry-level, ownership, and empowerment variables. Further, the research underpinning the model suggested that these variables operated in a progressive fashion. If this is indeed the case, then aquatic education programs focusing on the entry-level variables of awareness, knowledge, and angling skills should be the steppingstone that leads to ownership and empowerment and ultimately to environmental behavior change. As Kellert (1987) noted, the capacity to perceive oneself as an integral and obligate member of the ecological community requires a fundamental sense of affectation for and identification with nature. This can be accomplished through significant, positive contact with the outdoors over a long period of time (Chawla 1998, 2000).

As Knuth and Siemer (2004) point out, aquatic education programs focusing on entry-level variables are only the first step in stewardship development. Yet, it is a critical point because the initial awareness, knowledge and involvement in the environment facilitates movement to issue understanding and personal investment in aquatic resources (ownership variables) and responsible angling skills and perceived competence in using environmental action strategies and skills (empowerment variables). Hungerford and Volk (1990) and Knuth and Siemer (2004) both emphasize that pro-environmental behavior will be more likely to occur if all three levels of variables are included in an aquatic education program.

The research reported in this paper focuses on the first portion of the aquatic stewardship education model proposed by Knuth and Siemer (2004). I examine the relationships between entry-level variables (awareness, knowledge, and angling skills) and concern for the aquatic environment. Specifically, I examine the effects of youth participation in a multiweek fishing skills and angling education program on concern for aquatic resource conservation. I hypothesized that perceived improvement in fishing skills would lead to a greater interest in fishing, which in turn would lead to an increase in concern for aquatic resources.

Methods

The subjects for this study were students in school physical education classes conducting fishing education units funded by grants from the Recreational Boating and Fishing Foundation. Each unit contained modules on fishing skills, basic aquatic ecology, on-water fishing experiences, and discussions of aquatic resource conservation issues appropriate to grade level. Instructional time devoted to each module varied by school due to differences in curricula, resources, time, and grade level. However, curricula for all units contained content for each module.

Physical education students at 34 schools, in grades ranging from 4 to 12, completed a four-page questionnaire at the beginning and at the end of their fishing programs to assess changes in perceived fishing skill level, interest in fishing, and attitudes toward aquatic resource conservation. Permission to survey the students was obtained from school administrators and parents by the physical education teachers. Overall, 1,162 students were surveyed. Student names or identification numbers were not allowed for use on the survey instrument. As a result, student responses to the pre- and postunit surveys were matched using a combination of school identification number, date of birth, gender and grade in school. This matching procedure successfully matched 93% of the student pre- and postunit surveys. Unmatched surveys occurred when either the beginning or ending survey was absent. This procedure resulted in 1,080 matched responses. Students at all grade levels were administered the same survey. Survey instruments for this study are provided in Fedler (2004).

The preunit survey asked students about their previous fishing activity, perceived skill fishing level, interest in fishing, and aquatic resource concern. The postunit survey included the same skill, interest, and aquatic concern measures as the preunit survey, but added questions on perceived changes in fishing skills and interest.

Fishing skills were measured on a 5-point Likert-type self-rating scale ranging from "very weak skills" to "very strong skills." Students were also asked to describe their fishing skills after their fishing unit. Responses to this question ranged from "possibly worse than before the class" to "much better than before the class." Interest in fishing was also measured on a 5-point self-rating scale ranging from "very weak interest" to "very strong interest." Students rated how their interest in fishing changed due to the class. Responses to this question could range from "much weaker interest" to "much stronger interest."

Aquatic resource concern was measured using a five-item scale comprising statements that show concern for the aquatic environment and were replicated from an earlier study by Siemer and Knuth (1998). These statements, shown in Table 1, were rated on a 5-point scale ranging from "not at all important" to "very important." The items underwent a reliability analysis to assess the internal consistency of the scale. A variable representing aquatic resource concern was constructed by summing responses to each of the five statements for each student. This procedure resulted in scale scores ranging from 5 to 25.

Two possible confounding influences on the relationships among skills, interest, and aquatic resource concern were those of previous fishing experience and age. Previous fishing experience should be related to skill level in that students would have been exposed to some basic equipment handling and casting instruction if they had engaged in fishing previously. This experience could mask the true relationship of fishing skills with interest and aquatic resource concern. Previous fishing experience was measured at three levels: no experience, a few times, and many times. Likewise, grade in school could exert some influence on the relationships, particularly aquatic resource concern, because older students would have been exposed to and studied environmental issues to a greater degree than younger students. Thus, the effects of both variables on skills, interest, and aquatic resource concern were controlled during the analysis by using analysis of covariance (ANCOVA) when testing for differences among means.

Results

The Recreational Boating and Fishing Foundation awarded fishing program development grants to 42 school physical education programs for the 2003–2004 school year. Of these programs, three involved developmentally or mentally challenged students that were exempt from the evaluation survey requirement. An additional three school fishing programs began early in the school year before the evaluation program was established. The remaining two programs failed to administer both pre- and postunit surveys. The net result was 34 school programs providing both pre- and postunit evaluation surveys for the analysis.

The first step in the analysis was to construct the aquatic resource concern scale from the five scale items. Reliability analysis was conducted on the scale to determine the degree to which each of the items measured the concept of aquatic resource concern. Results of the analysis show that the five items were related (Table 1). The Cronbach's Alpha reliability statistic of 0.927 is very high and can be viewed much like a multiple-correlation coefficient. Each of the five item-total correlations is very high; deleting any of the five items would lower the overall scale reli-

TABLE 1. Composition and reliability statistics for the aquatic resource concern scale.

Scale item	Scale mean if item deleted[a]	Item-total correlation	Cronbach's alpha if item deleted[b]
Help take care of places in your area where aquatic plants and fish live	13.94	0.832	0.906
Think about how things you do might affect aquatic plants and fish	14.02	0.830	0.906
Use water efficiently	14.00	0.738	0.924
Help make sure that people in the future have clean water to drink	13.73	0.795	0.913
Help protect aquatic resources and habitats	13.79	0.850	0.902

[a] Overall 5-item scale mean = 17.37
[b] Overall scale alpha = 0.927

ability. Thus, the five-item scale provided consistent measurement of the concept of aquatic resource concern. Individual scores for the five statements were summed to produce a scale score representative of the individual's level of concern for aquatic resources.

The first relationship to be examined was between fishing skill level and interest in fishing. Among students in the physical education (P.E.) grant program, there was a very strong association between skill level and interest. As student skill level increased so did interest in fishing (Table 2). Although relatively few students reported their fishing skill level as weak or very weak (22%) following their fishing unit, most of these students rated their interest in fishing as weak or very weak. When students indicated their skills were average, a large majority indicated that their interest was average or strong. Among students reporting strong or very strong fishing skills, interest was strong or very strong. The differences in interest across the five skill levels was highly significant ($X^2 = 474.7$, $p < 0.001$). The mean rating scores in the right column of Table 2 provide another measure of the differences in interest among students with different skill levels. The ANCOVA (controlling for previous fishing experience and grade level) also was highly significant with posthoc tests, indicating that fishing interest was significantly different for each skill level ($F = 35.6$, $p < 0.001$). Previous fishing experience had a significant effect on the skill-interest relationship ($F = 3.49$, $p = 0.042$); however, this relationship was unaffected by grade level. The partial correlation (controlling for previous fishing experience) between skill level and interest in fishing was $R = 0.699$ ($p < 0.001$), indicating a strong relationship.

The impact of the P.E. fishing unit on student-perceived skills was very positive. Only 4% of the students indicated their skills declined, whereas 40% indicated their skills remained about the same. When examining the relationship between change in fishing skills and change in interest in fishing, it would be expected that as skills change became more positive, the change in interest would also increase. The data in Table 3 shows that this expectation was confirmed. For each level of skill change, the change in interest in fishing was significantly higher than the previous level. Thus, the students with the greatest change in skills also reported the greatest change in interest. Among students reporting their fishing skills declined, about one-fourth said their interest in fishing was stronger following participation in the fishing unit. Mean rating scores for each skill change level were significantly different from each other ($F = 47.51$, $p < 0.001$) (Table 3). Again, previous fishing experience also had a significant effect on the change in fishing interest. The partial correlation, controlling for previous experience, was 0.463 ($p < 0.001$), again indicating a strong positive relationship between skill level change and changes in fishing interest.

The next question to be addressed was whether a change in fishing skills and interest had any influence on concern for aquatic resources. For this analysis, the aquatic concern scale, described above, was used as the dependent variable. These scores, summed over the five statements in Table 1, could range from 5 to 25 with a midpoint of 15. As shown in Table 4, the few students who indicated their fishing skills declined or who said their skill level was similar to that before the class showed a moderate level of concern for aquatic resources, as their mean

TABLE 2. Relationship between fishing skill level and interest in fishing.

Skill level	Interest in fishing (%)					
	Very weak	Weak	Average	Strong	Very strong	Mean[a]
Very weak ($n = 90$)	71.1	15.6	8.9	2.2	2.2	1.58[1]
Weak ($n = 136$)	22.1	48.5	23.5	4.4	1.5	2.18[2]
Average ($n = 407$)	3.4	16.7	61.6	14.4	3.9	2.99[3]
Strong ($n = 228$)	1.8	1.8	42.1	42.1	12.2	3.60[4]
Very strong ($n = 156$)	1.3	1.3	15.4	28.2	53.8	4.26[5]

[a] $F = 97.80$, $p < 0.001$. Means with different superscripts differ at $p < 0.001$.

TABLE 3. Relationship of change in fishing skills to change in fishing interest.

| | Change in interest in fishing (%) | | | | | |
Change in skill level	Much weaker	Slightly weaker	About the same	Slightly stronger	Much stronger	Mean[a]
Probably worse than before (n = 44)	36.4	18.2	18.2	22.7	4.5	2.48[1]
About the same as before (n = 297)	14.1	10.1	53.0	14.6	8.2	2.91[2]
Somewhat better than before (n = 410)	1.5	5.9	46.3	38.0	8.3	3.48[3]
Much better than before (n = 166)	0..0	0.0	20.5	36.1	43.4	4.21[4]

[a] $F = 40.28$, $p < 0.001$. Means with different superscripts differ at $p < 0.001$.

scores were close to the midpoint of the scale. There was no significant difference in their scale ratings. Those students that reported an improvement in their skills showed greater concern for aquatic resources ($F = 18.26$, $p < 0.001$). Students indicating their skills were "somewhat better" following their fishing units had significantly higher concern ratings than those reporting no improvement. Students who indicated their skills were "much better" than before the unit started had the highest level of concern. As in the previous analyses, past fishing experience had a positive interactive effect on the relationship between skill level change and aquatic resource concern ($F = 10.84$, $p < 0.001$). The partial correlation between skill change and aquatic resource concern was 0.304 ($p < 0.001$), indicating a moderate relationship.

The final analysis concerns the relationship between change in fishing interest and aquatic resource concern. Overall, this relationship followed the same pattern as with fishing skills. Students reporting weaker fishing interest over the course of their fishing unit had aquatic resource concern ratings below the scale midpoint (Table 5). However, among those students whose interest remained the same or grew stronger, concern for aquatic resources increased. Moreover, as level of student interest in fishing grew stronger, concern for aquatic resources also increased ($F = 22.50$, $p < 0.001$). There was nearly a 10-point swing in aquatic concern ratings from students with very weak interest in fishing to those whose interest was much stronger. The effect of previous fishing experience on the relationship was not significant. The bivariate correlation between interest and concern was 0.404 ($p < 0.001$), which indicates a significant, yet moderate, positive relationship.

Conclusions

The stewardship education model proposed by Knuth and Siemer (2004) integrates several

TABLE 4. Relationship of change in skill level to aquatic resource concern.

| | Aquatic resource concern | |
Change in skill level	Mean[a]	n
Probably worse than before	14.53[1]	44
About the same as before	15.85[1]	297
Somewhat better than before	17.27[2]	410
Much better than before	20.73[3]	166

[a] $F = 16.87$, $p < 0.001$. Means with different superscripts differ at $p < 0.01$.

TABLE 5. Relationship of change in fishing interest to aquatic resource concern.

| | Aquatic resource concern | |
Change in interest level	Mean[a]	n
Much weaker	12.39[1]	76
Slightly weaker	14.18[2]	72
About the same	16.32[2]	425
Slightly stronger	18.48[3]	278
Much stronger	21.53[4]	132

[a] $F = 24.80$, $p < 0.001$. Means with different superscripts differ at $p < 0.001$.

strands of environmental education research to form a useful framework for both developing and evaluating programs. Empirical research supporting their model for aquatic education is relatively sparse. The need for more research to clarify linkages among entry-level, ownership, and empowerment variables is partially addressed in this research.

Results from this study clearly support the hypothesized relationship between involvement in outdoor activities and environmental concern. Students in the school physical education fishing programs increased both skills and interest in the activity. There were also very strong relationships among skill change, interest change, and level of aquatic concern.

One of the major improvements in studying the relationships among skills, interest, and aquatic concern is the long-term nature of the physical education programs in this project. The units typically ranged from 4 to 8 weeks with three or four class meetings per week. A few of the programs lasted from 4 to 6 months. These programs provided adequate time for teachers to include in-depth discussions of the biological, social, and political issues surrounding topics dealing with habitat protection, water quality, and management of fisheries. A few physical education teachers went so far as to coordinate their units with science and social studies programs in their schools to enhance the environmental components of their programs. While this type of integrated school program goes beyond what can be achieved in nonformal education settings, there are opportunities in full-day and multiday programs to involve students in science-based curricula supporting the development of environmental awareness and aquatic resource concern. The onus is on state fish and wildlife agencies to ensure their aquatic education programs include the components that build fishing skill, conservation support, and stewardship responsibility

While building the entry-level variables of fishing knowledge, skills, and interest was their primary focus, fishing education supported by the physical education grants program is likely contributing to the building of ownership as well. The strong relationship between interest in fishing and the components of the aquatic concern scale, such as helping care for places where aquatic plants and fish live, helping make sure people have clean water in the future, and thinking about how your actions might affect aquatic resources, all show a building of personal investment in the aquatic resources.

The challenge for aquatic education programs is devising strategies for stewardship development that move beyond entry-level knowledge and experiences to integrate ownership and empowerment components into curricula. This is a critical step, as Knuth and Siemer (2004) point out, that requires thinking beyond 1-day events to establishing more comprehensive education programs that provide opportunities for students to learn issue identification and environmental action strategies and skills. Without these opportunities, agency goals of having an informed, concerned, and involved constituency will not be achieved.

A second and equally important step that needs to be taken is the assessment of the long-term effects of educational programs like the one reported here. There is a conspicuous absence of research addressing this gap in our understanding. Multiyear evaluations that follow students over time and that monitor their continued interest and involvement in fishing and other outdoor activities, that track their aquatic issue awareness and personal investment in aquatic resources, and that measure their perceived competence in using environmental action strategies and skills should be given priority if we want to ensure that investments in aquatic education return the long-term benefits agencies are seeking.

References

Carson, R. 1962. Silent spring. Houghton Mifflin, Boston.

Chawla, L. 1998. Significant life experiences revisited: a review of research on sources of environmental sensitivity. Journal of Environmental Education 29(3):11–21.

Chawla, L. 2000. Life paths to effective education. Journal of Environmental Education 31(1):15–26.

Fedler, T. 2004. National Fishing and Boating Education Grant Initiative: 2003–2004 evaluation survey results. Recreational Boating and Fishing Foundation, Alexandria, Virginia.

Geisler, C. C., O. B. Martinson, and E. A. Wilkening. 1977. Outdoor recreation and environmental concern: a restudy. Rural Sociology 42:241–249.

Hines, J. M., H. Hungerford, and A. Tomera. 1987. Analysis and synthesis of research on responsible environmental behavior: a meta-analysis. Journal of Environmental Education 18(2):1–8.

Hungerford, H. R., and T. L. Volk. 1990. Changing learner behavior through environmental education. Journal of Environmental Education 21(3):8–21.

Kellert, S. R. 1987. Social and psychological dimensions of an environmental ethic. Pages 18–19 *in* Proceedings of the International Conference on Outdoor Ethics. Issak Walton League of America, Arlington, Virginia.

Knapp, D., T. L. Volk, and H. R. Hungerford. 1997. The identification of empirically derived goals for program development in environmental interpretation. Journal of Environmental Education 28(3):24–34.

Knuth, B. A., and W. F. Siemer. 2004. Fostering aquatic stewardship: a key for fisheries sustainability. Pages 243–255 *in* E. E. Knudsen, D. D. MacDonald, and Y. K. Muirhead, editors. Sustainable management of North American fisheries. American Fisheries Society, Symposium 43, Bethesda, Maryland.

Leopold, A. 1949. A Sand County almanac. Oxford University Press, New York.

Nabhan, G. P., and S. Trimble. 1994. The geography of childhood: why children need wild places. Beacon Press, Boston.

Palmberg, I. E., and J. Kuru. 2000. Outdoor activities as a basis for environmental responsibility. Journal of Environmental Education 31(4):32–36.

Siemer, W. F., and B. A. Knuth. 1998. Youth participant outcomes associated with local Hooked on Fishing – Not on Drugs programs. Cornell University, Department of Natural Resources, Human Dimensions Research Unit Series Publication 98–5, Ithaca, New York.

Tanner, T. 1980. Significant life experiences: a new research area for environmental education. Journal of Environmental Education 11(4):20–24.

PART IV   Future Directions for Aquatic Stewardship Education

American Fisheries Society Symposium 55:179–187, 2007

Advancing the Theory and Practice of Aquatic Stewardship Education

BARBARA A. KNUTH[1] AND WILLIAM F. SIEMER

Human Dimensions Research Unit, Department of Natural Resources
Cornell University, Ithaca, New York 14853, USA

Abstract.—The declining quality and quantity of desired aquatic resources requires attention. Those who benefit from aquatic resources should be engaged and empowered to promote and practice aquatic stewardship to help reverse these trends. Recreational anglers, boaters, and other citizens with a stake in the future of aquatic resources may be reached through aquatic stewardship education efforts undertaken by government, industry, and nongovernment organizations. In an effort to stimulate a discussion on the current state of the theory and practice of aquatic stewardship education and generate ideas for future advances, the American Fisheries Society, the Sport Fishing and Boating Partnership Council, and the Recreational Boating and Fishing Foundation invited leading aquatic stewardship education practitioners and researchers to share their insights and experiences. This book is a result of that effort, based on a symposium on the topic held at the 135th annual meeting of the American Fisheries Society in Anchorage, Alaska. Building on the information provided by practitioners and researchers in the previous chapters and during a panel discussion following the symposium presentations, a set of recommendations emerges regarding next steps for advancing aquatic stewardship education theory and practice. These recommendations include strategies for improving shared understanding of what aquatic stewardship means and what education should include, strategies for encouraging best practices in stewardship education programs, strategies for fostering evaluation, and strategies for strengthening partnerships to increase the impact that any one organization will be able to have.

Introduction

In North America, about 31% of native freshwater fish species are imperiled (Leidy and Moyle 1998). Freshwater systems have experienced much greater degrees of degradation, in general, than marine systems, primarily because of the concentration of humans within and around these freshwater systems (Abramovitz 1996). Habitat degradation to ponds, lakes, streams, rivers, wetlands, estuaries, and other waters is caused by a variety of human activities, including contaminant pollution from industry, municipal services, transportation, and individual use of chemicals (e.g., cleaning products, lawn fertilizers); agricultural practices (e.g., grazing, irrigation, pesticide

and fertilizer use); flood control efforts; energy generation; mining; and land-use practices that contribute to physical conversion of aquatic habitats (e.g., development for commercial or residential use). Turning the tide on these trends requires a concerted effort by individuals, groups, and governments at all scales.

Healthy aquatic resources have the potential to provide numerous benefits to human society, including economic, spiritual, gustatory, esthetic, recreational, and commercial. While all citizens of the planet are potential beneficiaries from these values, certain stakeholder groups have an obvious direct connection to aquatic resources. These include recreational anglers and boaters whose pursuits depend on available, quality aquatic resources, and citizens with an interest in the qual-

<hr>

[1] E-mail: bak3@cornell.edu

ity of their watersheds. This symposium focused on reaching these types of audiences through aquatic stewardship education programs. Although these stakeholder groups are the focus of this symposium and our recommendations, many of these concepts should be transferable to helping to achieve aquatic stewardship education goals among other citizen groups.

We invited leading aquatic stewardship education practitioners and researchers from across the United States and from a variety of organizations (government, nongovernment, industry, academic) to share their insights and experiences about current approaches to aquatic stewardship education, and suggest directions for the future. These leaders convened at the 135th annual meeting of the American Fisheries Society (AFS) in Anchorage, Alaska, in a symposium sponsored by the Sport Fishing and Boating Partnership Council and the Recreational Boating and Fishing Foundation, two organizations whose missions relate directly to fostering aquatic stewardship particularly among anglers and recreational boaters. The symposium concluded with a panel discussion with active audience involvement. In this chapter, we synthesize the observations shared by the authors of the preceding chapters and the panel discussion participants, and provide recommendations for advancing the theory and practice of aquatic stewardship education.

Aquatic Stewardship Education: The Challenges of Theory and Practice

Knuth and Siemer (2004) outlined the major components required in programs intended to foster aquatic stewardship, including awareness of and interest in aquatic systems; personal investment, such as recognition of the benefits derived from healthy aquatic resources; knowledge of the skills and behaviors necessary to be a good aquatic steward; and the ability to carry out those behaviors. They also highlighted the importance of targeting educational activities at three levels of outcomes: entry-level variables, empowerment variables, and ownership variables. Many speakers in our symposium reiterated the importance of this comprehensive approach to aquatic stewardship education, recognizing the associated challenges of focusing education inclusively,

consistently, and frequently on awareness, knowledge, attitudes, skills, and participation—in fishing, boating, and aquatic stewardship. The case examples provided in earlier chapters illustrate some of the challenges in translating theory into practice.

Wattendorf and Lyman (2007, this volume) identified one of the most important practical challenges for achieving aquatic stewardship goals—the dichotomy of state aquatic resource management agencies seeking to recruit new anglers (and thus increase participation in consumptive uses of the resource) contrasted with the goals of protecting, restoring, and conserving sometimes fragile resources. Without fishing (or boating) participants, from where will the political and financial will come for good stewardship of fishery (and aquatic) resources? Indeed, even the Clean Water Act, one of the premier pieces of environmental legislation in the world, promotes the goal of achieving fishable, swimmable waters. Support for such a goal into the future requires public concern and political commitment for maintaining the benefits those aquatic resources can provide; aquatic stewardship education can help inform this commitment.

Concerns over a future clientele are not limited to fishery management agencies. The boating and fishing industries also rely on quality aquatic resources to attract participants who, in turn, purchase products and services provided by those industries. Industry can adopt an active role in promoting aquatic stewardship by stimulating awareness and interest in aquatic resources and by providing the skills and technology needed for individuals to be good aquatic stewards (Fontaine et al. 2007; this volume). Partnerships are possible among a range of aquatic resource managers, educators, professionals, and beneficiaries. Such partnerships will be critical into the future, involving both professionals and volunteers.

Recommendations

Based on the symposium presentations and the subsequent panel discussion, we suggest future efforts to advance aquatic stewardship theory and practice should focus in four main areas: (1) increasing shared understanding of what aquatic stewardship involves and how it can be defined, promoted, and measured; (2) increasing the adoption of "best practices" for aquatic stewardship education throughout a variety of types of programs; (3) encouraging active evaluation that allows learning and improvement to occur; and (4) building partnerships among and across aquatic resource beneficiaries, involving professionals, volunteers, and resource users.

Strategies for improving understanding

Several definitions of aquatic stewardship were shared in this symposium, reflecting the range of stewardship definitions found in the literature and in practice. Siemer and Hitzhusen (2007, this volume) summarized the common themes in stewardship definitions as including (1) an ethic of personal responsibility, (2) behavior based on reverence for the earth, (3) an obligation to future generations, (4) a need for personal action and participation, and (5) a commitment to use resources wisely and efficiently. Loftus (2007, this volume) questioned the ultimate importance of voluntary commitment and personal responsibility, suggesting that what really matters for the applied practitioner of aquatic resource management is ultimately human behavior, whether or not that behavior is internally or externally motivated. Knuth (2007, this volume) suggested the importance of considering issues of scale (local versus global) and the range of human behaviors that ultimately have an impact on aquatic resources (e.g., choice of how to dispose of monofilament line; choice of greater-or-lesser polluting transportation and personal vehicle use). If aquatic stewardship includes more than the fish in aquatic systems, it seems reasonable to broaden considerations of aquatic stewardship behaviors to include those human behaviors with a demonstrated or likely impact on aquatic habitats, no matter the geographic scale. Definitions of aquatic stewardship and articulation of desired stewardship behaviors will help educators identify their educational goals more clearly and will help evaluators measure the extent to which education programs have been successful and aquatic stewardship goals have been achieved.

Recommendations to help advance shared understandings about aquatic stewardship include the following:

- Continue efforts to clearly define aquatic stewardship. Particularly important is determining the extent to which stewardship is adequate if it is characterized by a "feeling" or belief or sense of responsibility or whether authentic stewardship must include human behaviors.
- Clarify the implications of considering stewardship to exist only if it is internally motivated or whether externally motivated stewardship behaviors may achieve, or at least help achieve, ultimate aquatic stewardship goals, thus suggesting that externally motivated stewardship behaviors are reasonable outcomes at least in the short term.
- Clarify what behaviors constitute desired aquatic stewardship. Andrews (2007, this volume) noted the importance of agreeing on the definition and scope of environmentally responsible behaviors to be promoted through aquatic stewardship education programs, including the education elements that focus on knowledge, skills, empowerment, intentions, commitment, and sense of responsibility. Bruskotter and Fulton (2007, this volume) suggested 14 direct angling behaviors that could be equated with stewardship (e.g., following fishing rules and regulations, maintaining a clean environment, releasing fish only in waters in which they were caught, cleaning up litter, avoiding boating through spawning areas and vegetated areas, volunteering time to improve fish habitat). Loftus (2007) suggested specific boating-related stewardship behaviors (e.g., reducing marine debris, reducing sewage discharge). McMullin et al. (2007, this volume) included a much broader set of behaviors potentially indicative of stewardship (e.g., recycling, water and electricity conservation, making environmentally friendly consumer decisions, activism with policy makers). If education programs are to promote specific, desired stewardship behaviors, there should be agreement on what those behaviors are (which ones are truly environmentally responsible and what geographic scale(s) of impact should be targeted).
- Related to the points above, develop clear objectives for stewardship education pro-

grams, including identifying clearly who is to be reached and what behavior endpoints are to be encouraged (Day 2007, this volume).

- Conduct research regarding the linkages between entry-level, empowerment, and ownership variables, and the teaching/learning approaches that may result in the greatest success (Fedler 2007, this volume).
- Through research, improve understanding of the underlying values that influence human behaviors regarding natural resources (broadly or specifically) and how to shape those values (Bruskotter and Fulton 2007).
- Conduct research to identify more clearly the variables that influence stewardship norms within society and thus how those norms may be influenced (Bruskotter and Fulton 2007).

Strategies for encouraging best practices

Aquatic stewardship education programs, like all environmental education programs, are strapped for resources of time, money, and staff. Putting limited resources to work most effectively to achieve aquatic stewardship education goals requires commitment and the adoption and implementation of best practices developed over time based on both theory and empirical evidence.

Recommendations regarding the use of best practices in aquatic stewardship education include the following:

- Aquatic stewardship educators should review the best practices documents summarized in Andrews (2007) and implement as many as possible given the resources available.
- Organizations seeking to promote aquatic stewardship through education (e.g., state fishery management agencies, nonprofits with an aquatic stewardship mission, industry groups with an outreach commitment) should have at least one point person with familiarity with best practices who can train other educators and should make an organizational commitment at the highest levels to provide the resources and training necessary for staff to implement best practices in their aquatic education work.

- Nonprofit organizations and government resource management agencies should offer incentives to volunteers to implement best practices in education programs, and provide appropriate training for the volunteer educators (Blair 2007, this volume).
- Lead organizations (e.g., the Recreational Boating and Fishing Foundation, Association of Fish and Wildlife Agencies, American Fisheries Society, Aquatic Resource Education Association, National Marine Educators Association, and others) should distribute and publicize best practices guidance documents among the fisheries profession, aquatic resource educators, angling and boating groups, and watershed associations potentially engaged in aquatic stewardship education.
- Best practices are applicable not only for education programs, but also for industry, particularly in the products made available to and promoted with consumers. The availability of environmentally friendly products within the marketplace empowers individuals to be able to choose to be better aquatic stewards, helping individuals act on their motivation to be good stewards by providing the technology (and sometimes helping individuals learn the skills) needed. Industry practices that encourage positive aquatic stewardship are sometimes voluntary and sometimes in response to laws and regulations. Implementation of best practices within industry should be recognized (e.g., the National Marine Manufacturers Association's Environmental Innovation Award as in Fontaine et al. 2007).
- In addition to the existing best practices guidance documents, continue to explore and apply new tools, such as social marketing (Day 2007).
- Integrate aquatic stewardship education efforts with the needs of school systems and the requirements of state tests. Align stewardship education efforts with environmental education standards and specific subject area standards (such as specific content, and overall critical thinking and problem-solving skills). Stewardship education activities will be more likely adopted in schools where the link to teaching requirements is more

apparent (Grack Nelson and Matthees 2007; Tudor and O'Malley 2007; both this volume).

- Develop best practices for other types of aquatic stewardship activities, including, for example, citizen science on broad scales (Tudor and O'Malley 2007).
- Compile and disseminate case studies illustrating how best practices are applied in schools, informal education programs, industry, and other venues.

Strategies for improving evaluation

Evaluation is a critical component for program success and can take many forms. Siemer (2001) provided an overview of evaluation concepts for aquatic stewardship education, emphasizing the benefits of both formative and summative evaluation. Formative evaluation focuses on assessing the correspondence between program goals, theory, and planned activities. Is there a logical link among these elements? Summative evaluation focuses on the extent to which desired outcomes have been achieved, including desired change in knowledge, attitudes, skills, and behaviors associated with the entry-level, ownership-level, and empowerment-level variables critical to address in comprehensive stewardship education programs (Knuth and Siemer 2004). Symposium presentations provided examples of formal evaluation incorporated within aquatic stewardship education programs (Grack Nelson and Matthees 2007; Tudor and O'Malley 2007).

Recommendations regarding improving the use and impact of evaluation in aquatic stewardship education include the following:

- As noted above, develop acceptable and appropriate measures of aquatic stewardship, including desired behaviors as well as the likely intermediary variables of awareness, attitudes, knowledge, and skills. Valid and consistent measures will enable better preprogram and postprogram evaluation studies and will enhance the opportunity to compare evaluation results across programs.
- Researchers and aquatic stewardship educators should partner to create a survey evaluation framework that includes longitudinal evaluation data that can be shared and ex-

panded across geographic locations and over time. Consistent measures should be included. Also important are preprogram (baseline) and post-program (effects) assessments, with post-program effects being measured over time to determine the stability of those effects (e.g., how long do desired behaviors continue after an education program ends?). Longitudinal analysis of long-term impacts is necessary to truly understand the potential for aquatic stewardship education programs (Fedler 2007; Grack Nelson and Matthees 2007).

- Organizations promoting aquatic stewardship education goals and programs should sponsor and fund evaluation efforts that can lead to the improvement of stewardship education programs. Funding for evaluation of outcomes, not just activities, should be a component of every aquatic stewardship education program.
- Partnerships should be encouraged between aquatic stewardship education programs and interested groups who can provide consultation to ensure evaluation efforts are valid and statistically robust. These issues are of particular concern with grassroots aquatic stewardship education efforts. Logical partners include members of American Fisheries Society chapters who have appropriate quantitative and statistical expertise and local universities where graduate students or statistics instructors may be able to incorporate education program analysis into their learning programs.
- Best practices apply to evaluation as well (Seng and White 2007; this volume). Beyond basic assistance with statistical analysis, aquatic resource educators should partner with research institutions to incorporate research as an integral component of education program efforts. Evaluation should include all the theorized components necessary for a comprehensive stewardship education program—entry-level, ownership-level, and empowerment-level variables.
- Comprehensive evaluation of the impact of aquatic stewardship education programs should also include on-the-ground measures of the quality and quantity of aquatic habitat, status of fish populations, and so forth.

The ultimate goals of aquatic stewardship focus on improvement in fishery and aquatic resource conditions. Have those ultimate resource-related goals been achieved, and what has been the contribution to those goals from aquatic stewardship practices?

Strategies for strengthening partnerships

Throughout the symposium, the importance of partnerships was emphasized. Comprehensive aquatic stewardship education requires resources and involvement—by professionals and volunteers, given the magnitude of aquatic resource challenges we are facing. Several recommendations emerged regarding cultivating likely productive partnership opportunities:

- Strengthen partnerships between government agencies and among government and nongovernment organizations. Organizations such as the American Fisheries Society can play a lead role in helping foster the necessary connections (Burger and Barnes 2007, this volume).
- The American Fisheries Society should continue actively its commitment articulated in its strategic plan to provide aquatic resource policy leadership, engage in public education, and be active in resource conservation advocacy. These activities will have a greater impact if AFS develops partnerships with groups such as watershed organizations, land trusts, and community-based service groups (Burger and Barnes 2007). Such partnerships are relevant not only to the American Fisheries Society but also to other organizations seeking to promote aquatic stewardship.
- The American Fisheries Society can play a lead role in fostering greater dialogue among fisheries professionals about methods and venues to promote stewardship, including discussions of best practices for aquatic stewardship education, assisting aquatic resource educators with evaluation efforts, and recruiting volunteers to participate in education efforts. American Fisheries Society members should be encouraged to be involved in stewardship education and outreach.

- State fisheries management agencies should examine how the Aquatic Education component of the Federal Aid in Sportfish Restoration Program is administered within their states. Often, the program is not a core part of the fisheries agency; in such cases, efforts are required to foster cooperation and support between the fisheries professionals and aquatic resource educators to help ensure that their efforts are mutually supportive.
- Efforts should be made to promote the potential contribution of aquatic stewardship education to schools and other education programs (Grack Nelson and Matthees 2007; Tudor and O'Malley 2007), focusing on the benefits to students of improved understanding of field science, scientific inquiry, and the various methods used. As Tudor and O'Malley (2007) suggest, aquatic science concepts and activities can support learning about experimental hypothesis-testing, gaining problem-solving skills, and gaining experience with descriptive, correlative, and comparative skills.
- Bruskotter and Fulton (2007) noted that people access deeply held values to help determine appropriate behavior toward the environment. This emphasizes the importance of working with nonangling groups—for example, faith communities (Siemer and Hitzhusen 2007)—that may ultimately have more influence on the thoughts and behaviors of citizens than aquatic resource professionals will ever have.
- Efforts should be made to promote aquatic stewardship commitment and behaviors beyond anglers and other aquatic resource recreationists. As Bruskotter and Fulton (2007) noted, the high endorsement of stewardship behaviors among anglers implies anglers already perceive a strong obligation to care for aquatic resources. This suggests that partnering with community groups, civic associations, watershed groups, and other nonrecreational audiences may be particularly important to achieving goals associated with the quality and condition of aquatic resources.
- American Fisheries Society members and other aquatic resource professionals should

be encouraged to translate fisheries and aquatic science topics into popular media to extend our reach beyond the traditional clientele for these professions. These may include media targeted to specific audiences, such as boating media (Lydecker 2007, this volume), or less-specialized outlets that target members of the general public (with an interest in aquatic resources).

- Partnering at the local level is important for emphasizing the salience of aquatic stewardship. People may best respond to issues that are visible to them and affect their lives directly. Partnering at these levels can include providing grants to boating and angling groups for environmental-improvement projects and working with Cooperative or Sea Grant Extension educators (Lydecker 2007). Other opportunities include partnering with existing environmental awareness efforts (e.g., Storm Drain Painting as in Glick 2007; this volume) or with existing youth groups such as Girl Scouts, Boy Scouts, and 4-H. Grack Nelson and Matthees (2007) provided examples of working with these groups to help them identify correlations between aquatic stewardship lessons and the organizations' activity requirements so that the lessons (MinnAqua) would be used as a supporting tool, not a replacement for the organizations' educational materials.

- Aquatic stewardship educators should strive to take advantage of existing outreach opportunities to which stewardship concepts may be added, such as boating safety courses and trade shows (Lydecker 2007).

- Fisheries and aquatic resource professionals can increase efforts to work in partnership with other organizations at the national or local levels who share interests in aquatic resource stewardship. These include the Aquatic Resource Education Association, the National Marine Educators Association, the National Marine Manufacturers Association (e.g., NMMA Water Watch Program as in Fontaine et al. 2007), Tread Lightly, Fish America Foundation, Ocean Conservancy, Tampa Bay Estuary Program (Lydecker 2007) and the Pacific Education Institute (Tudor and O'Malley 2007).

- Industry should continue its involvement in developing technological solutions to aquatic resource environmental concerns, making them available through the marketplace to raise awareness about aquatic environmental issues, and enhances the abilities (empower through skills) of aquatic resource users to be good stewards (Fontaine et al. 2007).

Conclusions

As the condition of aquatic resources continues to decline, aquatic stewardship education can contribute to raising public and political awareness and stimulating behaviors and actions to stem this trend. Although fisheries and aquatic resource professionals may be charged most directly with the responsibilities to protect, conserve, and manage aquatic resources, achieving aquatic resource stewardship goals will require a concerted effort beyond the professions. The behavior of every citizen has the potential to affect aquatic resources in some way. Logical partners to engage in aquatic resource education include the most closely related stakeholder groups of anglers and boaters. The potential exists, however, to extend the reach of aquatic stewardship education programs beyond these groups and reach out to other educational, service, community, and civic groups whose missions and goals are compatible with aquatic stewardship goals. Clarifying what is meant by aquatic stewardship, implementing best practices in stewardship education and evaluation, and fostering productive partnerships are critical efforts required to achieve future advances in the theory and practice of aquatic stewardship education.

References

Abramovitz, J. N. 1996. Imperiled waters, impoverished future: the decline of freshwater ecosystems. Worldwatch Institute, Worldwatch Paper 128, Washington, D.C.

Andrews, E. 2007. Fostering aquatic stewardship with the help of best education practices. Pages 25–32 in B. A. Knuth and W. F. Siemer, editors. Aquatic stewardship education in theory and practice. American Fisheries Society, Symposium 55, Bethesda, Maryland.

Blair, D. 2007. The Trout Unlimited experience teaching aquatic stewardship to youth. Pages 79–84 *in* B. A. Knuth and W. F. Siemer, editors. Aquatic stewardship education in theory and practice. American Fisheries Society, Symposium 55, Bethesda, Maryland.

Bruskotter, J. T., and D. C. Fulton. 2007. The influence of angler value orientations on fisheries stewardship norms. Pages 157–167 *in* B. A. Knuth and W. F. Siemer, editors. Aquatic stewardship education in theory and practice. American Fisheries Society, Symposium 55, Bethesda, Maryland.

Burger, C. V., and M. E. Barnes. 2007. The role of the American Fisheries Society in fostering aquatic resources stewardship: past successes, future opportunities. Pages 117–123 *in* B. A. Knuth and W. F. Siemer, editors. Aquatic stewardship education in theory and practice. American Fisheries Society, Symposium 55, Bethesda, Maryland.

Day, B. 2007. Environmental education for aquatic stewardship. Pages 45–53 *in* B. A. Knuth and W. F. Siemer, editors. Aquatic stewardship education in theory and practice. American Fisheries Society, Symposium 55, Bethesda, Maryland.

Fedler, A. J. 2007. A test of aquatic education and stewardship relationships among youth. Pages 169–175 *in* B. A. Knuth and W. F. Siemer, editors. Aquatic stewardship education in theory and practice. American Fisheries Society, Symposium 55, Bethesda, Maryland.

Fontaine, M. W., M. P. Dunn, and D. Lijana. 2007. Overview of the recreational boating industry's aquatic stewardship through technology, innovation and education. Pages 55–72 *in* B. A. Knuth and W. F. Siemer, editors. Aquatic stewardship education in theory and practice. American Fisheries Society, Symposium 55, Bethesda, Maryland.

Glick, A. L. 2007. Government, nongovernment organizations, and industry: programs that foster aquatic stewardship. Pages 85–91 *in* B. A. Knuth and W. F. Siemer, editors. Aquatic stewardship education in theory and practice. American Fisheries Society, Symposium 55, Bethesda, Maryland.

Grack Nelson, A., and J. Matthees. 2007. Developing tomorrow's anglers and aquatic stewards: formative evaluation of MinnAqua's leaders' guide. Pages 33–43 *in* B. A. Knuth and W. F. Siemer, editors. Aquatic stewardship education in theory and practice. American Fisheries Society, Symposium 55, Bethesda, Maryland.

Knuth, B. A. 2007. Improving our understanding of the theory and practice of aquatic stewardship education. Pages 3–10 *in* B. A. Knuth and W. F. Siemer, editors. Aquatic stewardship education in theory and practice. American Fisheries Society, Symposium 55, Bethesda, Maryland.

Knuth, B. A., and W. F. Siemer. 2004. Fostering aquatic stewardship: a key for fisheries sustainability. Pages 243–255 *in* E. E. Knudsen, D. D. MacDonald, and Y. K. Muirhead, editors. Sustainable management of North American fisheries. American Fisheries Society, Symposium 43, Bethesda, Maryland.

Leidy, R. A., and P. B. Moyle. 1998. Conservation status of the world's fish fauna: an overview. Pages 187–227 *in* P. L. Fiedler and P. M. Karieva, editors. Conservation biology for the coming decade. 2nd edition. Chapman and Hall, New York.

Loftus, A. J. 2007. Measures of aquatic stewardship from the boating perspective. Pages 127–135 *in* B. A. Knuth and W. F. Siemer, editors. Aquatic stewardship education in theory and practice. American Fisheries Society, Symposium 55, Bethesda, Maryland.

Lydecker, R. 2007. Fostering boating-related aquatic stewardship: reaching the boater. Pages 73–77 *in* B. A. Knuth and W. F. Siemer, editors. Aquatic stewardship education in theory and practice. American Fisheries Society, Symposium 55, Bethesda, Maryland.

McMullin, S. L., K. S. Hockett, and J. A. McClafferty. 2007. Does angling or boating improve the stewardship ethic of participants? Pages 145–155 *in* B. A. Knuth and W. F. Siemer, editors. Aquatic stewardship education in theory and practice. American Fisheries Society, Symposium 55, Bethesda, Maryland.

Seng, P. T., and G. M. White. 2007. Measures of aquatic stewardship from a fisheries perspective. Pages 137–143 *in* B. A. Knuth and W. F. Siemer, editors. Aquatic stewardship education in theory and practice. American Fisheries Society, Symposium 55, Bethesda, Maryland.

Siemer, W. F. 2001. Best practices for curriculum, teaching, and evaluation components of aquatic stewardship education. Pages 18–36 *in* T. Fedler, editor. Defining best practices in boating, fishing, and stewardship education. Recreational Boating and Fishing Foundation, Alexandria, Virginia.

Siemer, W. F., and G. E. Hitzhusen. 2007. Revisiting the stewardship concept: faith-based opportunities to bridge from principles to practice. Pages 103–116 *in* B. A. Knuth and W. F. Siemer, editors. Aquatic stewardship education in theory and practice. American Fisheries Society, Symposium 55, Bethesda, Maryland.

Tudor, M., and M. O'Malley. 2007. Citizen science: stewardship education in Washington State. Pages 93–101 *in* B. A. Knuth and W. F. Siemer, editors. Aquatic stewardship education in theory and practice. American Fisheries Society, Symposium 55, Bethesda, Maryland.

Wattendorf, B., and J. Lyman. 2007. Reconciling fishing and boating with safe, sustainable use. Pages 11–21 *in* B. A. Knuth and W. F. Siemer, editors. Aquatic stewardship education in theory and practice. American Fisheries Society, Symposium 55, Bethesda, Maryland.